Anthony Burgess was born in Manchester in 1917. After six years in the Army he worked as an instructor for the Central Advisory Council for Forces Education and as a grammar-school master. From 1954–1960 he was stationed in the Far East, where he was an education officer in the Colonial Service.

He became a full-time writer in 1960, although he had already published three novels and a history of English literature, as well as composing several full-scale works for orchestra and other media.

His work includes *A Clockwork Orange* (later filmed by Stanley Kubrick), *Honey for the Bears*, *The Long Day Wanes*, *Time for a Tiger*, *Earthly Powers*, the Enderby novels and *The Kingdom of the Wicked*.

Anthony Burgess

FLAME INTO BEING

The Life and Work of D. H. Lawrence

First published in Great Britain by
William Heinemann Ltd 1985
Published in Abacus by
Sphere Books Ltd 1986
27 Wright's Lane, London W8 5SW

Printed and bound in Great Britain by
Collins, Glasgow

Per
Liana

Contents

Preface

This brief book had its origins in the intention to write a book even briefer — a centennial tribute to D. H. Lawrence which should be a sort of payment of a debt. We all, readers of books and writers of them, are grateful to literary genius for enriching our lives, but the writer has the duty and privilege of expressing his gratitude through his craft. Inevitably, as with all debts, he puts off payment, but he cannot evade the final notice of a centenary. In 1964, the quatercentenary of Shakespeare's birth, I produced at last a novel on the life and loves of the greatest English poet after many years of indecisive brooding. It might have been a better novel if I had prolonged its incubation, but the clock whirred and got ready to strike, and it was clear to me that if the book was not published on 23 April 1964 it might never reach publication at all. In 1982, James Joyce's centenary, there was broadcast — simultaneously from Dublin and London — my musical version of *Ulysses*, a tribute which some critics heard as a disparagement. I have, with the same expectation, set four of Lawrence's poems to music. I have also made a television film about him. I proposed also a brief homage to him in the medium which is my primary *métier*, and this book is the result.

I had wished merely to discuss certain selected works of his, but I discovered that it was not possible to separate Lawrence's work from his life. One could not choose a segment of his life — which, God knows, was short enough — and therefore one could not choose a segment of his work. What you have here, then, is a brief literary biography which may serve to introduce the man and his writings to those who know nothing of either — with the exception, naturally, of *Lady Chatterley's Lover* and the scandal which still clings to its author – or, knowing something of both, would like to know more. Lawrence wrote a remarkable amount in a life truncated by tuberculosis, and the reading of what he wrote should not be a matter of random choice: he needs to be read entire, and in an order dictated by the vicissitudes of his life. This may well be true of all imaginative writers, but it is overwhelmingly true of Lawrence.

I mentioned a debt, but this is not a literary debt – at least, not in the sense that I ever wished to write like Lawrence or that I have ever recognised in my own work, such as it is, any trace of his influence. There is a great disaffinity of culture and even blood between myself and him. I, mostly Irish, brought up in the north of England as a Catholic, of a pub and shop background, confront a Nonconformist Anglo-Saxon from the Midlands, proud of his puritanism, drawn to pre-Christian gods, the son of a miner. But I admire him as the sort of good Englishman I can never myself be, I admire his intransigence, and I sympathise with his sufferings on behalf of free expression. A hundred years after his birth, I consider that he has triumphed over his enemies (though, in the English-speaking world, one can never be sure), and that he stands for that fighting element in the practice of literature without which books are a mere décor or a confirmation of the beliefs and prejudices of the ruling class. I say at the end of my book that literature is essentially subversive, and that Lawrence is a witness (or martyr, which means the same thing) for that truth. He is a powerful exemplar of those virtues which all who write for a living, and at the same time to promote a pleasure in living, like to think inheres in the practice of their craft or art – energy, doggedness, desperate sincerity, delight in the daily struggle to make words behave.

In old age I wake up with surprise to find myself in the situation that Lawrence chose in his youth – namely, that of a British writer in exile (married, incidentally, to a foreign aristocrat), who feels more at home by the Mediterranean than by the Thames or the Irwell, using foreign languages more than English in daily discourse, trying to hear English and see the English the more clearly for not living with them. Voluntary expatriation never goes down well with my, and Lawrence's, fellow-subjects of the British crown: the novelist who lives abroad is trying to evade taxation or bad weather or both (in fact, he evades neither). What he is really trying to do is to get out of the narrow cage which inhibits the British novel, to acquire a continental point of view, to avoid writing about failed love affairs in Hampstead. He is also fulfilling the writer's right to live where he wishes, so long as he can get on with his work. The thing to remember about Lawrence's exile is that it enabled him to serve England, or at least England's literature, far better than if he had stayed at home.

As a preface is no more than a discardable lizard's tail, though fixed frontally, it may accommodate fancies that would be improper in the body of the work (which, having a certain organic life, is a sort of animal). Lawrence was the only great British writer to celebrate a centenary in 1985, a year devoted to musicians and, most of all, to Handel, who was born in 1685. There is a certain piquancy in the chance concelebration of the birth of a great German composer who became British and that of a great British writer who, marrying a German, abandoned Britain. Handel was adored by the British (when they were not adoring *The Beggar's Opera*); Lawrence was reviled by them. It would be highly fanciful to seek any community of aim and achievement in George Frideric and David Herbert. But I remember a passage in Samuel Butler's *The Way of all Flesh* where the narrator, seeing and hearing farm labourers singing a hymn in a country church, finds the tune of 'Here the ploughman near at hand/Whistles o'er the furrowed land', from Handel's setting of Milton's *L'Allegro*, getting into his head. He comments: 'How marvellously old Handel understood these people!' Read *The White Peacock* and *Sons and Lovers* and *The Rainbow* to see how marvellously Lawrence understood them too. All art is concerned with penetrating into the heart of life. Both Handel and Lawrence knew this, and they performed some marvellous acts of penetration.

A.B.
Monaco, April 1985

1

Lawrence and Myself When Young

D. H. Lawrence died in March 1930, when I was just thirteen
years old and too unliterary to notice. At that time I read juvenile
shockers in bed with a torchlight. I first became aware of the
subversive power of even subliterature when my father threw
into the kitchen fire my copy of the *Boy's Magazine* which was
just starting a serial about the end of the world. He would
undoubtedly have seen a brief notice of Lawrence's death in the
Daily Mail, knowing him vaguely, like the newspaper itself, as a
purveyor of dirt. 'Good riddance to bad rubbish,' he might have
said, in something like Lawrence's own boyhood accent. We were
a Lancashire family, and Lawrence had been born close enough
to Derbyshire to inherit a northern dialect. As a child I was called
'mardarse', and so apparently was he:

> – Eh, tha'rt a mard-arsed kid,
> 'E'll gie thee socks.

Further south, deeper into Nottinghamshire and certainly in
Leicestershire, the term is 'mardy bum'.

It was not until about 1934 that I began to know about Lawrence. What my father's generation, which was also Lawrence's,
called dirt I and my schoolfellows thought of as liberation. We
wanted the truth about sex more than we wanted literature. I
was more concerned with music than with poetry or the novel in
those days, and what literary discoveries I made I often made
obliquely through music. Grieg's *Peer Gynt* Suite led me to the
play itself and then to the whole of Ibsen, with Björnsen to

follow. I was attracted to the music of Delius and the songs of his young friend and adorer Peter Warlock. Reading about both, I learned that Peter Warlock, whose real name was Philip Heseltine, thought highly of a novelist named Lawrence but eventually became his enemy and was ridiculed in one of his novels. Delius had lived on an orange plantation in Florida, and there had been some talk of Lawrence's setting up a kind of pantisocratic colony there (I knew about pantisocracy through having Coleridge as a set book). I also learned that Heseltine appeared, exalted more than libelled, in a novel of Aldous Huxley's called *Antic Hay*. This novel led me to *Pointer Counter Point*, a promising musical title, and there I met Mark Rampion, who, I was told, was really Lawrence.

Those were great days for the young who looked for sex in books, and they can never be recovered in an age of permissiveness. Literature was the way into a forbidden world. Now it is all too open and the mystery has departed. I bought the collected works of Shakespeare for three shillings and sixpence and found plenty of eroticism in *Venus and Adonis* and *The Rape of Lucrece*. Then there was Boccaccio's *Decameron* which, in the editions then available, either left out the story about putting the devil in hell or presented it in the original Tuscan. The impulse to get hold of an Italian primer was great. Thus are we led to learning. *Gargantua and Pantagruel* in the Everyman edition was more lavatorial than erotic, but it left nothing out and it blew like a great clean dirty wind through my boyhood. Great literature bloomed all about us, and it was not a bit like *Black Beauty*. But, we heard, there were three modern works which said too much about sex and in consequence had been banned by the British state. These were *The Well of Loneliness*, *Lady Chatterley's Lover* and *Ulysses*. We had had *The Adventures of Ulysses* by Charles Lamb and his demented sister in the second form, and we were puzzled that the Greek hero should now have sailed into a forbidden zone of activity. We were inflamed with a desire to get hold of these books not merely because they were outlawed, like Robin Hood, but because the reactionary or popular press hammered at them so relentlessly.

James Douglas, one of Lord Beaverbrook's editors, led many of my generation to the pleasures of modern literature through the sheer bloody vehemence of his attacks. A headline spread over two pages of the *Sunday Express* greeted Aldous Huxley's

Brave New World with 'THE MAN WHO HATES GOD'. A *Daily Express* article rather untypically called for a flight of new young poets. These however were not to be seduced by the sordid un-intelligibility of Pound and Eliot (cited as the author of 'O the moon shines bright on Mrs Porter'). We were grateful to learn these names: hated by Douglas, they had to be good. Douglas would have preferred to see his children dead at his feet than contaminated by Radclyffe Hall. Joyce and Lawrence were, of course, unspeakable. Ivor Brown, a literary man who should have known better, confirmed the gutter-press prejudice against frankness in literature by publishing a book called *I Commit to the Flames*. The title mean what it said, and naturally Lawrence and Joyce were to be the primary combustibles. Those, as I say, were great days, the days of surgent Aryan cleanliness and the old Roman salute.

I was attracted to Joyce more than Lawrence at the time, chiefly because of my Irish blood and my Catholicism. This Catholicism was of a Lancashire variety that had produced at least one undistinguished family martyr, and it had been refreshed by mar-riage into immigrant families from Dublin and Tipperary. At the age of sixteen I was losing my faith, and I was told by my history master, an Irishman from Liverpool, that Joyce's *A Portrait of the Artist as a Young Man* might suggest a rational justification of a painfully irrational process. I did not know why I was apostas-ising, but apparently Joyce's hero did. When I read Father Arnell's sermon on hell I was, like Stephen Dedalus, scared back into being a good son of the Church and, for at least six weeks, kept away from the occasions of sin, meaning chiefly great literature. By the time I was seventeen I knew that hell was probably a fable. I could, I thought, now safely become a lapsed Catholic and read Joyce in a trance of aesthetic calm. My history master imported the Odyssey Press edition of *Ulysses* from Nazi Germany and I became, and have remained, a sort of Joycean.

You cannot, we are told, be a Joycean and a Laurentian as well. Richard Aldington, Lawrence's best biographer and one of his best critics, points out somewhere that the Joycean and Lau-rentian approaches to art and life are totally opposed. 'Joyce is concerned with being, Lawrence with becoming.' I take the point: there is a kind of medieval stasis about Joyce, and *Ulysses* is soaked in Aristotle and St Thomas Aquinas. Lawrence is on the move, molten, seeing beliefs as products of emotional or instinctual states which, of their nature, are highly changeable. Stylistically Joyce is drawn to economy and exactness, Lawrence to a diffuseness which looks for what he is trying to say while he is saying it. No potential writer would ever take Lawrence as a model; *Ulysses* is a textbook of literary technique.

Having discovered Joyce, I was not at first eager to read Lawrence. The style of such books of his as were available in the public library was not immediately attractive: he did not belong to the modernists as Joyce so spectacularly did (the pamphlet instalments of the book we knew as *Work in Progress* were coming out at the time). Indeed, the only book of Lawrence's that anybody wanted to read in the thirties was the one they were not permitted to read. Such Laurentians as Huxley and Aldington were more popular than the master himself. And the books that were written about Lawrence stressed the man and the pseudo-prophet over-reverently while ignoring the writer. Middleton Murry's *Son of Woman* was a slobbering affair. No major critic discoursed on his literary technique; when T. S. Eliot mentioned him in *After Strange Gods* it was to condemn him as a heretic. A reference to *The Man Who Died* in Huxley's *Eyeless in Gaza* led some of us to that brief masterpiece whose blasphemies James Douglas had unaccountably missed, but the Christ who rose from the dead to copulate, in rapid shuddering rooster fashion, with a priestess of Isis represented a shock to orthodox faith more than to one's literary sensibility. The authoress of *Gone With the Wind* had clearly read the story: her ending is identical with Lawrence's. (She had read *Ulysses* too: 'Gone with the wind. Hosts at Mullaghmast and Tara of the kings . . .') The literary historians confirm that, between his death and the outbreak of the Second World War, Lawrence was remembered as a doubtful prophet but almost totally ignored as a writer. He had written a dirty book and had his exhibition of dirty paintings raided by the police; the brilliance of *Sons and Lovers* and *Women in Love* had either not yet been acknowledged or had been occluded.

When I began to read for a degree in English at Manchester University in 1937, there were portents that Lawrence might soon be taken seriously as a stylist. The English department was under Professor H. B. Charlton, specialist in Robert Browning (1812–1889), who considered Gerard Manley Hopkins (1844–1889) a young upstart, but my tutor was L. C. Knights, a Cambridge doctor, a Leavis man, one of the editors of *Scrutiny*. The I. A.

Richards innovation, true to the scientific tradition of Cambridge, of examining a literary text under the critical microscope had been imported into Knights's seminars in Lime Grove, and once a week we got down to weighing words, assaying images and measuring rhythms in cyclostyled extracts from works unnamed so that reputation should not film the innocent eye. One of the passages was this:

> But heaven and earth was teeming around them, and how should this cease? They felt the rush of the sap in spring, they knew the wave which cannot halt, but every year throws forward the seed to begetting, and, falling back, leaves the young-born on the earth. They knew the inter-course between heaven and earth, sunshine drawn into the breast and bowels, the rain sucked up in the daytime, nakedness that comes under the wind in autumn, showing the birds' nests no longer worth hiding. Their life and interrelations were such; feeling the pulse and body of the soil, that opened to their furrow for the grain, and became smooth and supple after their ploughing, and clung to their feet with a weight that pulled like desire, lying hard and unresponsive when the crops were to be shorn away. The young corn waved and was silken, and the lustre slid along the limbs of the men who saw it. They took the udder of the cows, the cows yielded milk and pulse against the hands of the men, the pulse of the blood of the teats of the cows beat into the pulse of the hands of the men. They mounted their horses, and held life between the grip of their knees, they harnessed their horses at the wagon, and, with hand on the bridle-rings, drew the heaving of the horses after their will.

This, from the second page of *The Rainbow*, is part of a des-cription of life on the Brangwens' farm. We were not merely told it was good prose: we were encouraged to handle the pulse of the blood of the teats of the rhythm, finding organic honesty and other fine properties.

Heaven knows what good prose is. If it is, as seems likely, an organisation of words that fits the subject so closely that we have the impression of living skin rather than a glove, then Lawrence's skill here cannot be denied – so long as we are quite sure what the subject is. The subject is clearly not the dull labour of farming nor the rolling of the agricultural calendar: it is a sort of mystico-sensual relationship between man and the earth – specifically Laurentian man and the Laurentian earth – a little hard to accept and rather easy to parody (as in *Cold Comfort Farm*). It makes sense in terms of Lawrence's peculiar mysticism; its triumphs are those of a writer taking chances and trusting that daring will not be interpreted as nonsense (what is this 'pulse and body of the soil'? In what way is sunshine drawn into the bowels? How does the lustre of the corn slide along the limbs of the men who see it?); it is good prose only if *The Rainbow* works as a novel. Whether or not it worked as a novel was not a question to consider in a practical criticism seminar. But for me, moved by those 'organic' rhythms, the passage was a narrow way into the whole of the Lawrence country. I was given a copy of the unexpurgated *Lady Chatterley* and got Lawrence the sex-man out of the way; now I was free to read him seriously.

Others who were reading him seriously, and I felt this was certainly true of the Cambridge crowd, were seeking less joy and enlightenment than evidence that the proletarian novel existed. This was the time of what Orwell called the 'pansy left', the Spanish Civil War, revulsion at Tory, but not Marxist, rodo-montade, massive unemployment, Mass Observation, dis-satisfaction with what was called bourgeois literature. There was a confusion between the proletarian and agricultural subcultures among those who knew little of either. There was a nostalgia (exemplified in Q. D. Leavis's *Fiction and the Reading Public*) for a period in British cultural history that had probably never existed – a time of honest verbal values, when words were close to the lathe and the forge and the plough and muck in the byre. A term taken from Gerard Manley Hopkins, much used by the Leavis crowd, that seemed to denote a combined moral and aesthetic honesty was 'the thew and sinew of the language'. There were plenty of thews and sinews in Lawrence, as well as loins and ganglia. Lawrence told us in his novels and prophetic writings that Western industrialism was breaking down, that bourgeois Christianity was dead, that salvation lay in a return to the life of the loins and the instincts. William Blake had said similar things more than a century before, and he too had been a kind of pastoral proletarian.

When the war broke out in 1939 any prophet of doom was likely to be taken seriously, and prophecies of doom were discovered where no prophecies had been intended. The last great work to be published in peacetime was Joyce's *Finnegans Wake*, which looked like what Haydn, in his *Creation*, had called a Representation of Chaos but was actually a recipe for re-constituting any given world after its collapse. The world of the thirties did not, reasonably enough, collapse until Europe collapsed in 1940 and, after the deaths of Virginia Woolf and James Joyce in 1941, it seemed that the time had come, for those who could spare the time, to consider how far literature had prepared us for the bad times ahead. It proved possible to divide the literature of the past fifty years into movements corresponding to certain views of humanity, and Lawrence was found to fit snugly into a category labelled Natural Man.

The literature of Natural Man was a reaction against the doctrine of Progressive Man, whose major prophet had been H. G. Wells. Wells denied the validity of the Augustinian Christian view of humanity as a sick forlorn creation born into original sin and begging for redemption: man was perfectible and, with the aid of science, technology, rational education and a well-organised state, could realise a utopian life in which the ogres of disease, ignorance and want would be conquered, nationalism would wither away and, with nationalism, war. This optimism expressed itself differently in Wells's fellow-Fabian Bernard Shaw, who dreamed of a Superman whose span of Life Creative Evolution had prolonged to several centuries: far too young to overcome our existing problems, we must learn to grow up. Scientific liberalism, with evil as a mere product of imperfect environment and aggressive nationalism as one of humanity's growing pains, survived the First World War, despite the fact that Germany, the best-educated country in the world and the best-equipped to build the utopian state, destroyed Europe in four years of savagery that owed much to advanced science. It proved impossible for Wells to sustain his enlightened optimism when the Second World War came: *Homo sapiens* had failed and must now make room for some new, less suicidal life-form. 'You fools,' he cried. 'You *damned* fools.'

In the twenties it was Ernest Hemingway who seemed to be the voice of Natural Man reacting against exploded scientific liberalism: he produced a new kind of hero who had put off rational thought and relied on his nerves and instincts: not quite an animal, he accepted without question a juvenile code of honour

and a definition of courage as 'grace under pressure'. Hemingway
developed a literary style very well suited to this diminished (or
cleansed) image of man. Helped by Gertrude Stein, he saw that
the old complex sentence of the age of optimism had the wrong
resonances for an epoch of disillusionment. Prose must be stripped
and simple, repetitive, artless-looking while being the product of
very cunning art. It may be that Hemingway's prose is the biggest
stylistic innovation of our century. Both Eliot and Joyce rely on
the ironic evocation of dead forms, assuming in the reader a knowledge of the literatures of the past. Hemingway genuinely starts
again from scratch. Next to him Lawrence looks very old-
fashioned, but he was rejecting the rational civilisation which
foundered in the Great War while Hemingway was still a school-
boy. In a sense his cult of Natural Man is complementary to
Hemingway's: Hemingway's heroes are solitary men, often with
guns; Lawrence's fight with women in the intervals of loving
them. *Sons and Lovers* for the one, *Men Without Women* the
other.

A kind of fiction whose subject-matter was Imperfect Man
seemed, in the forties and after, to get closer to the real human
situation than either the Edwardian optimism of Wells or the
anti-intellectualism of Lawrence and Hemingway. Franz Kafka
was accepted as perhaps the major European figure, with his
strange allegories about inexplicable guilt and grotesque
punishment. Original sin came back. Huxley, who admired
Lawrence immensely while being too intellectual to follow him
all the way, had already satirised scientific progressivism in *Brave
New World*: in *Eyeless in Gaza, After Many a Summer, Time Must
Have a Stop* and *Ape and Essence* man is a poor forked creature
who has failed to put off the cravings of self; he needs the eternal
light and is told, at the great didactic length which is a kind of
legacy from Lawrence, how to reach it. Evelyn Waugh and
Graham Greene sought salvation in the Catholic Church, and
Greene found theological evil a useful fictional property.

In 1960, after a court case of some length and much fatuity,
Lady Chatterley's Lover was no longer a banned book, and Lawrence ceased to be a subversive author. His fangs were drawn and
he became a mild classic, meaning a writer wrapped in his period.
If you wanted fictional heroes who rejected society, you went to
the American Beats. Lawrence had, in a sense, done his work of
bringing about sexual liberation. He was accepted as a remarkable

if careless nature poet. His novels were transformed to the cinema screen so that their sexual messages could be shown without the obfuscations of a no longer viable prose style.

The various categorisations of Lawrence as a sex prophet, a voice of Natural Man, a wilful and foolish rejector of both religion and science seem to me to ignore his true essence. He is, like Tolstoy or Hardy, too large a writer to be relegated to a slot. No novelist or poet has been more concerned with the representation of human reality to the extent that, growing impatient with art, he seems to bypass it and interpose nothing between the reader and the vision. His writing does not seem to have emerged, lathed and polished, from the workshop: when we read him we are in that workshop, witnessing a hit-and-miss process of creation in which orthodox faults – prolixity, repetition, apparent absurdity – are idiosyncratic virtues. Lawrence is impatient with the techniques of literature; to read him is to feel oneself in contact with a personality which has broken through form and rhetoric and confronts one in a kind of nakedness.

The approach is at the opposite pole to that of James Joyce. Joyce wrote about the self-effacing artist, removed from his work like the God of creation, 'paring his fingernails'. Lawrence is always in his work and is irremovable: any survey of his writings has to be a survey of his life. What may be loosely termed his philosophy is bound up with the man himself. His heroes are always himself, just as his heroines are always the women in his life. But when one speaks of the Laurentian 'self', one never means an easily recognised unity. One of the big cries of the youth of our age has been about the need for finding an 'identity'. Lawrence knew that identity meant nothing; the important thing was entity, pure being. We recognise human individuals through physical trappings and reduce them to passport photographs: the 'personality' is a face attached to a body. Lawrence knew that within himself there was a multitude of people hardly ever at peace with each other. Walt Whitman had given him the right answer to those who accused him of inconsistency: 'Do I contradict myself? Very well, I contradict myself. I am large, I contain multitudes.'

If Lawrence was irrational, it was because he recognised how small a part reason plays in the business of living. The centre of his response to the external world was the solar plexus, not the cerebral cortex. He punched his solar plexus when rejecting the

doctrine of evolution, saying: 'I don't feel it *here*.' Well, there are
plenty of scientific truths which reason has to accept, but there is
no reason why our guts and instincts should have to bow to
them. Ordinary language says that the sun rises and sets: we have
no direct experience of the Copernican truth. I am told how
gravity, television and aeroplane engines work, but there is a part
of me that is not convinced. Radio, which we have had a long
time, still sounds like a daily miracle. Blake did not see the sun
sinking as a golden guinea dropping into the sea: he heard the
heavenly host singing 'Holy, holy, holy'. Lawrence was like that,
and reason said he was wrong. Of course, he was not merely
wrong but dangerous when he shouted his rational opponents
down with assertions about the wisdom of the solar plexus. He
would have been a very useful prophet to the Nazis, convincing
the world that the holy imagination was right when it saw Jewish
blood as different from Aryan blood, and to hell with the microscope.

The prescientific or antirational in Lawrence made him a
genuine primitive man, a sort of pagan. He was an animist, finding gods in nature, as prepared to believe in the Aztec Quetzalcoatl as in the Greek Aphrodite. If we were honest with ourselves,
we would accept that the ancient gods were not driven out by
Jewish monotheism: St Paul could not laugh off Diana of the
Ephesians by calling her an irrational figment: she was there,
many-breasted, and she had to be conquered. Joyce took Greek
myth as a template for his *Ulysses*, but the Greek gods are comic.
They are no joke with Lawrence: the world is too complex and
too vital not to be crowded with gods and goddesses whom no
gentle Jesus can drive out. When he was a dying man Bavarian
gentians were torches leading him to the nether halls of Pluto
and Proserpina: his poetry was never word-play; it was a statement of truth.

All this may be nonsense, but Lawrence never fails to make his
personal faith, or faiths, sound like a disturbing sort of sense. His
writings always disturb. He may seem, in *Women in Love* and
The Plumed Serpent, to be following the old fictional path of
realism, but he disturbs us by seeming to transpose his characters
to a mythical region where they cease to be ordinary human
beings and become gods and goddesses. In *The Plumed Serpent*
the three chief characters are literally made to join the Aztec
pantheon. In all the novels the characters wear clothes, smoke

cigarettes, discuss *Pelléas et Mélisande*, take tea, but sooner or later they behave oddly, their impulses overcome reason, they are naked not clothed, their voices speak from the unconscious. We recognise that they are behaving as gods and goddesses behave. One of the keys to understanding the Old Testament is the realisation that Jehovah is not rational, that human reason is a very feeble instrument with which to confront the divine, and that what is waking sense in heaven is sleeping sense on earth. Lawrence's world is the divine unconscious, and it sits strangely with the chairs, newspapers and ashtrays of the modern realistic novel. Perhaps Lawrence was intended to write *Paradise Lost* or Blake's prophetic books: he was born, fortunately one thinks, into a literary tradition which reduced poetry to the lyric and saw the novel as a substitute for the epic. Lawrence's entire output, made of fiction, drama, verse, philosophy, psychology and books on travel, to say nothing of his thousands of letters, adds up to a unity to be read rather as one reads the Bible (there is even a work called *Apocalypse*). It records the adventures of a personality, whatever that term means, and not a race, but it has, as one of its purposes, the redemption of a race. He wanted to bring his own people, the British, to a kind of promised land. Like all Britain's prophets, he preached to a wilderness.

2

Beginnings

Cyril, the somewhat colourless narrator of Lawrence's first novel, *The White Peacock*, speaks for his author:

> I was born in September, and love it best of all the months. There is no heat, no hurry, no thirst and weariness in corn harvest as there is in the hay. If the season is late, as is usual with us, then mid-September sees the corn still standing in stook. The mornings come slowly. The earth is like a woman married and fading; she does not leap up with a laugh for the first fresh kiss of dawn, but slowly, quietly, unexpectantly lies watching the waking of each new day. The blue mist, like memory in the eyes of a neglected wife, never goes from the wooded hill, and only at noon creeps from the near hedges.

To be exact, 11 September 1885. This is pastoral prose which owes something to Thomas Hardy, and yet Lawrence was the son of a miner working in Brinsley Colliery, Eastwood, about ten miles north-west of Nottingham. Poverty, squalor, industrial degradation should have been his themes, and these would have made him a true proletarian writer, but Eastwood looks on to fields and farms, and Lawrence chose to make himself a countryman.

Eastwood was full of miners' cottages, but it never became a slum. Today it is a decent lower-middle-class town, with chain groceries and videocassettes for hire, gentlemanly pubs, good-mannered people. The good manners falter a little when David

Herbert Lawrence is mentioned. 'We don't go much for him here,' a pub landlord told me. When I paid my first visit to Eastwood as a boy, there were old men who remembered Lawrence's father – 'a real old English gentleman' – while Bert Lawrence was a mardarse and a mother's lad. Lawrence had put Eastwood on the literary map, which is always a shameful thing in England, and he had produced the wrong sort of literature: Eastwood families had been libelled and presented in a context of filthy sex; his books had been banned; he himself had run away with a foreign woman, wife of a Nottingham professor. A few commercial enterprises have cashed in on Lawrence's reputation – a men's clothing store advertises its stock as being 'for sons and lovers'; a television rental shop is called Lawrenceville; a café in Walker Street is named the White Peacock – but he is otherwise near-invisible. Dublin still hates James Joyce, but it submits to the plastering of the city with commemorative plaques, Bloom's Hotel, the Anna Livia Bridge, the American Express bust of the author on Stephen's Green. I still find it hard to understand why Joyce, a most hermetic writer, earns this kind of homage, when Lawrence, a man of the people, is neglected. True, the cottage where he was brought up still stands and enjoys a measure of quasi-official protection, but nobody is proud of it. It does not excite pride, once you have subtracted the spirit of Lawrence: a wretched undersized hovel, it reminds us how the poor once had to live. In this rabbit hutch John Arthur and Lydia Lawrence brought up five children.

The Cyril of *The White Peacock* is surnamed Beardsall, which was Lydia Lawrence's maiden name. This reminds us of Shakespeare's giving a whole forest to the Arden family in honour of his mother, while his father has to be a mere shadow of the son. The Lawrence marriage was a mismatch, and David Herbert believed that he hated his father. John Arthur Lawrence was a miner's butty – a man in charge of a coalface, a sort of foreman of miners, while Lydia, whose father had been an engineering overseer at Sheerness Dockyard, clung to the myth that she was of gentle stock. She had taught at a private school, knew books, spoke standard English. Her husband, too old to have been netted into education by the 1870 act of parliament, spelt out the newspaper a letter at a time and spoke thick dialect. Lydia had been in love with a pious young man whose desire to join the clergy had been thwarted by his father and who had been too timid to declare his affection, though he gave Lydia a Bible she kept all her life. With the frustrated love affair four years behind her, she met John Arthur Lawrence at a party in Nottingham and fell for his physique. He was big, muscular, bearded, and fell in his turn for her gentleness, delicacy, aura of a refined world far away from his. The gods of genetics like to work through the attraction of opposites. It was a disastrous marriage, but it produced D. H. Lawrence.

Any miner, unless on strike, disdains to be regarded as one of the poor and downtrodden. John Arthur earned good money, but he spent a lot of it on drink. His wife was a total abstainer, a devotee of the Band of Hope, and she railed at the drunkard when he tottered in from the pub. David Herbert remembered:

Outside the house an ash-tree hung its terrible whips,
And at night when the wind rose, the lash of the tree
Shrieked and slashed the wind, as a ship's
Weird rigging in a storm shrieks hideously.

Within the house two voices arose, a slender lash
Whistling she-delirious rage, and the dreadful sound
Of a male thong booming and bruising, until it had drowned
The other voice in a silence of blood, 'neath the noise of the ash.

The father has come home, jovial and tipsily affectionate, but the mother rails like a harpy. It is a common sordid situation, as old as Noah's vineyard, but David Herbert has made it elemental and mythical: the two contending voices are joined in that of the tree, a world-tree, Yggdrasil (which was an ash), and life itself is the raging dialectic of man and woman. Lawrence's own married life was full of screaming and plate-smashing. Marital dissension may have scared him as a child, but men had to fight women before taking them to bed.

Although the boy took the side of the mother, the poet in him had to respond to the simple, sensuous, passionate nature of the father. It was a rough and brutal simplicity. No abstract idea, not even the vague theological ones of the Congregationalist chapel, had ever pierced the armourplate of his skull (strange that T. S. Eliot should say something similar of Henry James), his life was work, booze, rabbiting, odd jobs about the house, the sodality of the pub. As for passion (which used to be a very dirty word in the north), this was the cock-and-hen business which Lawrence seemed to approve. The mother was refined but narrow, rather anaemic, sanctimonious. Ambitious for her sons only in her desire to see them cleanly settled in the suburbs, with a pensioned desk-job (turning them into 'stool-arsed Jacks', the father called it), pious and teetotal, she would never be able to see that the life of the artist is closer to that of the miner than the bank manager.

The poet in David Herbert recognised too that his father, having toasted his breakfast bacon on the fire and caught the fat on his bread, walked through green country to become a daily part of subterranean myth. He entered the earth, like the Sicilian snake in the poem yet to be written, and became a kind of Pluto, a guardian of the dark mystery in which fire slumbered; bringing the coal home he was a sort of Prometheus. If the unconscious plays so large a part in Lawrence's work, it may be because, in his youth, it had a physical counterpart in the coalmines. There was a parodic Dantesque triunity, with the purgatory of the dull rough town, enlivened by the howls of the drunks, the paradise of the fields and the farms, and the place where the coal came from. His father is believed to have bequeathed him nothing, but Lawrence tended to glamorise the male community and the virtues of physical self-reliance. He lacked his father's animal muscularity, but he would have liked to be a good animal. Being a good animal is one of the aspirations of his first gamekeeper character, the one in *The White Peacock*.

Though Lawrence learned refined English from his mother, he was close enough to his father to respect the Derbyshire dialect. He mastered its entire linguistic system and wrote some of his best early poems in it. In later life he would use the dialect assertively – when overcome in argument, especially by his wife, or when encountering a pale respectability he must have associated with his mother. Although physically he was not a miner's son, being delicate, hypersensitive and no lover of rough sports, he had a certain defensive pride in his body. His body was beautiful because it was male, and one of the minor horrors of the Great War was the submission of this body to the weary or derisive probing of medical officers to see if it was fit for cannon-fodder. As a youth he lacked the strong animal glow of his father, but he was attractive in other ways: the blue eyes, the slim vigour, the intellectual enthusiasm, the mercurial changeability appealed to men as well as women. Towards the end of his life, when living in Mexico, he liked to think of himself as a condor or a mountain lion, but the natives saw him as a fox. They had picked on his russet colouring and his watchfulness. He was not pleased, but the natives had found the right totem. He ravaged the hen-roosts of the bourgeoisie, and he was pursued to his death.

In the sense that the 1870 Education Act sent Lawrence to school and taught him to put words together, he was a proletarian writer. But the British state was not concerned with the fostering of literary talent in its elementary schools; it seemed to want to produce a breed of ill-paid pen-pushers, stool-arse Jacks, to serve commerce and industry. You picked up literature on the side, out of the Bible, like John Bunyan. And it is a fact that Lawrence responded to the Bible, as he responded to the vigour of the Congregationalist hymns: the images of Galilee and Judaea fed a desire for the remote and mysterious. It was from the Congrega-tionalist minister, who was his godfather, that he got those rudiments of French and German that he parades in his first novels. He was quick to learn and had a remarkable memory. The capacity to remember, without the benefit of the little notebook that Samuel Butler said every true author keeps in his waistcoat pocket, is one of his most astounding traits. The sharp and retentive eye is always at work, as it is not in Joyce, who was dim-sighted and given to sounds. Lawrence was a man of great visual gifts whose first ambition was to be a painter. Those paint-ings of his that survive show a delight in colour but suffer from a lack of training in perspective and anatomy. Lawrence did not like to be taught techniques. He scorned the piano and mistrusted 'art' music: you had to learn scales to master the one and the other was full of harmonic and contrapuntal nonsense. On the other hand, you could write a poem or even a novel without being taught how. Lawrence's literary talent functions in spite of the strictures of art. You just let the stuff pour out.

He went to the Beauvale Board School and, at twelve, won a scholarship to Nottingham High School. He was not happy. He believed that the strain of the daily train journeys impaired his health, which was always delicate, and sowed the seed of the lung disease which was to kill him. At fifteen he was faced with the problem of finding a job and pleasing his mother by getting on in life as his elder brother William Ernest was already getting on. William Ernest was in London, earning ten pounds a month and likely to earn more. David Herbert agonised over the Situ-ations Vacant columns in the public library, foreseeing himself as 'a prisoner of industrialism' and one 'taken into bondage' but, still jobless, imagining that the people of Eastward sneered at him: 'I suppose he's living on his mother.' The job he eventually found was with Messrs Hayward of Nottingham, who manufactured surgical and orthopaedic implements. He worked for three months as a junior clerk at eight shillings a week. During this period a terrible event shook the Lawrence household and showed the folly of trying to get on in life. William Ernest had weakened himself with overwork (and with worry over an unhappy love affair). He developed pneumonia and erysipelas and died in his mother's presence in his shabby London lodgings. This broke her heart, made her withdraw from the world and her other children, sending her into a stupor of grief and self-reproach. She was shaken out of this by David Herbert's staggering home from Nottingham with the same pneumonia. The need to nurse him restored her sanity. The son too was saved – not only from the fate of his brother but from the anguish of an uncongenial job. The doctor (although the later Lawrence never admitted it) warned the parents of a tubercular condition and ordered six months' complete rest. All his life Lawrence remained tubercular, but he always refused to accept this, preferring to speak of bronchial trouble or an exceptionally bad cold or a dose of flu. Tuberculosis was a dreadful word. Nevertheless it was tuberculosis that was to kill him at the age of forty-four.

It was during the winter of 1901–2 that the interesting triangular situation developed which is the main theme of *Sons and Lovers*. Lawrence's devotion to his mother had always been reciprocated, but she had to divide love between her children (leaving none for her husband) and to give the major portion to her eldest son. During his convalescence David Herbert monopolised that love and entered into a relationship which some might regard as morbid. The morbidity of the mother's possessiveness comes out in her attitude to a friendship that Lawrence had already made and now had the opportunity to develop. He had paid a visit to a farm called the Haggs, run by the Chambers family which Mrs Lawrence knew from chapel, and met the daughter Jessie, a girl of fourteen, pretty, intelligent, shy, distant and with a 'rather superior manner'. The friendship with Jessie was of great importance to Lawrence and she is fixed firmly in his early novels – as Emily in *The White Peacock* and Miriam in *Sons and Lovers* – and some of the short stories. His mother,

sensing what Jessie meant to her son, disclosed considerable jea-
lousy. The whole story is, as we shall see, set out in *Sons and
Lovers*.

I am writing neither a comprehensive biography nor a scholarly
study of Lawrence's work. I am trying to record the impact of
that work on a temperament which, like his, was driven to literature. *Anch'io sono pittore*, as even the worst dauber can say when
speaking of Leonardo. One thing I am unable to take in comfortably is Lawrence's relationship with his mother. This is because, like a great number of the generation born during the
Great War, I lost my mother in the influenza epidemic that came
after it and thus never knew her. This means that the Oedipus
complex remains for me a matter of academic interest, and the
triangle in which Lawrence was involved is a configuration
imported from another planet. The mother–son nexus has played
no part in my life and I am inclined to discredit its importance.
As set out in *Sons and Lovers* it is, to me, a remote clinical record
transformed into a poem by Lawrence's literary genius. That
Lawrence was saved from a lifelong filial fixation by an accident
we shall come to later seems certain, but the relationship with
Jessie Chambers, which should have been emotionally and
sexually fulfilling, was thwarted from the start.

On the other hand, it was Jessie who encouraged the artist in
him, just as the farm itself, and her welcoming family, brought
him into contact with a natural productive rhythm remote from
the claustrophobic atmosphere of his home. He was, of course,
torn two ways. He loved the darkness of innocent sleep with his
mother, as well as the windy sunlit openness of the farm. Jessie
could have turned him into a man, but he wanted to remain his
mother's boy, even going so far as to refuse to shave when his
young beard began to sprout. If he wanted to turn Jessie into a
woman, it was only in the sense of release from the henyard and
the brutish bossiness of her farmer brothers and the entry into a
world of books and thought and culture. When, in 1903, Lawrence and his sister Ada went as pupil-teachers to the Ilkeston
training centre, Jessie went with them.

Lawrence was seventeen and becoming conscious of his intel-
lectual powers. At Ilkeston his essays were well thought of, with
Jessie he discussed books, his sister Ada played Chopin and
Brahms for him on the family piano, that link with gentility.
Teaching colliers' sons for half the week and being taught himself

the other half, giving out much of himself to unresponsive louts and getting little in return, either in money or the unquantifiable satisfaction of spreading a little light, he was in that frustrated and exhausted situation which is the state teacher's lot in a country where pedagogy has always been a despised trade. Pouring out words in the classroom to little avail, he had no urge to write in his free time. He was an amateur painter until he was twenty. It was in 1905 that he suggested to Jessie that they might try a little poetry together: he was too shy, too scared of the middle-class rebuff to a collier's son, to dare the public exposure of himself in words. His first venture into literature was collaborative in the sense that Jessie took on a kind of aesthetic responsibility for what he wrote: he did the work, but the burden of saying whether it was good or bad was wholly hers. He wrote poems, later stories. In 1907 a local paper offered a prize of three guineas for a short story: he sent in two under his own name and a third under Jessie's. They had no doubt of the respective values of these pieces: the one signed Jessie Chambers, conventional and sentimental, took the prize easily; the others, which essayed serious art, got nowhere. From the start Lawrence knew all about literary markets: literature had split into the genuine and the spurious, and this was one of the consequences of the 1870 Education Act, which produced the phenomenon of prolefeed.

While working, painting and trying to write, Lawrence was also preparing himself for entry to Nottingham University. He gained a King's Scholarship and was just twenty-one when he took up a two-year training course in what was called the Normal Department. Here he received instruction in French from Ernest Weekley, with whose wife he was later to run away. He also worked on his first novel, writing and rewriting with a care he rarely thought necessary in his maturer work. Then, achieving a teacher's certificate after an examination in which he gained distinctions in all subjects except English, he went south to teach in a school in Croydon. There he discovered *The English Review*, which was edited by Ford Madox Hueffer, and, in an agony of shyness and indecision masked by the arrogance of the artist whose work is too good for this world, thought he might as well send in some contributions. Or rather it was Jessie who was to send them in: if they were rejected, the blame would be all hers. Hueffer received three poems and the story called 'Odour of Chrysanthemums'. He had perhaps the greatest editorial flair of

his time, if not of the century, and it was enough for him to read
the opening paragraph of the story:

> The small locomotive engine, Number 4, came clanking,
> stumbling down from Selston with seven full wagons. It
> appeared round the corner with loud threats of speed, but
> the colt that it startled from among the gorse, which still
> flickered indistinctly in the raw afternoon, out-distanced it
> at a canter. A woman, walking up the railway line to
> Underwood, drew back into the hedge, held her basket
> aside, and watched the footplate of the engine advancing . . .

He read no further; he recognised quality. Lawrence was
launched. He and Jessie lunched with Hueffer in London and met
Ezra Pound. Probably without knowing it, Lawrence the poet
had, in his impatience with technique, rushed straight into
modernism, giving his poems the prose flavour that both Hueffer
and Pound knew was necessary to the process of killing 'Geor-
gianism' – tired romantic rhythms, 'poetic' inversions, second-
hand emotions. In his early work Lawrence was entitled to thee-
and-thou a little, since this was a legacy of dialect, and inversions
like 'sweet it is' were an unsure tribute to what the world at that
time termed poetic. But even the earliest poems are mature in the
sense that they know what they are doing: something has to be
expressed, and urgently; the poet has not merely decided that it
might be a good thing to compose a poem:

> I have opened the windows to warm my hands on the sill
> Where the sunlight soaks in the stone: the afternoon
> Is full of dreams, my love; the boys are still
> In a wistful dream of Lorna Doone.

> The clink of the shunting engines is sharp and fine
> Like savage music striking far off; and there
> On the great blue palace at Sydenham, lights stir and shine
> Where the glass is domed on the silent air.

Hueffer was eventually given the manuscript of *The White
Peacock*. Riding on a London bus with its author, he delivered
judgment: 'It has every fault that the English novel can have,'
but he added: 'You've got genius.' Lawrence's later grim
comment was: 'In the early days they were always telling me I
had genius, as if to console me for not having their own in-

comparable advantages.' That is the working-class boy speaking out: 'genius' excused his gaucherie in upper-class artistic society, possibly his unpatrician accent and his provincial education. He was accepted by the literary establishment, but with unspoken reservations, and he was always suspicious of what sounded like patronage. Still, he joined the Edwardian novelists. On Hueffer's recommendation, Heinemann accepted the book, and Lawrence was paid an advance of fifty pounds. Whatever my inferiority to Lawrence in the field of fiction, I am proud to record that I received precisely the same sum as an advance on my own first novel, and from the same publisher. That, however, was fifty years later.

Biographies of Lawrence usually have to disparage Hueffer for his supercilious approach to the first novel of a great writer, but we ought to remember that Hueffer, under his post-war de-germanicised name Ford Madox Ford, remains, after all his discardable hackwork churned out to earn bread, one of the great British novelists of the century. The tetralogy *Parade's End*, shamefully cut down in its British version to a trilogy (this is something which I can never forgive its editor, Graham Greene), is the best of the novels of the Great War and an astonishing survey of the decline of British society, of which that war was a symptom rather than a cause; *The Fifth Queen* is conceivably the best historical novel ever written; *The Good Soldier* is profound and technically innovative. Ford, working under the influence of the great French stylists, particularly Flaubert, was obsessed, as was his friend and collaborator Conrad, with the problems of fictional technique, and he saw in Lawrence, inevitably, a primitive who had never even thought of these problems. He admired the power, but he deplored what he saw as carelessness, repetitiveness, a truckling to narrative tradition and a disdain of modernist devices. He saw that first novel as little more than a mediocre piece of Edwardian fiction. Except, of course, for the 'genius'.

Meanwhile, Lawrence's mother was dying of cancer, and the fifty-pound advance went to a medical specialist who was called in too late. It became a matter of great urgency that Lawrence should be able to place a bound and jacketed copy of his book in the hands of the sick woman – not as the son's first major artistic achievement, but as an earnest of his beginning to 'make good'. If she had been able to read the novel, she would have seen in it

various indirect tributes to herself – a highly moral exposition of
the dangers of the demon drink, the elevation of the family she
raised to social heights never attainable in real life, the total rejection of the father who had begotten that family. She died,
knowing at least that her dearly loved son was making something
of his life. Dying, she plunged Lawrence into a despair that could
only be exorcised in the eventual forging of a masterpiece. If his
mother was to be brought vividly back from the dead in *Sons
and Lovers*, it was from the grave that she won her victory over
her rival Jessie. Any possibility of the long boy-and-girl
friendship's at last consummating itself into mature love was now
liquidated: Jessie belonged to his youth, when his mother had
been alive, and much of her reality had subsisted in the conflict
between the woman and the girl. Jessie should have fought
harder; her heroism was genuine, but it was saintly and negative.
She should have hit out at both the son and the mother; instead
she was the martyr or witness of a growing talent, nursing a
dumb love and at last cast off brutally. Lawrence met another
girl, Louie Burrows, and in a kind of mad abandon became
engaged to her. The engagement did not last and could not. A
stronger female force was needed to shake him into maturity and
cast off the spell of his mother. But his own writing did that too.

We will have to consider *Sons and Lovers* in its chronological
place. For the moment something must be said about the books
which are a preparation for it. *The White Peacock* was published in
1911 and, seventy-odd years later, its freshness and originality are
hardly at all impaired. Reviewers either ignored it or, which was
worse, patronised it. The only review remembered today, if it
can be called a review, is the comment of Lawrence's father, who
struggled with the first page and then gave up. 'And what did
they gi'e thee for that, lad?' – 'Fifty pounds, father.' – 'Fifty
pounds! An' tha's never done a day's work in thy life!' So brutal
and philistine a personage had already been judged and condemned in the novel itself. The Beardsalls are the Lawrences freed
from the eldest Lawrence, who is dying far away from them
with his kidneys shot to pieces through drink. He sends a maudlin
regretful final letter which excites no pity, and then he dies. The
Beardsalls come into four thousand pounds and live like small
gentry. Lettice (one of Ada Lawrence's baptismal names) prepares
for marriage to the son of a mine-owner. Lawrence, who is Cyril
in the book, had dreamt of a cottage and thirty shillings a week,

living with his mother and helping with the housework when not painting and reading Shelley. Here the dream is more than fulfilled. The mother is kept somewhat in the background while Lettice takes up much of the downstage area to flaunt her beauty, chic, and knowledge of foreign literature. It is, we may say, a rather snobbish vision, in which even the farming neighbours of the Beardsalls, based on the Chambers family, are purged of bucolic grossness, and also their dialect, in order to be fit company for Cyril and Lettice and their 'little mother'.

Lawrence's titles do not always mean much, and some readers have puzzled about the pertinence of this one, but there is a scene in the middle of the book where a white peacock perches screaming on a worn and discoloured gravestone angel and the gamekeeper Annable cries: 'The proud fool! – look at it! Perched on an angel, too, as if it were a pedestal for vanity. That's the soul of a woman – or it's the devil.' The bird moves off into the dark and he adds: 'That's the very soul of a lady, the very, very soul. Damn the thing, to perch on an old angel. I should like to wring its neck.' The patrician woman whom Annable married was a white peacock. He is a neat reversal of the gamekeeper Mellors in Lawrence's final novel, who is fulfilled by marrying a lady, whereas Annable has been ruined. Like Mellors he can switch from the local dialect to an educated King's English, but he has elected a rabbity life with an uneducated woman and a horde of children. He loves the rabbits on the estate which he protects, and they seem to have a significance for him (and for his author too) which goes beyond their mad capacity to breed. 'Be a good animal, true to your animal instinct,' he says desperately, as Lawrence's father might have said had he been able to comprehend the idea. Having delivered his philosophy and cursed the white peacock, he has not much else to do except be wiped out arbitrarily. This is so that we can better concentrate on the central figure, George Saxton, who is loosely based on one of the Chambers brothers.

He is a fully drawn character, ruddy, handsome, called pretentiously 'Mon Taureau' by Lettice, but prepared to have his animal nature softened through educative talks with Cyril. He wants Lettice, but she is far above him, another white peacock. She is going to marry Leslie, who is a preliminary sketch for the Gerald Crich of *Women in Love*, but she cannot resist leading George on merely to drop him. When she is very much a rising industrialist's lady, George has become the husband of Meg, daughter of a pub landlord. He does not do badly: he makes money out of horses and later becomes a minor voice of socialism, but he is uneasily aware that he has been left out of the great feast of life. Cyril and Emily, George's sister, go to tea at the inn he now manages and, through cruelty or stupidity, exhibit the cultural rift: 'Our very speech was clipped with precision, as we drifted to a discussion of Strauss and Debussy . . . George sat looking glum and listening to us. Meg was quite indifferent.' Lawrence does everything to show how far he, the miner's son, has climbed a cultural scale which will, by sleight of hand, seem to be an emanation of the social scale. Talk of the possibility of the proletarian novel was always empty: one of the uses of fiction is to affirm the values of the bourgeoisie. This work, with its Latin and French tags and burblings about classical music, is full of Lawrence's (or his mother's) genteel wish-fulfilment. This does not, of course, make it a bad novel. Far from it.

George, whose white peacock has fluttered away from the broken angels, takes to drink. Lawrence, a paid-up member of the Band of Hope, draws on memories of his father to show the wretched process of his decline. He lives with his sister Emily, having deserted his wife and children, and Emily is married to Tom Renshaw, twenty-nine years old, a former soldier, 'a well-built fair man, smoothly, almost delicately tanned', who is managing his father's farm. Cyril has thought of himself marrying Emily a little too late: it is Lawrence making a declaration for Jessie which, to his relief, he does not have to follow up. With his instinct for the right summary of degradation, Lawrence shows hungover George taking breakfast at midday. The maid serves him and despises him.

> 'It's fried white-bait,' she said. 'Shall you have that?' He lifted his head and looked at the plate. 'Ay,' he said. 'Have you brought the vinegar?'

It is one of those episodes from literature which stick in the mind. I did not realise I was recalling it when, in my third novel about Malaya, I showed a drunkard in a Chinese coffee shop proposing, though not getting, the same dish for himself. It is the physical particularity of Lawrence which holds us.

And this novel, without the portentous heaviness of Hardy, is brilliantly particular in its evocation of the English countryside. I am, like Saul Bellow's Charles Citrine, a city boy, and flowers are to me a closed book or an unintelligible botany primer. Joyce, also a city boy, said he disliked flowers, which was another way of saying he knew nothing about them. There was, according to Ben Jonson, an Elizabethan inn-sign painter who could paint only a rose. '"For," said he, "there is no flower like a rose."' That is very nearly my position. There used to be a story about someone telling Thomas Hardy that a new young writer had appeared who, on the strength of a novel called *The Black Peahen* or something, exhibited far more knowledge of wild flowers than did the Wessex master. Hardy flew into a rage and cried: 'I know a *million* wild flowers. There's old man's bethany and stinking ragwort and that long purple thing and – I know a *million billion* wild flowers.' There is a competitiveness among wild flower lovers which strikes the city boy as absurd, and Lawrence showed it from start to finish. In *The White Peacock* we have a rich compendium of the idle man's country lore combined with very exact knowledge of the life of the farm. And the humour and compassion are notable:

> I met George tramping across the yard with a couple of buckets of swill, and eleven young pigs rushing squealing about his legs, shrieking in an agony of suspense. He poured the stuff into a trough with luscious gurgle, and instantly ten noses were dipped in, and ten little mouths began to slobber. Though there was plenty of room for ten, yet they shouldered and shoved and struggled to capture a larger space, and many little trotters dabbled and spilled the stuff, and the ten sucking, clapping snouts twitched fiercely, and twenty little eyes glared askance, like so many points of wrath. They gave uneasy, gasping grunts in their haste. The unhappy eleventh rushed from point to point trying to push in his snout, but for his pains he got rough squeezing, and sharp grabs on the ears. Then he lifted up his face and screamed screams of grief and wrath unto the evening sky.
>
> But the ten little gluttons only twitched their ears to make sure there was no danger in the noise, and they sucked harder, with much spilling and slobbing. George laughed like a sardonic Jove, but at last he gave ear, and kicked the ten gluttons from the trough, and allowed the residue to the eleventh. This one, poor wretch, almost wept with relief as

he sucked and swallowed in sobs, casting his little eyes apprehensively upwards, though he did not lift his nose from the trough, as he heard the vindictive shrieks of ten little fiends kept at bay by George. The solitary feeder, shivering with apprehension, rubbed the wood bare with his snout, then, turning up to heaven his eyes of gratitude, he reluctantly left the trough. I expected to see the ten fall upon him and devour him, but they did not; they rushed upon the empty trough, and rubbed the wood still drier, shrieking with misery.

'How like life,' I laughed.

How, to be more specific, like the literary life.

The White Peacock is, among other things, a study of a very English aspiration which was later to be termed hypergamy – marrying into a social class above one's own. There are perils in attaining this, as the story of the gamekeeper shows, but there are equal perils in the frustration of not attaining it. It is men who suffer: women are capable of very easy social adjustment. Women, in fact, are at home in the world, and men have to resent this. There are a number of judgments to be made about Lettice, but the narrator refrains from making them. The book is remarkable for its narrative restraint. First novels usually brim with the author's view of the world, which is all the material he so far has: Lawrence, always an egotist, presents little of himself, reserving the qualities of a first novel to his third. Cyril–Lawrence is an observer whom this most visual of novelists never permits us to see clearly (it is only towards the end, and very incidentally, that we learn he wears glasses). We have what looks at first like a pastoral idyll, in which beneficent nature teems all around us (even an adored mother is swallowed up in it: look again at the citation which begins this chapter), but a Darwinian struggle is going on, with animals spilling enough blood, and men set traps: so do women. It is a very mature novel and, despite Ford Madox Hueffer's implied strictures, not without subtleties of form. It is even an important novel, but nobody saw that when it first appeared. I am not sure that many see it now.

3
The Denial of Life

Anybody can write a first novel. If an author can jump the hurdle of his second he can settle, without too much trouble – except for shortage of money, creative agony, and the hostility or indifference of the critics and the public – to a kind of career. Lawrence wrote his second novel, *The Trespasser*, with healthy speed in the summer of 1910. Heinemann agreed to publish it, though with misgivings. Hueffer said: 'It is a rotten work of genius. It has no construction or form – it is execrably bad art, being all variations on a theme. Also it is erotic.' Lawrence was later to ask, very sensibly, what was wrong with paying homage to the god Eros (whose effigy, after all, stands in Piccadilly Circus). For the moment Hueffer's imputation upset him more than it upset Heinemann. *Erotic* was a dangerous word, and one that a Croydon schoolmaster had to be scared of seeing attached to his off-duty scribblings. The big erotic scandal of the day had been fomented by what now seems to us a very harmless book – Wells's *Ann Veronica* – and Lawrence feared that *The Trespasser* might be discussed in 'an *Ann Veronica* fashion'. He withdrew the manuscript and started work on the first draft of *Sons and Lovers*, which brought his mother back to life but at the same time exacerbated his misery over her death. He wrote poems about her:

> My little love, my dearest,
> Twice you have issued me,
> Once from your womb, sweet mother,
> Once from your soul, to be

Free of all hearts, my darling,
Of each heart's entrance fee.

He was living a lonely life, torn by grief, estranged from Jessie, comforted chiefly by letters from Edward Garnett, who was then a reader for Duckworth: Garnett saw his worth and urged him to go on writing. There was a market for short stories in those days, though not for Lawrence's. Nevertheless he turned out a number: they mostly stand midway between his poems and his novels, trying out themes to be developed in the longer fictional form, aiming to fix emotions against solidly realised country backgrounds. He was also working hard in the classroom, and he was not well.

It was just a year after his mother's death, in November 1911, that he broke down with tubercular pneumonia in both lungs. The Croydon school did not accept liability for the illness of its employees, and moreover made it clear that Lawrence was not to come back and breathe germs over its pupils. That sensible enough hygienic principle generally applied, and Lawrence, deprived of practising the trade for which he had been trained, was now forced into the profession of letters. First, though, he had to wrestle with death, watched over by his sister Ada, but his natural vitality won through. His doctor sent him to convalesce in Bournemouth, an un-Laurentian place full of military widows and palm court trios, and there he rewrote *The Trespasser*. He also charmed his staid fellow-boarders in the lodging-house which he could barely afford. He always had charm when he wished to have it; he also had great courage and a capacity for hard work. When *The Trespasser* was finished it went not to Heinemann but to Garnett at Duckworth's. Authors, we are told, ought not to change their publishers, especially so early in their careers, but Lawrence always had to publish where he could. There are novelists, such as Sir Hugh Walpole and Dame Agatha Christie, who can settle comfortably with one publisher. This is known as loyalty, meaning that the publisher may always expect work of ever-increasing saleability and no danger of aesthetic or moral shocks to a public that is, in its turn, encouraged to be loyal.

The Trespasser is a very brief novel, which many second novels are (do not wait too long for the follow-up to your first), and it could be termed erotic if sexual frustration came under that heading. It is not a novel about the social world Lawrence knew, nor does it exploit the Nottinghamshire proletarian-pastoral ambience. It is set mostly on the Isle of Wight, which Lawrence had visited and liked, and its characters are musicians. Lawrence, as we know, professed to disdain 'art' music, but three of his heroes – here, in *Mr Noon* and in *Aaron's Rod* – either compose it or play it. Siegmund in *The Trespasser* has an aggressively Wagnerian name, and he plays the violin in an opera house. He is gifted with absolute pitch, as is his loved one Helena, and Lawrence does not comment on the extreme rarity of this faculty. Siegmund comes home nightly from his fiddling to a somewhat sordid suburban home. His wife Beatrice does not look after him.

> The room was drab and dreary. The oil-cloth was worn into a hole near the door. Boots and shoes of various sizes were scattered over the floor, while the sofa was littered with children's clothing. In the black stove the ash lay dead; on the range were chips of wood, and newspapers, and rubbish of papers, and crusts of bread, and crusts of bread-and-jam. As Siegmund walked across the floor, he crushed two sweets underfoot. He had to grope under sofa and dresser to find his slippers; and he was in evening dress.

There again we have the physical particularity. The mess is not something remembered from his mother's tidy home, but the situation of the unwanted husband and father is that of the despised and brutal miner's butty transposed into a higher social key.

Siegmund's sin is greater than that of Lawrence's father, who did nothing worse than come home drunk. Siegmund is an adulterer, or is trying to be one. He has fallen in love with his former pupil Helena and she has said: 'You are so tired, dear. You must come away with me and rest, the first week in August.' This was while he lay with his head in her lap in Richmond Park.

> She stroked his face, and kissed him softly. Siegmund lay in the molten daze of love. But Helena was, if it is not to debase the word, virtuous: an inconsistent virtue, cruel and ugly to Siegmund.

And now they are to spend a few frustrating days on the Isle of Wight. It is as near to a foreign territory as Lawrence can reach,

symbolising a forbidden zone into which Siegmund is to trespass.
He is, we must say today, not much of a trespasser. He never
achieved sexual consummation with the girl who, after all, has
lured him into the forbidden zone. She permits kisses which,
according to the narrative, grant her enough sensual satisfaction:
she is one of those 'dreaming women', whatever they are, whose
erogenous excitability is limited to the lips. Like the Isle of Wight,
she is safely close to the mainland of Edwardian respectability.
Siegmund, naturally enough, tries to go further than morality
permits. He is a married man with children, but chaste now and
sensitive, considerate, a musician of skilled and delicate touch, her
response to which is, by our standards, highly hysterical:

> She began to sob, dry wild sobs, feeling as if she would go
> mad. He tried to look her in the face, for which she hated
> him. And all the time he held her fast, all the time she was
> imprisoned in the embrace of this brute, blind creature,
> whose heart confessed itself in thud, thud, thud ... Her
> sobbing was like the chattering of dry leaves. She grew
> frantic to be free. Stifled in that prison any longer, she would
> choke and go mad. His coat chafed her face: as she struggled
> she could see the strong working of his throat. She fought
> against him; she struggled in panic to be free.
>   'Let me go!' she cried. 'Let me go! Let me go!' He held
> her in bewilderment and terror. She thrust her hands to his
> chest and pushed him apart. Her face, blind to him, was
> very much distorted by her suffering. She thrust him
> furiously away with great strength.

With similar strength she has, on previous occasions, drawn him
to herself, permitting a tumescence which neither literature, religious morality, nor the precepts of home have prepared her for,
to say nothing of the birds and the bees. What does she think a
man has down there?

Today there are harsh names to call her, of which the gentlest
is *allumeuse*. But she is not exceptional and she is not to blame.
The whole ethos of the time was dedicated to promoting sexual
ignorance and attaching deadly sin to the sexual impulse. It was
the lower middle class that suffered most. Country copulatives
could writhe in the fields and the aristocracy keep mistresses, but
the victims of hypocrisy were the dwellers in mean streets with
the chapel bell tolling over them. John Keats is an archetypal

victim, too poor to marry, sick from syphilis after his one daring
brothel visit, both Fanny Brawne and himself debarred even from
mutual masturbation and the use of the condom. There is not
even room in the literary tradition that Lawrence has inherited
for a frank discussion of the real problem. The girl's virginity,
her 'trump card' as they used to say in the great game of securing
a husband, must be identified with her 'chastity', which, as
Lawrence was to show, meant something rather different from
the fear of sex. Young people today must be incredulous of
Helena's hysteria, finding the whole situation remoter than the
Isle of Wight, but their permissiveness had to be fought for, and
Lawrence was the chief of the warriors.

Siegmund goes home, like Lawrence's comparatively virtuous
father, to sullen children who despise him and a wife who dutifully puts his cold dinner on the table. He is in love with another
woman, and that love cannot be fulfilled in marriage, let alone in
a discreet liaison. He has failed to sin by Edwardian standards,
but his household treats him as a sinner. He has committed
adultery in the rigid Christian sense of looking on a woman with
lust in his heart, if lust can properly designate a complex of
tenderness and most considerate desire. Siegmund sits in his room
wretchedly, contemplating his next engagement – playing in the
pit for a vapid operetta. He decides that life is no longer worth
living and he hangs himself with his leather belt. This is the only
instance of suicide in all Lawrence's fiction. He may have thought
of it himself after the death of his mother and cautiously determined to try it out in fiction first. But he was too much of a
fighter to give in so tamely to the pressures of life, though we are
not entitled to despise Siegmund for making this second and final
trespass. It is the measure of Lawrence's own distaste for a life-
denying world that he should impose this nasty quietus on his
alter ego. Lawrence knew all about sexual frustration, and that
suicide is, paradoxically, a symbol of the struggle to bring about
a cleaner state of affairs. At the end of the book Helena still wants
little more than 'rest and warmth', and her new lover Byrne,
another allomorph of Lawrence, is ready to give it. We may guess
that he will give something else first. Meanwhile Siegmund's
violin lies mute, the bow slackened.

In early 1912, a Georgian and no Georgian, Lawrence thought
of taking a trip much further away than the Isle of Wight. It
has been suggested that the new urge to travel represented a

restlessness that was part of the tubercular syndrome, but there was a practical motive. He did not see how he could live on his writing and, barred from teaching under the Board of Education, he considered it might be possible to teach abroad – specifically in Germany. Germany had become a centre of culture and enlightenment for the British as long ago as the period of the Romantic Revival, when writers began to despise their Latin roots and think more highly of their Teutonic. Two more years and all that would change; meanwhile Lawrence saw Germany as full of *Gemütlichkeit* and respect for talent, perhaps even tolerance for the free sexual impulse; moreover, he had a Leicester aunt who had married a Krenkow in Waldbröl on the Rhine: family connections might be a help. But first he consulted his old French teacher, Professor Ernest Weekley, who had academic connections in Germany and had even married a German wife. In April 1912 Lawrence had lunch with the two of them, and his life changed. He fell heavily in love with his hostess and she reciprocated. Siegmund had already met Sieglinde in Jessie, sister and lover but mainly a sister; now he met Brünnhilde.

Brünnhilde was Emma Maria Frieda Johanna, Baroness von Richthofen, daughter of Baron von Richthofen, a Prussian army officer wounded in the Franco-Prussian war and now governor of Metz, today a French town but then part of the Reich. Her mother had been born a Marquier, one of an aristocratic family that had escaped from France during the revolution and settled in the Black Forest. Frieda's cousin was the von Richthofen later to be known as the Red Baron, scourge of the Royal Flying Corps and comic dream villain of the Peanuts cartoons. Frieda was six years older than Lawrence; her husband, Professor Weekley, was a good deal older than his wife and positively patriarchal to his old pupil: his dates – 1865–1954 – show that the marital tragedy which was about to strike did him no lasting harm. For that matter Frieda died at the ripe age of seventy-seven, remarrying at seventy. Contact with Lawrence seemed to promote longevity; himself he could not save.

Frieda's life with the professor, which produced three children, seemed happy enough. Weekley was no dry stick. Remembered among the literary as Lawrence's cuckold, he retains honour among philologists as the author of *The Romance of Words* and *Adjectives and Other Words*, learned but highly readable books which, before the science of linguistics had been launched, helped to promote an interest in language among the merely literary. I was reading him with pleasure while I was looking for *Lady Chatterley's Lover* and had no knowledge of the connection between the two authors: that connection was kept discreetly quiet in the reference books until Weekley's death. It has sometimes been asked why an evidently lively and very unprovincial young German lady of great blonde beauty and emancipated ways should marry a small English academic and be willing to bring up three children in dull Nottingham. Probably the Richthofens, when Weekley met them in Germany, assumed greater social distinction in the rank of a British professor than Britain itself would allow: *professor* has always been a word of disdain in England, whereas in Germany it is still an honorific of high import. Frieda came down in the world when she married Weekley, but she was to sink to the lowest possible social depths when she ran away with a penniless miner's son who was trying to be a writer. She was easy-going and had too much of the natural aristocrat and child of nature in her to have to mount a high horse. She was a great taker of lovers, and such sexual escapades as Nottingham could offer must have filled in pleasantly enough such time as she could spare from looking after her three children and warming Ernest's slippers.

Lawrence told her they had to run away together; and they did. The story of the elopement and the anguish it caused was set down almost immediately by Lawrence in a play entitled *The Fight for Barbara*, in which the author appears as himself, though renamed Wesson, and Frieda has become the daughter of English aristocracy, with Weekley as her distinguished doctor husband pleading his lost cause very eloquently and reviling the proletarian seducer in good round Laurentian terms. The story is more fully told in what amounts to a newly discovered novel, *Mr Noon*, published as late as 1984, though its first half had appeared posthumously in *A Modern Lover* (1934) and then, in 1968, collected in the second volume of miscellanea collectively called *Phoenix*. It was common practice for Lawrence to write half a novel, abandon it, and then pick it up again with no great concern for plausible continuity: when in doubt change your main character's character, though retaining the name, and make him or her start a new life somewhere, preferably in Italy. This happened with both *The Lost Girl* and *Aaron's Rod*.

Lawrence wrote what we may term *Mr Noon 1* as a complete

story, then produced *Mr Noon 2* but left it incomplete. There were good reasons why he did not want *Mr Noon 2* published in his lifetime, and these were mostly to do with the laws of libel. The carbon copy of the typescript of *Mr Noon 1* got to the literary agent Curtis Brown in 1934 and was put into print. *Mr Noon 2* disappeared until 1972, when it was auctioned, along with other Lawrence papers, by Sotheby Parke Bernet, bought by the Humanities Research Center of the University of Texas, and, somewhat belatedly one would have thought, made available for publication fifty years after *Mr Noon 1*. The entity, *Mr Noon* unnumbered, is more than a curiosity. It is, with all its faults – most of them willed, perverse, and very Laurentian – quite entrancing. It is as though *Love's Labour's Won* had been unearthed and found quite as good as *Much Ado About Nothing*.

The Gilbert Noon of Part I seems to be based on a certain George Henry Neville, whom Lawrence knew in Eastwood. He was a schoolmaster and eventually a fellow teacher, but he caused a scandal by having to contract an insufficiently hasty marriage. His child was born less than three months after the wedding, and he had to resign from his post at Amblecote, Stourbridge. Lawrence is less interested in the man himself than in the twin themes of sexual incontinence and provincial sanctimoniousness. His hero is a mathematician and a musician – a highly skilled one, apparently, since he is working on a violin concerto and, in Part II, is assembling the materials for a symphony. Like all provincial young men he spoons, and Lawrence is very informative about spooning. Boys wait for girls after church or chapel on Sunday evenings and then kiss and cuddle them in dark doorways. We do not know whether Lawrence himself did this, but his information seems first-hand. Sometimes the loveplay demands a sequel, and Noon goes the whole hog in the woodshed of the father of a certain Emmy. The father is enraged, reports Gilbert to the governing board of the school where he teaches, and in effect compels his resignation. Reports that Emmy has 'neuralgia of the stomach' get through to Gilbert Noon, who assumes pregnancy. He goes off to Germany to study for a doctorate. Here Part I ends.

It is brilliantly comic, pathetic and very sharp in its observations of provincial mores before the Great War. It will stand, as it once had to, well on its own, but it is minor art. With the addition of Part II, we have something very like a major novel and one of

immense autobiographical interest. For Gilbert Noon is no longer
G. H. Neville but D. H. Lawrence. Noon's name was once funny
and pathetic, rhyming with *spoon* and signifying that its owner
had reached the limit of his provincial possibilities and must
henceforth decline. But Noon in Germany, where Part II begins,
is *nun* or now, and Gilbert becomes a creature of urgent im-
mediacies. He turns into a kind of priapic force who upsets an
aristocratic German family, a subverter of the Teutonic order
which is stiffening itself to destroy Europe.

The story is an almost unembroidered account of the elopement
of Lawrence and Frieda. The whirlwind affair is transferred from
Nottingham to Munich. Johanna von Habenitz, married to an
English academic in Boston, Massachusetts, comes home to
Germany to see her family, insists on sleeping with Noon after a
mere two hours of conversation, and then next morning finds, as
he does, that the world has changed. Her family has to be told
that she proposes to run away with a penniless Englishman, so
the two of them go to Metz, which Lawrence rechristens Detsch,
a place clanking with soldiery and creaking with starched Teutonic pride. Johanna and Gilbert want divorce, which in Germany
will take three years to arrange; the Baron and Baroness revile
the low-born Nottinghamshire seducer, appeal to all the gods of
stability, succeed only in stiffening the resolve of its subverters,
then see their daughter and her lover go off into the night – over
the Austrian Alps into Italy.

Lawrence's descriptive powers are at their finest in Part II. He
captures the atmosphere of a German garrison town, sees into the
gemütlich German soul which is ruining itself with dreams of
order, then takes off into the mountains and forests, recording
everything – which was his special gift – as though recovering
from an illness (which in a sense he always was) and seeing the
natural world as for the first time. Johanna, whom we get to
know physically as well as any heroine in literature, is adorable
but maddening – is, in a word, Frieda. The intimacy between the
bizarrely ill-assorted two is presented candidly but without lu-
bricity. When Lawrence sails off into his harangues to the reader
about sex mysticism he knows in time when to leave off. He is
never without humour or irony.

His technique is cheeky, even insolent. He is always addressing
the dear reader, whom he does not permit to be male, and in no
ingratiating spirit. He is ready sometimes to revile the reader's

presumed prudishness in front of a WC door. His attitude to the
lovebirds is mockingly affectionate. Johanna has slept around; the
sleeping around has led her to Gilbert, but it does not stop with
him. She confesses that she has been 'had' by an American friend
picked up on their Alpine trek. Gilbert forgives her. Lawrence
knows that forgiveness is not in order nor, indeed, is any sympathetic but sorrowful response to what the world calls infidelity.
Gilbert has a lot to learn about women and we watch him
learning. Lawrence is candidly watching his past self.

In terms of a style which Lawrence had, in 1912, still to develop
(Ford Madox Ford would regard it as a jettisoning of even those
minimal artistic traits shown in *The White Peacock*) I have leapt
ahead. Soon, in terms of subject-matter, I shall have to leap back
again to the unemancipated days of his Eastwood youth. For the
moment we must look at Lawrence the transformed man. One
element in his new nature is a large inconsistency which he
nurtured rather than tried to lose. The married Lawrence became
the great sex-prophet who believed in fidelity and, when circumstances enforced it, a fierce chastity (*Lady Chatterley's Lover* is as
much about chastity as amorous abandon): he stood, with an
almost Christian puritanism, for the value of marriage, forgetting
that he had disrupted one matrimonial union. Standing also for
certain 'natural' rights, he scorned Frieda's pining for her children,
whom the very unnatural rigidity of the laws of Britain now
prevented her from seeing. His work shows an intense love of
children, as of all living beings not yet corrupted by civilisation,
but, accepting a childless marriage for himself with equanimity,
he was not prepared to indulge his wife's maternal emotions. He
became intolerant, dogmatic and rather unlikeable.

On the other hand, he had too much natural charm and vitality
to make reservations about his worse side assume much importance. Frieda caught the charm and the lovability early. She
watched him playing with her children in Nottingham, totally
absorbed in floating paper boats to give them pleasure: 'suddenly,'
she records, 'I knew I loved him. He had touched a new tenderness in me.' There is no doubt that, in good Shavian fashion,
it was Frieda who made the decision to run off with him, while
allowing him to carry the manly pride, misgivings and responsibility for the elopement. The elopement took them, as *Mr
Noon* relates, to Munich, the Tyrol, eventually to Lake Garda.
They settled for their first winter in Riva, then an Austrian town.

Here Lawrence had to get down to work, for neither of them had any money. This meant not only writing but the house chores he had learned from his mother and father together, or separately. He scrubbed, cooked, laundered, mended, while Frieda lay in bed smoking a cigarette or demanded to be amused. He was one of those writers rare and admirable in their work habits, demanding neither silence nor seclusion. He never really owned a house so never had the luxury of a book-lined study. He would leave his writing in the middle of a sentence to look at a pie in the oven or rescue Frieda from a Laocoön of wet and tangled bed linen. In finishing *Sons and Lovers*, he had his inner vision on the past, but his outer vision took in a new paradisal world. His first travel book is full of the sunlight of Austria and Italy, despite its title (the publisher's, not his). *Twilight in Italy* shows love spilling over from an ecstatic ménage that was not yet a marriage to encompass the glory, human and natural, of a new life.

As for the old life, he had had enough of it. The writing of *Sons and Lovers* took him back to a sort of Edenic time but reminded him of the huge commercial and industrial machine that was wearing down so many but which he had been lucky enough to escape. A fine line of anti-British vituperation begins in Germany in the summer of 1912. He writes to Edward Garnett:

> Curse the blasted, jelly-boned swines, the slimy, the belly-wriggling invertebrates, the miserable sodding rotters, the flaming sods, the snivelling, dribbling, dithering palsied pulse-less lot that make up England today. They've got white of egg in their veins, and their spunk is that watery it's a marvel they can breed. They *can* nothing but frog-spawn, the gibberers! God, how I hate them! God curse them, funkers, God blast them, wish-wash. Exterminate them, slime ... Why, why and why was I born an Englishman! – my cursed, rotten-boned, pappy-hearted countrymen, *why* was I sent to *them*. Christ on the cross must have hated his countrymen. 'Crucify me, you swine,' he must have said through his teeth. It's not so hard to like thieves also on the cross. But the high priests down there – 'Crucify me, you swine.' – 'Put in your nails and spear, you bloody nasal sour-blooded swine, I laugh last!' God, how I hate them – I nauseate – they stink in sourness.

They deserve it that every great man should drown
himself. But not I (I am a bit great).

This bad temper had a lot to do with Weekley's refusing, for the
moment, to divorce Frieda. It also reflected his failure to force his
fellow-countrymen to read him (*The White Peacock* went into a
second printing but then trickled out of print; his first volume of
poems sold a hundred copies). As for his wishing he had not been
born an Englishman, he did not really mean that. The truth was
that, from his various outposts of exile, he saw it as his duty to
affirm his Englishness and persuade Englishmen to be English in
just his way. Richard Aldington said that he was as English as a
wet Sunday in Hull. In a letter to Edward Garnett's son David,
written three weeks after the one just quoted, and inviting him
to come and stay in Icking bei München, he says: 'It will be
awfully jolly to see you . . . I must explain to you first that I am
living with a lady who is not my wife . . . I look fearfully English,
and so I guess do you, so there is no need for either of us to carry
the Union Jack for recognition.'

'Awfully jolly . . . frightfully English . . . a ripping girl' and so
on. Not only frightfully English but sometimes anxious to
conform to what he saw as genteel English usage, though his
slang was usually a bit out of date. He was also proud to be a
product of the English working class. He was also, as the letter to
Garnett *père* indicates, turning himself into Jesus Christ. One of
the disturbing features of *Twilight in Italy* is his tendency to deliver sermons from the mount in which the symbology of the
religion he had abandoned is distorted into being the vehicle of a
new vague faith of his own. This was a faith of blood and instinct
and somatic consciousness and other imponderables. But Frieda
was always ready to deride his portentousness. She was even ready
to drag him out of the sacred gloom which he brought to the
writing of *Sons and Lovers*, whose working title was *Paul Morel*.
She proposed the addition: 'or, His Mother's Darling'. This did
not please Lawrence.

4
Son and Lover

David Herbert Lawrence was called Bert as a boy; he did not like his first name. For all that he wrote, towards the end of his career, a very fine biblical play entitled *David*, in which he seems to imply a personal identification. The prophet Samuel, annoyed with Saul for not slicing Agag to ribbons, mischievously inverts the succession to Saul's rule and picks on a shepherd lad who slays the Philistine giant and, when a grown man, so desires another man's wife that he arranges for her husband to be killed. He also sings psalms to the harp. One cannot miss the David Herbert here. When Lawrence went off with Frieda he became Lorenzo. But, as this new Lorenzo, writing about his past self, what name was he to give that self? He decided on Paul Morel. Joyce's *A Portrait of the Artist as a Young Man*, which appeared three years after *Sons and Lovers* and is the other great *Bildungsroman* of the epoch, has habituated us to looking for symbolic significance in names. 'Stephen Dedalus' drips with meaning: the first artistic martyr is also the fabulous builder of a labyrinth and the inventor of flight. But one looks in vain for resonance in 'Paul Morel'. *Morel* means black and may have something to do with the hero's diving into the black places of his own soul, but clearly the choice of name derived from Lawrence's snobbishness: he knows the name is French; the coal-miner's family gains a little exotic distinction from it. As for the first name, Paul in the novel is sometimes called 'Postle, but it is no good looking for buried references to the conversion of the Gentile. This novel is very important, but it is not constructed on modernist principles. The modernism lies not in its form but its content.

The content is Lawrence's own youth, the locale Bestwood or Eastwood, the technique is plain as anything in Wells or Bennett. Until, that is, the first of the climactic quarrels between the brutal miner and his refined wife. He shuts her out of the house. She fears the chill of the night, not for herself but for the unborn Paul 'boiling' within her. Then external nature takes over:

> The tall white lilies were reeling in the moonlight, and the air was charged with their perfume, as with a presence. Mrs Morel gasped slightly in fear. She touched the big, pallid flowers on their petals, then shivered. They seemed to be stretching in the moonlight . . . She bent down to look at the binful of yellow pollen; but it only appeared dusky. Then she drank a deep draught of the scent. It almost made her dizzy.
>
> Mrs Morel leaned on the garden gate, looking out, and she lost herself awhile. She did not know what she thought. Except for a slight feeling of sickness, and her consciousness in the child, herself melted out like scent into the shiny, pale air. After a time the child, too, melted with her in the mixing-pot of moonlight, and she rested with the hills and lilies and houses, all swum together in a kind of swoon.

'Herself melted out . . .' We are being told, early in the book and almost casually, of the shakiness of human identity. And where, in *The White Peacock*, flowers and moonlight have a mostly decorative function, they are here being drawn into the drama. There is something else also that is new, and that is the almost hallucinatory exactness of notation. In their next quarrel Morel hurls a table-drawer at his wife, who has the baby Paul in her arms. He hits her forehead and it bleeds.

> He was turning drearily away, when he saw a drop of blood fall from the averted wound into the baby's fragile, glistening hair. Fascinated, he watched the heavy dark drop hang in the glistening cloud, and pull down the gossamer. Another drop fell. It would soak through to the baby's scalp. He watched, fascinated, feeling it soak in; then, finally, his manhood broke.

'His manhood broke': the phrase is epic, and not mock-epic either. We are into a world beneath traditional realism. It owes something to the naturalism of Thomas Hardy, where the gods of nature are interested in men and women as material for torture, but nature in Lawrence is rarely anthropomorphic, and people are damnably free to hurt themselves and each other. There is in him a level at which men and women reach beneath identity. We must take that term 'manhood' seriously.

But the characters have an easy and often humorous commerce with the daily world, drab but never dull. It is a world which, for us, has a piquant historical interest – Morel's medicines, for instance: 'He had hanging in the attic great bunches of dried herbs: wormwood, rue, horehound, elder flowers, parsley-purt, marshmallow, hyssop, dandelion, and centaury. Usually there was a jug of one or other decoction standing on the hob, from which he drank hugely.' These people are the servants of the new industrialism, but they are still doggedly close to the fields and woods which the mines and canals are beginning to despoil. With this background very fully set up, we are ready for the entrance of the young Paul: 'Paul would be built like his mother, slightly and rather small. His fair hair went reddish, and then dark brown; his eyes were grey. He was a pale, quiet child, with eyes that seemed to listen, and with a full, dropping underlip.' Who says he is? Who is the observer? We are up against the narrative problem with which Ford Madox Ford wrestled. *A Portrait of the Artist as a Young Man* solves it by the lyrical method – maintaining the point of view of the central character, whom we never see from the outside. Lawrence does not recognise the problem. Though we remain mostly with his hero, there are sudden rapid cuts to other viewpoints. This is old-fashioned, but it permits a critical approach necessary to Lawrence's method: Paul Morel is too mercurial, exasperatingly shifting in his sentiments, to be entrusted with the entire narrative.

The young Paul touches his apostolic namesake only by burning his sister's doll Arabella as though it were a heathen goddess and praying fervently – for his father either to die or to stop drinking. It is one of the paradoxes of literature that detestable characters tend to engage our sympathy rather more than virtuous ones. Walter Morel is the disruptive force that crashes in, drunk, dirty, selfish, aggressive, at the end of each idyllic day, but he is not really antipathetic. He breaks easily in crisis, he is comically repentant, his dialect is more engaging than the cold English of rebuke that Mrs Morel levels at him. Like Falstaff, he 'grows old' and shuffles out of the picture. But, in his careless

vigour, he represents a principle about which Lawrence always
maintained a strong nostalgia – a rough and beautiful masculinity
which stands out against female domination. Set against him, the
young Paul is seen to yield too easily to the female in himself. He
is also pretentious and a subtler bully than his father. Here he is
with Miriam, at the beginning of what is termed their 'lad-and-
girl love':

> 'Why are you always sad?' he asked her.
>
> 'Sad!' she exclaimed, looking up at him with startled,
> wonderful brown eyes.
>
> 'Yes,' he replied. 'You are always sad.'
>
> 'I am not – oh, not a bit!' she cried.
>
> 'But even your joy is like a flame coming off of sadness,'
> he persisted. 'You're never jolly, or even just all right.'
>
> 'No,' she pondered. 'I wonder – why?'
>
> 'Because you're not; because you're different inside, like a
> pine-tree, and then you flare up; but you're not just like an
> ordinary tree, with fidgety leaves and jolly –'
>
> He got tangled up in his own speech; but she brooded on
> it, and he had a strange roused sensation, as if his feelings
> were new.

Very well; here we have a youth emerging out of his class and
assuming attitudes he does not yet understand. He cannot find a
solidity analogous to that of the miner's butty who is his father.
His mother recognises his pliability and starts to play on it. Of
Miriam she says to herself: 'She is one of those who will want to
suck a man's soul out till he has none of his own left, and he is
such a gaby as to let himself be absorbed. She will never let him
become a man; she never will.' Such words could never be spoken
of her unsatisfactory husband.

The conflict between Mrs Morel and Miriam for the possession
of Paul now begins.

> 'She exults – she exults as she carries him off from me,' Mrs
> Morel cried in her heart when Paul had gone. 'She's not like
> an ordinary woman, who can leave me my share in him.
> She wants to absorb him. She wants to draw him out and
> absorb him till there is nothing left of him, even for himself.
> He will never be a man on his own feet – she will suck him
> up.' So the mother sat, and battled and brooded bitterly.

Soon Lawrence very carefully sets up the erotic scene in which Mrs Morel proclaims her own will to absorb. The sequence begins with the father's washing himself in the scullery:

> He had still a wonderfully young body, muscular, without any fat. His skin was smooth and clear. It might have been the body of a man of twenty-eight, except that there were, perhaps, too many blue scars, like tattoo-marks, where the coal-dust remained under the skin, and that his chest was too hairy.

The wife remembers him as he was:

> 'You've had a constitution like iron,' she said, 'and never a man had a better start, if it was body that counted. You should have seen him as a young man,' she cried suddenly to Paul, drawing herself up to imitate her husband's once handsome bearing.
>
> Morel watched her shyly. He saw again the passion she had had for him. It blazed upon her for a moment. He was shy, rather scared, and humble. Yet again he felt his old glow. And then immediately he felt the ruin he had made during these years. He wanted to bustle about, to run away from it.

After this arousal, we will soon be ready for another. Paul's mother goes out to shop, leaving him to look after the loaves in the oven. Miriam comes in, 'with her dark eyes one flame of love.' Paul does not want this flame and is happier to flirt, in Miriam's presence, with a girl named Beatrice who somewhat arbitrarily enters. She kisses him on the cheek cheekily and he says, 'I s'll kiss thee back, Beat.' Then he remembers the bread, which is burnt. Miriam has come to be given a French lesson, Beatrice leaves, Paul loses his ebullience in shame: 'He only knew she loved him. He was afraid of her love for him. It was too good for him, and he was inadequate. His own love was at fault, not hers.' Love is shunted off into a line of Baudelaire – *'Tu te rappelleras la beauté des caresses.'* Then Paul takes Miriam home. He comes back to find his mother in her rocking-chair, the burnt bread discovered. Paul is rebuked not for his carelessness but for his apparent devotion to Miriam. Paul has to say: 'No, mother – I really don't love her. I talk to her, but I want to come home to you.'

He had taken off his collar and tie, and rose, bare-throated, to go to bed. As he stopped to kiss his mother, she threw her arms round his neck, hid her face on his shoulder, and cried, in a whimpering voice, so unlike her own that he writhed in agony:

'I can't bear it. I could let another woman – but not her. She'd leave me no room, not a bit of room –'

And immediately he hated Miriam bitterly.

'And I've never – you know, Paul – I've never had a husband – not really –'

He stroked his mother's hair, and his mouth was on her throat.

'And she exults so in taking you from me – she's not like ordinary girls.'

'Well, I don't love her, mother,' he murmured, bowing his head and hiding his eyes on her shoulder in misery. His mother kissed him a long, fervent kiss.

'My boy!' she said, in a voice trembling with passionate love.

Was it Jocasta who did the seducing? When Morel comes home, tipsy, he says, 'venomously': 'At your mischief again?' What mischief is he thinking of? He goes to the pantry to steal the wedge of pork pie Mrs Morel has bought for her son and, rebuked, hurls it in the fire. Father and son put up their fists against each other, the mother faints, the scene is over. 'The elderly man began to unlace his boots. He stumbled off to bed. His last fight was fought in that home.' Oedipus has taken possession.

But, needless to say, the year of publication being 1913, this is not a drama of physical incest. Mrs Morel does not see in Miriam a narrowly sexual rival: she and we are concerned with a female possessiveness on both sides which is not easy to define. We are into the darkness now, where words cannot follow. It is a kind of secondary sexuality which the mother arouses in the son: he wants her to be young and smart, able to climb stairs vigorously when he takes her on a trip to Lincoln. But he is also thinking of conducting an affair with the suffragette Clara Dawes, a friend of Miriam's and a married woman estranged from her husband. She is working in the same firm of makers of orthopaedic appliances as Paul himself. We are, as far as the externals are concerned, out

of autobiography now. We need unity of place to allow the
personal drama to stand out: Lawrence does not have his hero
change jobs; the agonies of the classroom will be reserved for *The
Rainbow*. And we do not need to have a Paul who, like his
creator, ambitious to write, might start writing the book that
Lawrence is writing: he might learn to understand too well what
is going on in his soul. Paul is becoming a successful painter and
is even selling his pictures. This justifies his sharpness of eye, which
is so remarkable a feature of the book. His mother learns about
Clara and does not seem to mind too much his contemplation of
an affair:

> She would have been glad now for her son to fall in love
> with some woman who would – she did not know what.
> But he fretted so, got so furious suddenly, and again was
> melancholic. She wished he knew some nice woman – She
> did not know what she wanted, but left it vague. At any
> rate, she was not hostile to the idea of Clara.

No: she has it in only for Miriam. A 'nice woman' would not
have Miriam's dangerous emotional and, for that matter, intellectual depths. Miriam might become the woman she herself
wanted to be and, married to a fellow aesthete and intellectual,
achieve a happier marriage than her own. She will conquer
through gentleness and an appearance of passivity. Paul would
certainly never again be his mother's boy: better for him to spoon
with some ordinary 'nice woman' who could never take his
mother's place. She is very pleasant to Clara when she comes to
tea.

We know who the real-life Miriam was; where did Clara come
from? She is a mixture, owing something to an Eastwood friend,
Alice Dax, a well-known pioneer of feminism. She is beautiful,
blonde, rather heavy in build, a town girl who is, as it were,
pulled towards the earth, while Miriam of the farm yearns
upwards towards the light, the *lux clara*. We cannot help seeing
elements of Frieda's physique in Clara: Frieda, equally beautiful
and blonde, was no sylph. There is no similarity of temperament, but Clara is a married woman whom Paul wins from a
void of sexual indifference induced by her husband, and she is
thirty while Paul is 'going of twenty-three'. It would be absurd
to see anything of Ernest Weekley in the brutal Baxter Dawes,
a poorer version of Paul's father, but Paul's feelings towards

Dawes have been learned from Lawrence's towards the cuckold Weekley:

> There was a feeling of connection between the rival men, more than ever since they had fought. In a way Morel felt guilty towards the other, and more or less responsible. And being in such a state of soul himself, he felt an almost painful nearness to Dawes, who was suffering and despairing, too. Besides, they had met in a naked extremity of hate, and it was a bond. At any rate, the elemental man in each had met.

This sinking beneath identity to the 'elemental' is what Lawrence's books are about. But first identities have to be created. Like Clara's.

We do not know how much of this book was composed during that hard writing winter on Lake Garda. There is only one episode which we can confidently date as belonging to Lawrence's first stage of exile, and that is the scene in the pub where Paul has to appear unlikeable and bumptious, somewhat justifying Dawes's sneers, insults, and eventual physical attack:

> 'The aristocracy,' he continued, 'is really a military institution. Take Germany, now. She's got thousands of aristocrats whose only means of existence is the army. They're deadly poor, and life's deadly slow. So they hope for a war. They look for war as a chance of getting on. Till there's a war they are idle good-for-nothings. When there's a war, they are leaders and commanders. There you are, then – they *want* war!'

We are told that 'he irritated the older men by his assertive manner and his cocksureness.' He irritates the reader too, not for the first time, but Lawrence usually knows what he is doing. He cannot easily resist the puritanism of his upbringing, and Paul is, after all, a snob, a know-all, and a seducer. No character based on the author himself ever imposes his own shaky standards on the world Lawrence presents. That is the measure of his sanity.

This question of Clara's real-life origin is not important. The opposed roles of the dark and the fair woman had become a commonplace in the British novel when Lawrence was writing. The blonde–brunette polarity can be traced back to Madame de Staël's *Corinne*, and its *locus classicus* in the nineteenth-century British novel is *The Mill on the Floss*. The dark Miriam, whose

name, that of the sister of Moses, connotes a kind of Hebraic
prophetic power, an asexual intensity, is a version of Maggie
Tulliver without the tomboyishness, while Clara is a kind of Lucy
Deane brought low. Lawrence, who owes something to George
Eliot, owes nothing to her in the twisted sexual situation which
follows some plain speaking from Clara about Miriam. Paul tells
Clara about his relationship with the other girl:

> '. . . She sort of wants me so much that I can't give
> myself.'
> 'Wants you how?'
> 'Wants the soul out of my body. I can't help shrinking
> back from her.'
> 'And yet you love her?'
> 'No, I don't love her. I never even kiss her.'
> 'Why not?' Clara asked.
> 'I don't know.'
> 'I suppose you're afraid,' she said.
> 'I'm not. Something in me shrinks from her like hell –
> she's so good, when I'm not good.'
> 'How do you know what she is?'
> 'I do! She wants a sort of soul union.'
> 'But how do you know what she wants?'
> 'I've been with her for seven years.'
> 'And you haven't found out the very first thing about
> her.'
> 'What's that?'
> 'That she doesn't want any of your soul communion.
> That's your own imagination. She wants you.'
> He pondered over this. Perhaps he was wrong.
> 'But she seems –' he began.
> 'You've never tried,' she answered.

So now he tries. Miriam 'gives herself'. He is stunned by the
beauty of her nakedness, and he loves her, physically at last, 'to
the last fibre of his being'. But nothing is simple with Paul Morel.
'As he rode home he felt that he was finally initiated. He was a
youth no longer. But why had he the dull pain in his soul? Why
did the thought of death, the after-life, seem so sweet and con-
soling?' Why indeed? There are no easy answers, though the
obvious one is that Paul has defied a sort of incest taboo, since
Miriam has always stood in a sisterly relationship to him: incest,

clearly, has nothing to do with blood. There is also the question of Miriam's passivity, which accepts without welcoming. 'It would come all right if we were married,' she says in excuse. Meanwhile he is learning that sex is not a matter of diving into one's own impersonal darkness: there has to be a joint darkness, in which two people learn to shed identity. Shedding his own turns him into a beast: 'He had always, almost wilfully, to put her out of count, and act from the brute strength of his own feelings. And he could not do it often, and there remained afterwards always the sense of failure and of death.' Marriage would only perpetuate the condition. His eventual rejection of Miriam is vicious, but it startles her out of her passivity. 'She hated her love for him from the moment it grew too strong for her. And, deep down, she had hated him because she loved him and he dominated her.' She snarls at the infant in him, 'which, when it had drunk its fill, throws away and smashes the cup', saying angrily: 'You are a child of four.' To which he replies: 'All right; if I'm a child of four, what do you want me for? I don't want another mother.'

There is little of the mother in Clara, with whom neither possessiveness nor, for that matter, talk about Corot and Verlaine gets in the way of what an unequivocal chapter-heading calls 'passion'. But she refuses to remain a superb object of physical love. Paul discusses her with his mother. He says: 'I think there must be something the matter with me, that I *can't* love. When she's there, as a rule, I *do* love her. Sometimes, when I see her just as *the woman*, I love her, mother; but then, when she talks and criticises, I often don't listen to her . . . I love her better than Miriam. But *why* don't they hold me?' He knows the answer: 'I never shall meet the right woman while you live.'

His mother has not long to live. It was while Lawrence was wrestling on Lake Garda with the remembered agony of his own mother's incurable cancer that Frieda unfeelingly came up with the facetious secondary title 'His Mother's Darling'. We know how he responded, but he was keeping a cold eye on his craft and was able to dissociate himself from his alter ego: the 'mother's darling' gibe had come too late to be appropriate. Lawrence had always, so to speak, a good hand with death, approaching it in terms more Flaubertian than Dickensian. When William, Paul's elder brother, dies from pneumonia and erysipelas, his last words (he has worked in a shipping office) are: 'Owing to a leakage in the hold of this vessel, the sugar had set, and become converted into rock. It needed hacking −' The disease of a cargo serves for his own. Paul decides to hasten his mother's death with an overdose of morphia pills and takes his sister Annie into his confidence. 'They both laughed together like two conspiring children. On top of all their horror flicked this little sanity.' That tone is correct. The murder, or euthanasia, has no origin in the reality of Lawrence's mother's death, but it is managed with superb skill. But, after the death, there is some faltering of tone: 'The weeks passed half-real, not much pain, not much of anything, perhaps a little relief, mostly a *nuit blanche*.' That French touch is absurd in a situation so elemental. Later, in his cold Nottingham lodgings, Paul cries 'Mater!' as though he were Coriolanus. He is broken in himself, but at least he can suggest the mending of Clara's broken marriage. As for Miriam, she visits him, takes his head on her bosom, and proposes that they marry. Does he want it? 'Not much,' he says, with pain. But what he might accept is her saying 'with joy and authority, "Stop all this restlessness and beating against death. You are mine for a mate." She had not the strength. Or was it a mate she wanted? or did she want a Christ in him?' That goes too far, it elevates Paul to a suffering icon for worship. She says she has to go. 'By her tone he knew she was despising him.' We will despise him too, crying 'Mother!', if he is going to end the novel like that. But the last paragraph is exactly right:

> But no, he would not give in. Turning sharply, he walked towards the city's gold phosphorescence. His fists were shut, his mouth set fast. He would not take that direction, to the darkness, to follow her. He walked towards the faintly humming, glowing town, quickly.

Lawrence must have wondered where to place that final adverb. 'He walked quickly,' would have been too decisive. It is right that it should dangle nervously at the end of the sentence.

If, in that bare summary, I have concentrated on one son and lover, I must now let Lawrence's own account of the book justify the plurals of the title − a title it did not yet have when he sent the manuscript to Duckworth from Gargnano on 14 November 1912. Writing to Edward Garnett, he says of the mother:

. . . as her sons grow up she selects them as lovers – first the eldest, then the second. These sons are *urged* into life by their reciprocal love of their mother – urged on and on. But when they come to manhood, they can't love, because their mother is the strongest power in their lives, and holds them . . . as soon as the young men come into contact with women, there's a split. William gives his sex to a fribble, and his mother holds his soul . . . The next son gets a woman who fights for his soul – fights his mother. The son loves the mother – all the sons hate and are jealous of the father. The battle goes on between the mother and the girl, with the son as object. The mother gradually proves stronger, because of the tie of blood. The son decides to leave his soul in the mother's hands, and, like his elder brother, go for passion. He gets passion. Then the split begins to tell again. But, almost unconsciously, the mother realises what is the matter, and begins to die. The son casts off his mistress, attends to his mother dying. He is left in the end naked of everything, with the drift towards death.

He adds: 'It is a great tragedy, and I tell you I have written a great book. It's the tragedy of thousands of young men in England . . . I think it was Ruskin's, and men like him.' And again: 'It's a great novel.'

Lawrence's evaluation is just. When the book was published in May 1913, there were the expected objections to its candour, and certain libraries and shops refused to handle it, but the intelligentsia saw its power and originality, heard a new voice, greeted Lawrence as the coming man. Henry James was, God help him, to place Lawrence 'in the dusty rear', putting his homosexual protégé Hugh Walpole well ahead, but James may well have been frightened by *Sons and Lovers*. It still has the power to frighten less exquisite sensibilities, and the elements of pity and terror almost justify Lawrence's description of it as a tragedy, though there is more of a Sophoclean starkness in his plot-summary than in the florescent, leafy, pullulent book itself. Some intellectuals were delighted by what looked like evidence that the author had read Freud and had written a novel to explicate the Oedipus complex, but Lawrence only heard about the master of 19 Berggasse fairly late – from Frieda, who had a psychoanalyst friend and had done some reading on her own account in, naturally, the original German.

To call *Sons and Lovers* a Freudian novel could mean one of two things – that it contained knowledge of the Oedipus doctrine, which it does not; that, like *Hamlet*, there is a mystery of motivation which only Freud could explain, or Jones, or Ferenczi. But Freud died knowing that every nursemaid, or Eastwood miner's wife, had long known what was to him an epoch-making discovery: that the power of the mother over her sons and daughters entered the forbidden zone of sex, disabling adolescent love and grimly wrecking marriages. There is nothing tragic about it: it is a fact of love (my typewriter decided on that instead of *life*; it seems to know what it is doing), and even, in the mother-in-law joke, a staple of Donald MacGill picture postcards. If, as Lawrence says, 'thousands of young men in England' were sufferers from a filial fixation, how much worse is the situation in matriarchal cultures like the Jewish or Italian or that of Negri Sembilan in Malaysia. In *Sons and Lovers* the fact of love is set out with the intensity of genius, and the mother–son relationship owes its unique power to the nature of the son who is also the author, who is wrecked more because of his sensibility than the voracity of the maternal possessiveness. The novel could not have been written very much later. By the time the Oedipus doctrine was well disseminated it would have been obligatory for the author of such a book to view its content in self-consciously Freudian terms. The greatness of a book does not lie in its theme, only in the treatment of that theme. With his post-factum discovery of Freud, Lawrence's own attitude to his mother should have changed, but it did not. He was still writing elegiac poems about her on his honeymoon. But his immense stroke of luck in finding a woman like Frieda dragged him out of the state of being 'naked of everything, with the drift towards death'. The answer to the Oedipal problem is marriage to a woman like Frieda (or honest adultery waiting on the pleasure of the law). The real tragedy would have been for Paul to marry Miriam, or Lawrence Jessie Chambers.

Here is the last letter Lawrence wrote to his old partner in lad-and-girl love. It was sent from Gargnano in the early spring of 1913:

> I'm sending you the proofs of the novel, I think you ought to see it before it's published. I heard from Ada that you were in digs again. Send the novel on to her when you've

done with it . . . This last year hasn't been all roses for me. I've had my ups and downs out here with Frieda. But we mean to marry as soon as the divorce is through. We shall settle down quite quietly somewhere, probably in Berkshire. Frieda and I discuss you endlessly. We should like you to come out to us some time, if you would care to. But we are leaving here in about a week, it's getting too hot for us, I mean the weather, not the place. I must leave off now, they're waiting for me . . .

According to Jessie's own memoir of Lawrence, this letter 'suffocated' her. She sent it back to him without comment.

5
Coming Through

Lawrence, as that letter to Jessie shows, was no respecter of feelings. He was also arrogant, dogmatic, messianic, inconsistent; yet he was lovable. The self-portrait in *Sons and Lovers* allows no concessions to the conventional view of a fictional hero; in this respect Lawrence is close to the Joyce of *Ulysses*, who makes his autobiographical Stephen Dedalus sneer, pick his nose, refuse to take a bath, snub Leopold Bloom, show off his learning, and generally behave like the unlicked whelp he is. Paul Morel does not catch a louse from behind his collar, but there is enough uncleanliness in his inner life to render him detestable. He may be a good son but he is a wretched lover. His author is displaying a kind of honesty new in fiction, and he is warning the reader, as Joyce was to do a few years later, that there is no obligation to like a central character: what is important is the discipline of loving him. We love *malgrado*, *malgré*, *trotz* (as the new polyglot Lawrence would put it, showing off), in spite of. We have to love Paul, while excoriating him for his damnable treatment of Miriam, because of his poor forked nakedness. The important thing to remember about his author is that he knew his own faults and bore no ill will to anyone who flung them at him. He had no pious preconceptions about what a human personality ought to be like. Faults were the spume of identity; reality lay deeper.

Lawrence, in the two fantastic philosophico-psychologico-moralistic books he published after the Great War – *Psychoanalysis and the Unconscious* and *Fantasia of the Unconscious* – stressed a well-known truth – that the child may be the sum of the parental genes but his individuality comes from nowhere. Neither Lawrence's mother nor father made the great writer, but the great writer could not deny that he was a combination of his mother's fastidiousness and his father's aggressiveness. He was also a product of his environment. Members of the bourgeoisie do not scream at each other and throw saucepans, as did the old working class: their aggressions are tamed by upbringing and purged in school games. Lawrence was no games-player, and a traditional upbringing in a collier's hovel was not concerned with the hiding of emotions. But a small domestic space and a large family do not conduce to the bearing of grudges. In a middle-class home a first-class row can be stilled by one of the participants leaving the room and maintaining a long coldness. There could be none of that in a miner's family. A great purgative rage would be followed by manifestations of undying love. Lawrence brought this pattern into his life with Frieda; Frieda, being an aristocrat and not a bourgeoise, understood it better than, say, Katherine Mansfield would have done. A working-class boy should always marry into the aristocracy and preferably a foreign one. The middle-class English are cool and have taught restraint to their own traditional rulers. In a Silesian or a Tuscan good family there is, or was, no buffer between the life of an uninhibited peasantry, which lay all around, and a whip-cracking bottle-emptying class of *rentiers*. Lawrence did not marry into respectability, which is a middle-class invention.

The aggressiveness which forbade either Lawrence's or his father's taking a back seat manifested itself, in the young Bert as in the mature Lorenzo, in a desire for taking charge of things. Bert Lawrence led childhood excursions into the countryside, organised the commissariat, marched the weary party to the nearest railway station. He took charge of Christmas games and was the creative bullying force in charades. Lawrence never lost his love of charades. Having no strong belief in the solidity of human identities, he could act, mimic, turn himself into a frog or fish. Some of his animal poems are a kind of charade, in which he boasts an inner understanding of what no human soul can ever hope to understand – the inner sadness of a donkey or the water-honey blood of a trout. He would say, in effect, 'This is the way things are: I *know*', and no one could contradict him. If anyone dared, he would lose interest in his own thesis. He did not understand rational argument, or even wish to: it was a kind of weak concession to reality, which had to be approached through visceral conviction and not the pale reductions of ratiocination.

To be the dominant partner in his life with Frieda was something he had inherited from the Eastwood tradition in which the breadwinner was literally called 't'master', but he had his own heaven-given propensity to bully, which was intensified by Frieda's unwillingness to be bullied and her zest in fighting back. This was fascinating, and it had to be encouraged by more bullying. Too many other women were inclined to submit and worship, like the Jessie Chambers whom Frieda was supposed to be so anxious to meet. There were, in fact, only three women in the whole of Lawrence's life who would stand no nonsense and hence earned his undying respect. They were all mothers – his own, Frieda's, Frieda herself. Frieda's mother, inheritrix of two aristocratic traditions which combined in detestation of the *canaille*, began by treating him as the unwashed whippersnapper who had dragged her daughter down to the level of a *Kellnerin* or barmaid (she was too aristocratic to conceive of anything lower). He appreciated this. Later she learned to love him, as nearly everybody did, but love was best preceded by a damned hard kick on the *Arsch*.

This propensity to take charge, to bully, or merely to be cocky in the manner of his father, becomes important with the publication of *Sons and Lovers* and its warm reception in the ranks of the British intellectual middle class. He now came into contact with a number of people who, being his social superiors, would have to submit to the cycle of Laurentian amicality – ingratiating and deferential charm; bullying for a good they could not usually see; bitter rejection with the coda of satirical eternisation in whatever novel he happened to be writing. Some of these new acquaintances were distinguished – the Honourable Herbert ('Beb') Asquith and his wife, Lady Cynthia; E. M. Forster, the great if unproductive novelist; Lord Glenavy, who became the Director of the Bank of Ireland; Dikran Kouyoumdjian, who changed his name to Michael Arlen and wrote *The Green Hat*, thus virtually creating Mayfair; Amy Lowell, the American poetess who persuaded the poet Lawrence that he was an Imagist; Sir Edward Marsh, editor of the *Georgian Poetry* anthologies, who persuaded the poet Lawrence that he was a Georgian; John Middleton Murry the literary critic and Katherine Mansfield the New

Zealand short story writer, at first Murry's mistress, later his wife;
Lady Ottoline Morrell, a noted hostess and lover of artists, whose
Oxfordshire home Garsington was a refuge for such of them as
were directed to agricultural labour during the Great War; Philip
Heseltine the composer and his composer–musicologist friend
Cecil Gray; Bertrand Russell, philosopher and pacifist, later to
be Lord Russell. There was also Samuel Solomonovich Koteliansky, whom Lawrence called 'Kot', an expatriate from Kiev
who translated Russian literature into English. Lawrence, still
with much of the Croydon schoolmaster in him, would 'touch
up' the translations. ('Touching up' other people's work was a
hobby that later resulted in a novel called *The Boy in the Bush*,
written by M. L. Skinner but so thoroughly Laurentianised as to
have got into the Lawrence canon.) With 'Kot' he rarely quarrelled, since he was a foreigner.

Lawrence met some of these people when he and Frieda paid
a visit to England in the summer of 1913. The volume *Love
Poems and Others* had been published in the February, *Sons and
Lovers* in May, so he took with him a double reputation. From
Broadstairs, Kent, in July he demonstrated his fawning skill in
a letter to Edward Marsh: 'What joy to receive £3 out of the
sweet heavens! I call that manna. I suppose you're the manipu-
lating Jehovah. I'll sing you a little *Te Deum*. I wish you had
the publishing of one's work – soon I should have a fur-lined
coat.' He knew that Marsh knew little about poetry. He also
showed his generosity, which was considerable when it came to
non-aesthetic or non-pseudo-philosophical matters, by offering
to lend Middleton Murry five pounds so he could come to
Broadstairs. There was a friendship growing there, soon to
ripen, later to decay. But the Lawrences had not been driven
to England to make friends: Frieda was desperately anxious to
see her children, which could not be done legally. Instructions
had been given to the son Monty that 'he was not to talk to
people who came to the school to see him'. Lawrence wrote
to Garnett: 'Weekley is an unutterable fool. He wrote the most
hideous letter to the Frau Baronin – is altogether acting the
maniacal part of the "*mari trompé*".' So, frustrated, Frieda
wanted to go home to Germany. 'We are settled down again
here now. Frieda is getting better of her trouble about the children, for the time being, at least.' That qualification is important: Frieda never got over her trouble. Lawrence wanted

her to be his wife, not the mother of somebody else's children. That was the primary cause of the dissension between them.

During the war Lawrence published a volume of verse entitled *Look! We Have Come Through!* This is the most felicitous of all his titles, and it is attached to a poem-cycle which tells a story. It is a kind of novel in which surface identities defer to heroic generalities, but it is full of sharp observation, emotions that touch deep despair and ecstatic exaltation, and it is about Lawrence and Frieda. Here is the 'Argument':

> After much struggling and loss in love and in the world of men, the protagonist throws in his lot with a woman who is already married. Together they go into another country, she perforce leaving her children behind. The conflict of love and hate goes on between the man and the woman, and between these two and the world around them, till it reaches some sort of conclusion, they transcend into some condition of blessedness.

In a long free verse effusion written at Beuerberg, the man calls the woman 'Lot's wife!':

> The pillar of salt, the whirling, horrible column of salt, like
>   a waterspout
> That has enveloped me!
> Snow of salt, white, burning, eating salt
> In which I have writhed.

Frieda has dared to look back to England, where her children are, and, in the wonderful illogicality of poetry, has to be identified with another woman who looked back. Lot's wife was turned into a static pillar of salt, leaving Lot free to trek on and be seduced by his daughters, but Lawrence has to suffer from a saline whirlpool which hurts him more than it hurts Frieda. And even the term 'wife' is to be wrested from her:

> Lot's Wife! – Not wife, but Mother.
> I have learned to curse your motherhood,
> You pillar of salt accursed.
> I have cursed motherhood because of you,
> Accursed, base motherhood!

Only, presumably, his own mother was to be permitted motherhood. On Lake Garda, schooled by Frieda in the Oedipus complex, he can write, necrophilously, like this:

> To you, my little darling,
> To you, out of Italy,
> For what is loveliness, my love,
> Save you have it with me!

He is still an unsatisfactory lover, and not willing to concede that his situation is precisely that of Frieda – an unwillingness to kill the past. But Frieda's concern is at least with the living.

He is not always self-righteous:

> Since you have passion for me,
> as I for you,
> does not that passion stand in your way like a Balaam's ass
> and am I not Balaam's ass
> golden-mouthed occasionally?
> But mostly, do you not detest my bray?

It is clearly, as Lawrence reminds us in this sequence, one of the tasks of poetry to record moods, even dangerous ones. Some of the moods here are very dangerous:

> For I am quite indifferent
> To your dubious state,
> As to whether you've found a fortune
> In me, or a flea-bitten fate.
>
> Make a good investigation
> Of all that is there,
> And then, if it's worth it, be grateful –
> If not, then despair.

But the lovers come through the slough of despond and the valley of darkness, though physical ecstasy is delayed ('The night was a failure/but why not – ?') and the man has some damnable reluctance to being physically wanted:

> 'Don't touch me and appreciate me.
> It is an infamy.
> You would think twice before you touched a weasel on a fence
> as it lifts its straight white throat.'

Lawrence is, to use Saul Bellow's term, a *noli me tangerine*. A kind of pride in his body resists its becoming a mere instrument of pleasure. When he comes through it is in the spirit of Donne touching America in his mistress, but with less humour, more pretension:

> My God, but I can only say
> I touch, I feel the unknown!
> I am the first comer!
> Cortes, Pisarro, Columbus, Cabot, they are nothing, nothing!
> I am the first comer!
> I am the discoverer!
> I have found the other world!

We have to take that last line seriously. It was otherness Lawrence was after. In the act of physical love he was able to shed the obsessions of a powerful ego that could not be subdued by the exercise of the will. If a saint could subdue selfhood through meditation, prayer, flagellation, the new Laurentian man was to find the holy vision and the divine peace through the body of the beloved. He never glorified sex as an impersonal pleasure, and he was far above the middle-class Englishman's sniggering about 'indoor games'. The love of a person was to be expressed in a fusion that dissolved both persons involved. Frieda and Lawrence are woman and man, or it may be the other way round.

> The Lord of Hosts and the Devil
> Are left on Eternity's level
> Field, and as victors we travel
> To Eden home.
>
> Back beyond good and evil
> Return we. Even dishevel
> Your hair for the bliss-drenched revel
> On our primal loam.

The body of the loved one can be frankly glorified as she takes her morning bath:

> She spreads the bath-cloth underneath the window
> And the sunbeams catch her
> Glistening white on the shoulders,
> While down her sides the mellow
> Golden shadow glows as
> She stoops to the sponge, and her swung breasts
> Sway like full-blown yellow
> Gloire de Dijon roses.

And, with the coming of spring, things come right for ever, and
the poet relaxes into being Bert Lawrence:

> It is gorgeous to live and forget
> And to feel quite new.
> See the bird in the flowers? – he's making
>   A rare to-do!
>
> He thinks the whole blue sky
> Is much less than the bit of blue egg
> He's got in his nest – we'll be happy,
>   You and I, I and you.
>
> With nothing to fight any more –
> In each other, at least.
> See, how gorgeous the world is
>   Outside the door!

I have had difficulty in copying out those lines because of the
tears. The response to poetry, so A. E. Housman said, should
always be physical – whiskers bristling to impede the razor, a
shudder down the spine, a tightening of the scrotum, tears. It is
not necessarily the most elevated poetry that produces these
effects, but they have to be respected more than mere cerebral
responses. I cry in reading those lines because they express the
simplest desires on earth – to live, to love, to be happy. They are
desires generally thwarted.

I can never understand why *Look! We Have Come Through!*
did not make a larger impact on the poetry-reading world of the
teens and twenties. Much of it is, by the stern standards of T. S.
Eliot, clumsily composed, but much of it too is as modern as *The
Waste Land*, though less allusive: Lawrence's southern Europe does
not come out of books. A poetic sequence which celebrates the
triumph of love presumably embarrassed a public more at home
with drying combinations and a river sweating oil and tar. In the
Victorian age *An Angel in the House* and its obverse, *Modern Love*,
were not regarded as being in the best of taste, and the Georgians
must have been shy of Lawrence's parade of sexual love and hate.
He describes female breasts many times too, and not in a nutritive
context. He does not go so far as to admit the existence of pubic
hair (the discovery of which, and not his mother's dominance,
made Ruskin demented), but we cannot doubt that there is naked

love-making going on. What the sequence celebrates is modern love and an angel in the house, this angel being, as Brangwen explains in *The Rainbow*, a new sort of entity made up of man and woman.

In the autumn of 1913 this angel was settled in Lerici, where the poet Shelley had drowned, and half of it was hard at work, chiefly on short stories and plays, to say nothing of housework. Pagan love had its puritanical counterpart, which was expressed in scrubbing floors and cooking. Frieda did nothing except be herself, namely, apart from the *mater dolorosa*, a beautiful pagan. She watched Lawrence tie his braces round his waist and wield the scrubbing brush. 'Lord, to see the dark floor flushing crimson, the dawn of deep red bricks rise from out this night of filth, was enough to make one burst forth into hymns and psalms.' So writes Lawrence to Lady Cynthia, demoting her to 'Mrs Asquith'. He was, in a way, educating her. Sometime in that autumn Lawrence managed to get as far as the three hundred and fortieth manuscript page of a new novel – provisionally entitled *The Sisters*. This, when finished, was to be separated out into *The Rainbow* and *Women in Love*.

In July 1914 Lawrence and Frieda were in London. The divorce had gone through and, on the 13th, they were married at the South Kensington Registry Office. A couple of weeks later the Great War erupted and they were trapped in England. A four-year nightmare began for many people, and a nightmare not so prolonged for those who died in the Europe from which the Lawrences felt exiled. In nobody did the nightmare bite so sharply as in Lawrence. What comes next is very painful to write.

6

Dementia

Several times during the Great War Lawrence felt he was going mad. To those who served in it, which Lawrence never did and never could, that must have seemed like an intellectual luxury: to have to face the daily squalor and inanity of service life and the risk of being blown to pieces in Flanders was, in a sense, a safeguard against thinking too much and contemplating with horror the destruction of civilisation. But Lawrence could stand far enough back from the mass suicide to see it as a demented defection from a great salvatory principle, the one implied in his poems and novels: man belonged to the cosmos and was fulfilled through his natural instincts, of which love was the greatest; he had used reason to erect a vast mechanical complex which was now destroying him. War was the natural outcome of aggressive industrialism; technology was presented as a mode of human fulfilment but always turned into a device of destruction. These notions are commonplace now, but poets and visionaries were needed in those days to warn mankind about the futility of war, any war. If Lawrence sometimes seems to be writing like a madman from his retreat in Chesham, Buckinghamshire, it is because he was, in a sort of desperation, trying to hammer together a philosophy which might bring men and their governments to their senses, and the philosophy was, Lawrence being what he was, based not on reason but visceral conviction. This bred a kind of wild prophet whom nobody would listen to, and frustration made the prophecies even wilder. Lawrence fell into that dangerous trap which always awaits poets of his kind.

'Poets are the trumpets that sing to battle,' Shelley wrote. 'Poets are the unacknowledged legislators of the world.' That is nonsense and always was, but too many poets believe it. Ezra Pound believed it, ranting on Rome radio. Lawrence believed it.

He had to keep on with his trade of writing in order to earn a living, since prophets cannot eat air, but it proved dangerous for him to attempt anything outside the field of fiction. Fiction, with its characters locked into a plot and its concern with the down-to-earth, stopped Lawrence from philosophising overmuch, but once he started to write a book on a fellow-novelist, Thomas Hardy, he allowed ideas to breed, and ideas begot more ideas, and Hardy was soon left far behind. A publisher of a book on Hardy had a right to expect its author to keep to his subject, which Lawrence was too distracted or demented to do. The book was unpublishable, as Lawrence saw, and what he wrote of it came out posthumously in the collection of his fugitive writings called *Phoenix*. It is Lawrence writing prose of extreme beauty but making little sense. To write an unpublishable book was no way to earn a living. There was not merely the need to pay the rent and the grocery bills but the business of finding £150 to settle the divorce lawyer's fees. His inability or unwillingness to pay for Frieda's release from Weekley's toils resulted in his being declared bankrupt. That was an augury of the poverty he was to endure for the next four years.

One of the virtues of Ford Madox Ford's *Parade's End* is its power to remind us that a great war does not, except with a bomb, liquidate our private lives. Private agonies seem nothing against the background of burning cities and cadavers in no-man's-land, but they do not lose their capacity to agonise. So Frieda's agony over her children went on. Lawrence, in a letter to Amy Lowell, tried to distance himself from that agony in well-wrought dialogue. Frieda is Frieda and Weekley the Quondam Husband:

> Frieda: I came to see you about the children.
> Quondam Husband: Aren't you ashamed to show your face where you are known? Isn't the commonest prostitute better than you?
> Frieda: Oh no.
> Quon. Husb.: Do you want to drive me off the face of the earth, Woman? Is there no place where I can have peace?
> Frieda: You see I must speak to you about the children.

> Quon. Husb.: You shall *not* have them – they don't want to
> see you . . . If you had to go away, why didn't you go
> away with a *gentleman*? . . . Don't you know you are the
> vilest creature on earth? . . . Don't you know, my soli-
> citors have instructions to arrest you, if you attempt to
> interfere with the children?
> Frieda: I don't care.

Lawrence could philosophise and prophesy, but Frieda had to
face her suffering with little comfort from the husband who had
written about Lot's wife. Moreover, Frieda was a German sur-
rounded by rabid British patriots quite ready to immolate Henry
James's dachshund Max. Meanwhile Lawrence preached:

> I believe there is no getting of a vision . . . before we get our
> sex right: before we get our souls fertilised by the *female*. I
> don't mean the feminine: I mean the female. Because life
> tends to take two streams, male and female, and only some
> female influence (not necessarily woman, but most obviously
> woman) can fertilise the soul of man to vision or being.
> Then the vision we're after, I don't know what it is – but it
> is something that contains awe and dread and submission,
> not pride or sensuous egotism and assertion . . . We want to
> realise the tremendous *non-human* quality of life – it is
> wonderful.

So it is. But these words, from a letter to Gordon Campbell or
Lord Glenavy (as he became), had to ring with a large irrelevance.
There was a war on.

There was a kind of cashing in on the war with the publication
of a volume of Lawrence's short stories in December 1914. The
title, *The Prussian Officer*, is the title of the most memorable, and
most topical-seeming, story in the collection. It deals with the
instinctive enmity between a German infantry captain and his
orderly, resolved by the orderly's killing his officer and eventually
dying himself. It is a brilliant piece of writing, evocative of
the southern Germany that Lawrence knew and suggesting an
inside knowledge of German army life more appropriate to Erich
von Remarque than the tubercular miner's son from Nottinghamshire. Lawrence had a great capacity to see into things, to
guess and be proved right. The story is disturbing not because it
shows military brutality (which the British naturally liked to

believe was monopolised by the German enemy), but because of its very Laurentian ability to dig to a level below identity, in which nerves and instincts and unconscious forces drive men, even Prussian officers, into directions unmapped by the conscious mind. There is a hint of homosexuality turned rotten, an obsession with the male body, a sense of elements at work which must have made Lawrence's readers uncomfortable. It was not the kind of story to publish in wartime, when issues were becoming over-simplified and literature meant Rupert Brooke's sonnets, and there was talk of suppressing the volume, though this came to nothing.

A story of the following year, 'England, My England', is worth considering in the context of Lawrence's outstanding talent for always saying the uncomfortable thing. The germ of the story was the death of Lady Cynthia Asquith's brother at the front, but the narrative of a decent Englishman, so Anglo-Saxon as to carry the name Egbert, who loves his country deeply, as Lawrence did, and yet is unhappy about fighting for it, could not easily be interpreted as part of the literary war-effort. Here are two sub-versive paragraphs:

> . . . When the war broke out his whole instinct was against it. He had not the faintest desire to overcome any foreigners or to help in their death. He had no conception of Imperial England, and Rule Britannia was just a joke to him. He was a pure-blooded Englishman, perfect in his race, and when he was truly himself he could no more have been aggressive on the score of his Englishness than a rose can be aggressive on the score of its rosiness.
>
> No, he had no desire to defy Germany and to exalt England. The distinction between German and English was not for him the distinction between good and bad. It was the distinction between blue water-flowers and red or white bush-blossoms: just difference. The difference between the wild boar and the wild bear. And a man was good or bad according to his nature, not according to his nationality.

True but dangerous words. There are some who are convinced that the persecution of Lawrence during the war and after had more to do with his rejection of that war's spurious justice than the alleged immorality of *The Rainbow* (to which we shall come in good time). What his patriotic readers missed, of course, was the central truth of a story like 'England, My England', which had more to do with Lawrence and Frieda than with Lawrence and bigger, public issues. Egbert in the story duly goes off to die, because he has been told this is the right thing to do, but his death is a way out of an impaired marriage: his wife has turned into a mother, specifically a *mater dolorosa* after an injury to her child which Egbert's carelessness has probably caused, and the husband has the taste of salt in his mouth. In the same way 'The Prussian Officer' is about something profounder than the behaviour of a captain to his orderly.

Lawrence could be a very fine writer of short stories which must be termed, in the *Saturday Evening Post* sense, uncommercial. They do not have the superficial slickness of Scott Fitzgerald's contributions to that august and high-paying journal. While Fitzgerald wrote for money, aware that he had become an 'old whore', Lawrence tried to work out some of the themes in a small space which he expatiated on, often in a sprawling fashion, in the novels. They are serious art, and the limits set by the form were a curb on Lawrence's prolixity. *Sufflaminandus erat*, as Ben Jonson said of Shakespeare, and the short-story shape sufflaminated his fellow-Midlander. Never having succeeded in the genre myself, I am inclined to think that the short story is usually a waste of a good novel: by the time the setting and the characters have been set up, it is almost time to leave them. There are many who do not hold this view and, as far as Lawrence is concerned, believe that he did his best work in the form. This, to me, is like preferring Beethoven's bagatelles to his sonatas.

In 1915, Lawrence and Frieda lived in a cottage lent them by Viola Meynell, daughter of the poet Alice Meynell ('She walks, the lady of my delight,/A shepherdess of sheep': what else could she be a shepherdess of?). This brought them near to Lady Ottoline Morrell, which meant meeting Bertrand Russell. Lawrence, apart from rewriting his long novel and deciding to divide it into two, began to express two opposed ideas, expanded into manifestos. He wanted to establish a colony of like-minded souls, of which he should be the leader. He wrote fervently to Lady Ottoline about this:

> I want you to form the nucleus of a new community which shall start a new life amongst us – a life in which the only riches is integrity of character. So that each one may

fulfil his own nature and deep desires to the utmost, but wherein tho', the ultimate satisfaction and joy is in the completeness of us all as one. Let us be good all together, instead of just in the privacy of our chambers, let us know that the intrinsic part of all of us is the best part, the believing part, the passionate, generous part. We can all come croppers, but what does it matter? We can laugh at each other, and dislike each other, but the good remains and we know it.

Nothing would be more certain than the dislike, but, for Lawrence, the charm of the enterprise would consist in slapping people's heads and treating them as fractious children who must be reconciled in love of the head of the household. It would be Lawrence having his own way more successfully than seemed possible with fiery Frieda. The name of the visionary community was to come from Koteliansky, 'who groaned Hebrew music – *Ranani Sadekim Badanoi*'. Rananim, the society of friends, survives as a name on the gate of a cottage in Cornwall; it proved, inevitably, a lost cause.

The other project, no less visionary, was a reform of British society and, by extension, the whole world. He wrote long and earnest letters about this to Bertrand Russell, whom he even visited at Cambridge ('Cambridge made me very black and down. I cannot bear its smell of rottenness, marsh-stagnancy. I get a melancholic malaria. How can so sick people rise up? They must die first.' He was often very glib about people dying). The letters nag unmercifully:

> Can't you see the whole state is collapsing. Look at the Welsh strike. The war is going to develop into the last great war between labour and capital. It will be a ghastly chaos of destruction, if it is left to Labour to be constructive. The fight must immediately be given a higher aim than the triumph of Labour to be constructive ... or we shall have another French Revolution. The deadly Hydra now is the hydra of Equality. Liberty, Equality and Fraternity is the three-fanged serpent. You must get this into your lectures, at once. You are too old-fashioned. The back of the serpent is already broken.

And again:

I rather hated your letter, and am terrified of what you are putting in your lectures. I don't want tyrants. But I don't believe in democratic control. I think the working man is fit to elect governors or overseers for his immediate circumstances, but for no more. You must utterly revise the electorate. The working man shall elect superiors for the things that concern him immediately, no more. From the other classes, as they rise, shall be elected the higher governors. The thing must culminate in one real head, as every organic thing must – no foolish republics with foolish presidents, but an elected King, something like Julius Caesar. And as the men elect and govern the industrial side of life, so the women must elect and govern the domestic side. And there must be a rising rank of women governors, as of men, culminating in a woman Dictator, of equal authority with the supreme Man.

Russell was later to denounce Lawrence as a fascist – safely, posthumously. Lawrence hurt him badly:

I believe in your inherent power for realising the truth. But I don't believe in your will, not for a second. Your will is false and cruel. You are too full of devilish repressions to be anything but lustful and cruel . . . The enemy of mankind, you are, full of the lust of enmity. It is *not* the hatred of falsehood which inspires you. It is the hatred of people, of flesh and blood. It is a perverted mental blood-lust. Why don't you own it.

Let us become strangers again, I think it is better.

So much for Lawrence's treatment of the most brilliant philosophical mind of the age. Lawrence does not come well out of any of this utopian phase of his life (mega- and micro-). It is absurd of him to suppose that his gifts as a poet and novelist qualify him to deliver blueprints for perfect societies, in which King Lorenzo and presumably Königin Frieda are to preside over a Blakean Jerusalem (a release of the senses and the imagination) equipped with a socialist bureaucracy looking after nationalised industries. Fortunately the dream did not last. Unfortunately it was dispelled by an event that threatened not Lawrence's future as a remaker of society but his future as a writer.

This was the suppression of *The Rainbow* after its prosecution on the charge of obscenity by the Public Morality Council or, as Richard Aldington puts it, 'one of its jackals'. Lawrence had worked hard on this book. In February 1914 he said that he was starting to rewrite it 'for about the seventh time'. The final version was not completed until a year later and publication took place on 30 September 1915. On 5 October the *Daily News* reviewed it under the headline THE DOWNFALL and described it as a 'monotonous wilderness of phallicism'. The author of the review was Robert Lynd, who loved Charles Lamb and wrote for *Punch*. It was read by Clement Shorter and James Douglas (who, as we have noted, was still fighting for literary purity in the thirties): these eagerly sought dirt in the book, found it, and published brief notices which confirmed Lynd's imputation of obscenity. They roused the puritan activists, and the book went to trial in a police court. No defence was presented by the publisher, Methuen, who excused himself as a mere commercial exploiter of the printed word who did not quite realise how far he was corrupting the public. A prosecution witness, Mr Muskett, fired shots to the effect that *The Rainbow* was 'a mass of obscenity of thought, idea and action throughout, wrapped up in a language which he supposed would be regarded in some quarters as an artistic and intellectual effort'. No mitigation of this opinion was permitted by an artist or intellectual, a defence based on aesthetic merit not being admissible under British Law. Certainly Lawrence himself was not called on to give a horse's mouth account of what devil had driven him to wasting years of sweat, ink and paper on a pernicious production. The publisher meekly apologised, withdrew the book from sale, and agreed to its destruction. The magistrate, a Mr Dickinson, regretted that Methuen had been 'soiled by the publication of this work', ordered its burning or pulping, and imposed a fine of ten guineas. Nobody regretted the disaster this meant to the author, who lost his copyright, had to return his advance, was publicly stigmatised as an obscene writer with no chance of a rebuttal, and effectively was prevented from publishing anything under his own name until the war was over and lesser obscenities forgiven.

The suppression of *The Rainbow* meant that its sequel, *Women in Love*, could not be published until after the war, giving the reader the erroneous impression that it is a post-war novel. When Ken Russell made a film of the book in the seventies, he set it firmly in the twenties, complete with cloche hats, short skirts and

'I'm Forever Blowing Bubbles'. We have the impression that, after a debilitating war, its young survivors, 'fagged and near the thirties' (as H. G. Wells puts it in *Christina Alberta's Father*), are trying to make a new life appropriate to a new age. The book is timeless enough to survive the reader's misapprehension, but it was not permitted to make the impact that would have been so salutary for wartime intellectual Britain, to say nothing of those friends of Lawrence's who had now become enemies and were punished by highly satirical treatment in the work itself. The failure of Lawrence's friends and disciples to stand by him during and after the suppression of *The Rainbow* soured him somewhat. Indeed, the whole literary establishment comes badly out of the affair. Arnold Bennett, who had already anonymously sent the penurious Lawrence £40, gamely protested, as he was to do some years later over the persecution of *Ulysses*, but the Society of Authors did nothing. Philip Morrell MP, Lady Ottoline's husband, asked a question in Parliament and received no answer: after all, there was a war on. Appeal to a higher court or libel actions against the calumniating journalists was, to a man without money, out of the question. Lawrence let the matter drop, saying: 'I am not very much moved: am beyond that by now. I only curse them all, body and soul, root, branch and leaf, to eternal damnation.' That 'all' included friends as well as enemies; the 'only' implies a talent for anathematisation so rich that he can afford to curse with a minimum of breath. There were bigger things to think about.

When we read *The Rainbow* now, we not only see nothing even faintly offensive in it, but we wonder how, on its first publication, it could conceivably have shocked anyone except the sexual pervert. There is, true, sexual passion in it, but this is wholesomely protected by holy matrimony. The novel is a paean to marriage, and one of the titles considered and dropped was *The Wedding Ring*. That title might have made matters worse, implying that the horrors of the joys of the brothel had been transferred to prim, if rural, British households. But Lawrence was seriously attempting to show how the ethos of marriage was sustained during the Victorian and Edwardian periods and, in the modern age, encountered difficulties. He takes a family, the Brangwens, who keep a farm on the borders of Derbyshire and Nottinghamshire, and presents their life. That lyrical paragraph already cited, the one set for 'practical criticism' when I was a student, is of such poetic beauty that any sensible critic should have seen in it a guarantee of literary seriousness not to be confused with pornographic titillation. The pages that follow, summing up the hierarchy of rural life, the work and the aspirations, could even – if the critic did not particularly want literature – be accepted as admirable social history.

The first marriage presented is that of Tom Brangwen, a prosperous farmer who falls in love with a Polish widow who has settled in the district and lives at the vicarage. Here there is a Lawrence–Frieda situation, since Tom is drawn into both exogamy and hypergamy. Anna Lensky is of a superior class to his own, as he recognises. She is also six years older than Brangwen, and she has a daughter by her previous marriage. Brangwen accepts the girl into his household, and it is as though Lawrence is trying out possible sensations when, as a married man with Anna in his bed, he has the child looking at Tom coldly and telling him to go away. What Lawrence's response would have been to a child of Frieda's so treating him we can only guess. Tom Brangwen is tolerant, good-humoured, even loving. The development of the relationship between him and the stepchild Anna is beautifully presented, and it has a humour, affection and compassion which should have softened the heart even of a James Douglas. But cause for puritanical censure seems to appear when Brangwen's marital passion finds lyrical expression:

> He waited and waited till she came. And as he waited, his limbs seemed strong and splendid to him, his hands seemed like passionate servants to him, goodly, he felt a stupendous power in himself, of life, and of urgent, strong blood.
>
> She was sure to come at last, and touch him. Then he burst into flame for her, and lost himself. They looked at each other, a deep laugh at the bottom of their eyes, and he went to take of her again, wholesale, mad to revel in the inexhaustible wealth of her, to bury himself in the depths of her in an inexhaustible exploration, she all the while revelling in that he revelled in her, tossed all her secrets aside and plunged to that which was secret to her as well, whilst she quivered with fear and the last anguish of delight.

A page later her pregnancy is announced, so it is obvious what they have been up to.

Young Anna grows up and falls in love with her step-cousin

Will Brangwen. He represents a cultural step up from his uncle, being a Ruskinian who loves church architecture and practises the craft of wood-carving. He carves for Anna a butter-stamper with, upon it, 'a mythological bird, a phoenix, something like an eagle, rising on symmetrical wings, from a circle of very beautiful flickering flames that rose upwards from the brim of the cup'. He has also, we may note, carved this effigy for Lawrence himself, who has it on his tomb and the collected edition of his works. To the buyers of the Brangwens' butter it is merely outlandish and uncouth: the world of the byre and that of the larger aspirations do not meet; nevertheless, there is a phoenix on the butter. Another Laurentian symbol appears with the wedding of Anna and Will, one we have already met:

> The marriage party went across the graveyard to the wall, mounted it by the little steps, and descended. Oh, a vain white peacock of a bride perching herself on the top of the wall and giving her hand to the bridegroom on the other side, to be helped down! The vanity of her white, slim, daintily-stepping feet, and her arched neck. And the regal impudence with which she seemed to dismiss them all, the others, parents and wedding guests, as she went with her young husband.

This white peacock does not ruin her husband, however. She rejoices in the marital rites, prolongs the days and nights of the honeymoon, shocks the puritan reader with a delight in sex. The puritan publisher is in evidence when she cries: 'Come back to bed, quick.' In the Penguin edition we read: 'He put off what little clothing he had on and sat beside her in the bed.' The Heinemann edition leaves out the reference to undressing.

The theme of marital nakedness is sustained:

> When he was a child, he had thought a woman was a woman merely by virtue of her skirts and petticoats. And now, lo, the whole world could be divested of its garment, the garment could lie there shed away intact, and one could stand in a new world, a new earth, naked in a new, naked universe. It was too astounding and miraculous.
>
> This then was marriage! The old things didn't matter any more. One got up at four o'clock, and had broth at tea-time and made toffee in the middle of the night. One didn't put

on one's clothes or one did put on one's clothes. He still was
not quite sure it was not criminal.

There were critics enough in 1916 to put him right on that point.
And to point out the blasphemy in what follows:

> But it was a discovery to find one might be so supremely
> absolved. All that mattered was that he should love her and
> she should love him and that they should live kindled to one
> another, like the Lord in two burning bushes that were not
> consumed.

The second married pair have their problems. 'She pressed her
hand over her womb in anguish, while the tears ran down her
face. And why, and why? Why was he like this?' And why, it
must have been asked, did Lawrence seek to corrupt with that
anatomical reference?

There is still a shock, though totally of an aesthetic nature,
when Anna rejoices in her pregnancy and dances in her swollen
nakedness as though she were a female David. 'She danced in
secret before the Creator, she took off her clothes and danced in
the pride of her bigness.' Lawrence develops the biblical parallel
at some length, with Anna Victrix, as the chapter-heading names
her, exulting in the female's creative superiority to the plodding
male. 'Who was he, to come against her? No, he was not even
the Philistine, the Giant. He was like Saul proclaiming his own
kingship. She laughed in her heart. Who was he, proclaiming his
kingship? She laughed in her heart with pride.' If these pages,
parading a 'strange, lifted belly' before the Lord, give offence, it
is of the kind that Lawrence is always ready to give, turning his
characters into gods and goddesses or symbols of elemental power
when the reader has expected nothing more frightening than a
straight story.

There are attempts on the husband's part at extramarital love
which get no further than struggles in the park with a girl met in
a music hall. But whereas in *Mr Noon* spooning is treated quasi-
humorously, here Lawrence throws the whole weight of super-
charged language at us – 'Her cry had given him gratification . . .
His veins fused with extreme voluptuousness . . . When his
fondling had come near again, his hot living desire despising her,
against his cold sensual desire, she broke violently away from
him.' But Will Brangwen's sensuality is soon resanctified in the

marriage bed: ' "To-night I shall know the little hollow under her ankle, where the blue vein crosses." And the thought of it, and the desire for it, made a thick darkness of anticipation.' There is a great deal of this. It stimulates the reader, but not in the manner of pornography. The rhythms are the rhythms of poetry, not of rut, and the physicality of sex is raised to what may be termed a sacramental level. The scabrous reader, looking for obscenity, has to be content with what he can vaguely call bad taste, always a difficult term to define, or the representation of an amorous transport as too ecstatic to be other than blasphemous.

The younger Brangwens have two daughters, Ursula and Gudrun, the sisters of Lawrence's original title for the entire chronicle which, checked halfway with the suppression of *The Rainbow*, restarts with a more 'modern', less traditional, tone in *Women in Love*. Ursula and Gudrun are the heroines of this sequel, but they are not quite the grown women we leave at the end of *The Rainbow*. Ursula is to take on later some of the qualities of Frieda Lawrence, while Gudrun is to be seen as a sublimated Katherine Mansfield. In *The Rainbow*, after the halfway mark, Ursula is a palpitating girl who falls in love with the young Pole Skrebensky, thus, in a sense, seeming to round off the exogamic pattern, though she is herself, of course, half-Polish. She does not marry Skrebensky; he ditches her after a night of love. The intensity of passion is maintained in the third generation:

> But hard and fierce she had fastened upon him, cold as the moon and burning as a fierce salt. Till gradually his warm, soft iron yielded, and she was there fierce, corrosive, seething with his destruction, seething like some cruel, corrosive salt around the last substance of his being, destroying him, destroying him in the kiss. And her soul crystallised with triumph, and his soul was dissolved with agony and annihilation. So she held him there, the victim, consumed, annihilated. She had triumphed: he was not any more.

Ursula's love-life in the sequel is to find its fulfilment in Birkin, who is Lawrence himself. She is thus reserved for better things than an amorous Pole.

It is because of the lack of a plot in the traditional sense that

The Rainbow seems to have no other function than to glorify sexual love. What is the story? The story is no more than a chronicle of three generations of a family in which the important events are biological. A 1916 reader would have expected manipulations, surprises, knots and their unravelling. And he would not have expected, in a mere novel, such poetic intensity: he would have thought that sort of thing to have gone off with Thomas Hardy (condemned for pessimism, not obscenity, and virtually driven out of the preserve of the novel). *The Rainbow* has something of Hardy in it, especially in the wedding party scene, where a heavy bucolic humour steps in to mitigate the intensity. The last part of the book, where Ursula suffers and eventually succeeds as a teacher, belongs to the new Wellsian mode, in which a young woman makes her way in a man's world, but the outcry against industrial 'progress' is straight from Lawrence's throat:

> Hatred sprang up in Ursula's heart. If she could she would smash the machine. Her soul's action should be the smashing of the great machine. If she could destroy the colliery, and make all the men of Wiggiston out of work, she would do it. Let them starve and grub in the earth for roots, rather than serve such a Moloch as this.

She dreams, in her innocent youth, of a transformed world, of the industrially oppressed breaking out of their cerements, and of a new covenant with life. That is where the title comes in – 'a band of faint iridescence colouring in faint colours a portion of the hill . . . the world built up in a living fabric of Truth, fitting to the overarching heaven.'

Unless, which we cannot, we can relate Ursula's vision to a kind of redemption through physical love, *The Rainbow* fails to hold as an artistic unity. There has to be more, and we get the more in *Women in Love*, but the two novels do not cohere. They are very different entities. One is tempted to rate *The Rainbow* higher than it deserves the better to throw scorn or derision on its persecutors, and indeed it is easy enough to point to its great virtues – the solidity of the characters and the settings, the intensity of the feelings, the poetic verve of the writing. The trouble with it seems to be that the characters are moved less by their own volition than by their glands. The novel is a working model of determinism (something, again, vaguely Hardyesque).

Like *Finnegans Wake*, the work it least resembles, it presents life as a cycle. The novel, whether we like it or not, has to be a linear form – a progression from event to event and a kind of conclusion. It is not enough to lift the heart with a rainbow in the sky (one of the strengths of *Finnegans Wake* is that it accepts, with Wordsworth, that the 'regginbrow' comes and goes and is a very unreliable signature of covenant). This is not a great novel, but its author is clearly a great novelist. Its first detractors must have recognised this, resented it, and denied it in the easiest way available.

7
Westward

Lawrence wished to get out of England his England, and he cannot be blamed. It was not just a matter of the suppression of *The Rainbow*, though that was symptomatic of moral anaemia, hypocrisy, life-hatred, and other ingrained English ailments; it was also a matter of war hysteria and the patriotic fervour of popular rags like Horatio Bottomley's *John Bull*. Bottomley was a typical hero of the time: he was eloquent about sending young men to the trenches, and he made a fortune out of his recruiting speeches; his weekly journal was chauvinistic, bloodthirsty, sentimental, philistine, and ill-written. After the war Bottomley was tried and imprisoned for fraud; during it, Shaw's O'Flaherty VC could say 'that we shall never beat the Boshes until we make Horatio Bottomley Lord Leftnant of England'. Later *John Bull* was to rage against the obscenity of *Women in Love*.

Lawrence wished to go west, like the persecuted puritans before him, and Florida (whose heat would have impaired his lungs as surely as an English winter) looked like the promised land to which he could lead a handful of like souls. The young Philip Heseltine, one of them, had suggested the decayed orange plantation of Frederick Delius as a refuge, but Delius was rightly sceptical of a band of intellectuals' being able to live in its ruins. Like the Pilgrim Fathers, the pioneers of Rananim matched vision with unpracticality. There was also talk of Fort Myers, a millionaire resort not really suitable for penurious idealists. Still, Lawrence did not merely talk of going west; he raised money (including £5 from G. B. Shaw) for his and Frieda's passages.

But he did not realise, until the government put him right on the matter, that the only way out of England was with a rifle and pack. He and Frieda went west, but only to Cornwall, which could be glossed as not really England; they went as far west as they could, almost to Land's End. In a group of cottages between St Ives and Penzance they tried to set up Rananim.

When the Lawrences were more or less settled in the deep west, John Middleton Murry and Katherine Mansfield were summoned to join them. Lawrence regarded Murry not merely as his closest friend but also his blood-brother. He had become a believer in *Blutbrüderschaft* and proposed a kind of Teutonic or Red Indian ceremony in which bloods were literally mingled and undying mutual allegiance was sworn. It is difficult to understand this Laurentian hunger for male friendship too intense to be wholesome, especially as he was quick to shriek against the chosen brother and complain that he was sucking him dry. He did this with Murry and drove him away. Lawrence certainly never proposed a homosexual relationship, though there may have been deeper erotic motives than he was prepared to realise. It seems rather that an innate power-hunger, cognate with the creative urge, had to be exercised over some chosen man, since it did not work with the chosen woman, and this was implausibly presented as a mere longing for fraternal love.

Murry loved Lawrence sincerely enough, but he refused to be dominated. His later Judas-avowal – 'I love you, Lorenzo, but I do not promise not to betray you' – has been remembered better than his hard work on behalf of a genius he fully recognised. As editor of *Rhythm*, *Adelphi* and *Athenaeum*, he provided an outlet, sometimes scornfully rejected, for Lawrence's writings. He was a good editor and, as *The Problem of Style* still shows, sixty-odd years after its first appearance, an intelligent critic. He is supposed to be the original of Gerald Crich in *Women in Love*, but he is better known in his satirical transformation into Denis Burlap in Aldous Huxley's *Point Counter Point* – slimily spiritual, grasping, a patient seducer of women attracted to his soul. With his self-pity and hysterical streak he does not come well out of his autobiography *Between Two Worlds*. There is a more balanced and sympathetic portrait in his son's biography, *One Hand Clapping* (not to be confused with my homonymous novel).

Philip Heseltine was equally close to Lawrence in those days of western exile, a very young man whose musical genius was still to come to flower. As Peter Warlock, a bearded Elizabethan, he wrote the finest songs of the century; as Heseltine he became a great scholar of Tudor music. His literary taste was exquisite, as the songs show (the taste of most of our pre-Britten composers has been atrocious), and he was the first to display unqualified enthusiasm for Lawrence's genius. After the suppression of *The Rainbow*, he proposed printing and distributing the book on his own initiative, but this came to nothing. Lawrence evidently never followed Heseltine–Warlock's later career (he died in the same year as Lawrence, probably through suicide), and merely regarded him as a mouldable disciple. Both the Lawrences, believing powerfully in marriage and demonstrating this by smashing plates on each other, tried to arrange matrimony for their friends, invariably to unsuitable partners. Heseltine grew angry at being so manipulated and became an enemy: he was punished for his defection by being satirised in *Women in Love* as the spineless aesthete Halliday. Laurentians have never forgiven him for destroying the only manuscript of 'Goats and Compasses', Lawrence's essay on homosexuality. According to Cecil Gray, Heseltine's friend and biographer, he used the sheets 'in the discharge of a lowly but necessary function'. Gray was himself a musician, a composer who did not mind whether his compositions were played or not, a fine music critic, and the author of an excellent history of music. Both his *Peter Warlock* and his autobiography *Musical Chairs* are violently anti-Laurentian. Though drawn, through Heseltine, into Rananim, he grew tired of what he termed Tolstoyan impertinences like 'What do you think of yourself?' and 'Do you love your wife?' Lawrence could be exasperating in his moral and spiritual probing, what time the Cornish rain blew in from the Atlantic.

At first Lawrence loved Cornwall, especially when the spring came. The winter was always hard for him, though he swore that he suffered from no more than a passing irritation of the bronchii (the tuberculosis belonged to the past, a kind of filial remorse). Spring was a convalescence he imposed on a nature that had been shivering and coughing its heart out. He wrote to Russell in March 1916 ('Are you still cross with me for being a schoolmaster and for not respecting the rights of man? Don't be, it isn't worth it'):

We have taken a tiny cottage here, for £5 a year, which we shall furnish. We shall live very cheaply, because we are

going to be very poor indeed. But just under the wild hills
with their great grey boulders of granite, and above the big
sea, it is beautiful enough, and free enough. I think we can
be obscure, and happy, like creatures in a cave . . . One must
learn to be happy and careless. The old world never tumbles
down except a young world shoves it over, heedlessly. And
I'm sure the young world must be jolly.

This can be called prevernal optimism. At Higher Tregerthen,
Zennor, still an exquisite spot in the swing of the sea, he got
down to the scrubbing of floors and the writing of *Women in
Love* – which meant the reprocessing of the unfinished second
half of *The Sisters*. This was a long job, and the work was not
completed until November 1916. It was, as was to be expected,
unpublishable. Lawrence, finding no hope in England, sent it to
Maunsel & Co in Dublin, a firm famous for not having published
Joyce's *Dubliners*: he got it back in ten days. At the same time he
brooded over the Celtic imponderables of the old duchy. His
view of what Laurentian man should be like had been partly
moulded in Italy, as the publication of *Twilight in Italy* in July
1916 was to remind him. He found it convenient to ignore that
the laughing white-toothed uninhibited peasants he had known,
noble savages swilling wine and sucking in pasta, were very anxious to be crushed by the industrial machine Lawrence abomin-
ated. Here, in Cornwall, was pre-Arthurian man, close to the
ancient gods, breathing in magic from the loam, a people 'most
unwarlike, soft, peaceable, ancient'. He suffered for the rural
Cornishmen dragged into the mesh of war, but he suffered also
for himself. He had to go to Bodmin for an army medical examination. He was rejected because of the condition of his lungs,
but the mauling of his naked body was an affront to human
dignity. By this time he had grown a beard, a gesture of defiance
to those who would make clean-shaven cannon-fodder of him,
his doomed chin scraped sorely in icy water. In the Bodmin
barracks he was told: 'That'll have to come off tomorrow, dad.'
It never came off. It remained to the end, mark and blazon of a
free man who did not have to conform to the tyranny of King
C. Gillette.

  Lawrence's disgust and anger at the reduction of his proud
flesh into a mere thing for probing and deriding is fully set out in
the 'Nightmare' chapter of the novel *Kangaroo*. He is outraged

not only for himself but for his race and sex, and it must seem to some readers that he goes too far. My generation had to accept the indignity of more than the MO's cold fingers. Of course, Lawrence's rage is equivocal: his body, after the mauling, was found not to be good enough. He was not afraid of war (he was afraid of nothing), but he was entitled to cry out at war's insanity and, worse, its intrusion on the divine dignity of male privacy. Other men could good-humouredly accept that the cause of individual freedom might be served only by a temporary denial of it, and so, as a thinking man, could Lawrence. But the rest of him could no more help protesting than his chest could help coughing. To those of us in the war of 1939–45 who carried books in our kitbags, Lawrence was a comfort. He encouraged us to defy petty despotism – snarling back at lance-corporals, waylaying drill-sergeants in the dark between pub and barracks. He was our great prophet of subversion. But, of course, you cannot run an army that way.

His rage and nausea made Lawrence incautious in talking against the war to local Cornishmen. Ragged and poor, publishing only a poem here and a story there, he was living practically the life of a farm labourer: he had opportunity for intimate impieties about the whole bloody shambles. Cornishmen who listened and then talked in pubs decided they were patriotic Englishmen as well as primordial Celts. In the late summer of 1917 Lawrence and Frieda began to come under the surveillance of the authorities. She, as was well known, was a German, cousin to the Red Baron: the white scarf round her neck that flapped in the wind of the sea–cliff was a signal to U–boats, the washing she hung on the line was an elaborate semaphore. The enemy was nudging round the coast; a coastal vessel was actually torpedoed. All this had something to do with Lawrence's defiant singing of German folk-songs, his carelessness in letting lights blaze from the windows, his tarring of the chimney. On 12 October 1917, the police raided his house and began looking for incriminating documents and being cautious about a wrapped block of salt that Frieda had bought. Frieda, unwisely, jeered, and Lawrence whispered: 'For God's sake, stop it.' He must have reflected on the irony that, back in Metz, he had been under suspicion as a spy for England; now he was working for the Hun. Nothing could be proved against either of them, but they were given three days to get out of Cornwall. Black with a sullen hopelessness more than

with rage, he went with Frieda to stay at the house of Richard
Aldington's wife – the Imagist poet H.D., who has left a fictional
record of the brief sojourn at 44 Mecklenburgh Square. He began
to write a new novel, *Aaron's Rod*. He protested to the War
Office about his eviction from Cornwall and asked permission to
return: this was, with remarkable promptitude, refused. The
Criminal Investigation Department began to follow him around,
Lawrence the marked man. The publication of *Look! We Have
Come Through!* in November 1917 (under his own name: nobody
read poetry unless it was by the late Rupert Brooke) must have
struck with bitter irony: they had not come through, far from it.

In May 1918 Lawrence and Frieda went to stay at Mountain
Cottage, Middleton-by-Wirksworth, Derbyshire. His father, in
lonely retirement, was living not far away, and he did two strange
things for, or to, his son. He resoled a pair of boots for him in
cast-iron; he lighted a huge bonfire outside Mountain Cottage,
just as night was falling. This was Lawrence signalling Zeppelins,
also the father perhaps having a twisted revenge on the creator of
Walter Morel. One hand of authority not caring what the other
was doing, Lawrence received fifty pounds from the Royal
Literary Fund. On 11 September, his birthday, he was medically
re-examined at Derby and graded for 'secondary work', whatever
that was. *New Poems* came out in the October, then he was in
London on 12 November for an armistice party. So much for
Lawrence's war, except for its cruel aftermath, influenza, which
caught him but which a strong will to live withstood. Now came
the difficulty of leaving England, this time virtually for ever. The
Lawrences did not receive passports until October 1919. Then,
like the heroine of *The Lost Girl*, they watched the heavy grey
coffin of England descend into the dark waters. This time they
had really come through. Millions of others, of course, had not.

Lawrence's voluntary exile has always been held against him,
as it has been held against other British artists who preferred to
live and work abroad. An English writer should stay in England,
as Chaucer, Shakespeare and Milton did. But, matters of health
and tax avoidance aside, a writer can sometimes do his best service
to his country's literature by seeing his country, and hearing its
language, against the foil of an alien culture. Joyce could hardly
have written *Ulysses* in Dublin (for one thing, he would not have
met his Leopold Bloom there: he found him, through Italo Svevo,
in Trieste). Lawrence never failed in his love for England, or

what was left of it when he had subtracted its government and its *canaille*, and the sharpness of his observation of his native Midlands, as in *Sons and Lovers*, owed a good deal to his being able to evoke them against a foreign setting. But there was another thing. Lawrence increasingly found his audience in America, not Britain, and this put him in the situation of a self-consciously international writer whose subject-matter might as well be the whole world, not just an offshore island. Besides, he had the urge to make what one of his biographers called a 'savage pilgrimage', a search for old cultures which had not yet been wounded or quelled by industrialism, and this was to lead him, by way of the east and the antipodes, to the most un-English culture available, that of the Mexican Indians. He cannot be blamed for not staying home and writing like Miss Mitford. If he had left England to join the Anglo-Florentines, there might be cause for murmurs, but he never built a cosy nest in the heart of a sybaritic culture. He left England's rigours for worse rigours. As for the Anglo-Florentines, they have never been thought ill of, except by Lawrence.

What did he accomplish during a war that made him ill and nearly drove him mad? The writing of *Women in Love*, along with such odd literary jobs as would secure a subsistence not much above starvation, took him almost to the end of 1916. And then what looked at first like a desultory hobby emerges in the historical perspective as one of the most astonishing things that Lawrence ever did – namely, the creation of a new academic discipline. There was an educational Lawrence towards the end of that war busily but sometimes fruitlessly at work. After all, he had been a teacher. *The Times Educational Supplement* requested articles but did not publish them. A textbook called *Movements in European History* was written and revised and re-revised and eventually published under the pseudonym H. L. Davidson. I discovered this book when I was in the sixth form in 1934 and preparing for the Higher School Certificate in modern European history. I found it useful; Lawrence helped me to pass. I did not at the time realise how Laurentian it was. The 'movements' of the title is misleading, for the emphasis is on personalities with gut-convictions who changed the world, men like Luther and Calvin. It is scholarly, sober, but one has the sensation of banked fires.

That merely useful book cannot be compared with one that changed America's attitude to its own literature. In his wonderful little study of Nathaniel Hawthorne, published two years before Lawrence was born, Henry James said:

> ... The flower of art blooms only where the soil is deep ... it takes a great deal of history to produce a little literature ... it needs a complex social machinery to set a writer in motion. American civilization has hitherto had other things to do than to produce flowers, and before giving birth to writers it has wisely occupied itself with providing something for them to write about. Three or four beautiful talents of trans-Atlantic growth are the sum of what the world usually recognises, and in this modest nosegay the genius of Hawthorne is admitted to have the rarest and sweetest fragrance.

Lawrence's aim, in his *Studies in Classic American Literature*, was to show that the 'modest nosegay' was in reality a whole garden, if not a forest of Brazilian richness. In a letter to Robert Mountsier, his American agent, we find the germ of the idea at work in a list of books by Herman Melville, Fenimore Cooper, Walt Whitman, Jean de Crévecoeur, Hawthorne, Emerson, Benjamin Franklin, Edgar Allan Poe, as well as the speeches of Lincoln. He was starting his reading as early as January 1917. There is no irony in the fact that the same letter deplores Mountsier's treatment by Scotland Yard's Special Branch as an undesirable alien tied up with Lawrence's own suspicious behaviour at Zennor. 'Pah, but one is sick of the show. I think the best thing would be for us all to go to America ... I have *finally* decided that it is only possible to live out of the world – make a sort of Garden of Eden of blameless but fulfilled souls ...' The new interest in American literature was clearly cognate with Lawrence's realisation that his future audience lay further west than Land's End. At the same time, in his contradictory way, he was ready to blazon the glories of the English tradition in literature as opposed to what he thought of as the overratedness of the Russians to whom 'Kot' had introduced him. But English literature had made a fresh start in America, and Lawrence, first fascinated by his chance reading of *Moby-Dick* (from which he may have got, impressed by Ishmael and Queequeg, the notion of blood-brotherhood), went on to see a large field virtually ignored by the critics and the academics. Today it is taken for granted, even in European universities, that American literature is no mere annexe to that of the mother country but a vital and rewarding study in its own right. Without Lawrence's pioneer work this would still have happened, but it would have happened much later.

The *Studies* are no orthodox exercise in literary history or criticism, designed (like the European history book) for cautious teachers and students who have examinations to pass. It hectors and bullies, though this time not the British; very logically, the fellow countrymen of Whitman, Melville, Dana and Hawthorne are his target: the Americans have to learn about their destiny and see what their literature says about it. Discussing Fenimore Cooper, he says:

> . . . You have there the myth of the essential white America. All the other stuff, the love, the democracy, the floundering into lust, is a sort of by-play. The essential American soul is hard, isolate, stoic, and a killer. It has never yet melted.

And who or what is Moby Dick?

> He is the deepest blood-being of the white race; he is our deepest blood-nature.
>
> And he is hunted, hunted, hunted by the maniacal fanaticism of our white mental consciousness. We want to hunt him down. To subject him to our will. And in this maniacal conscious hunt of ourselves we get dark races and pale to help us, red, yellow, and black, east and west, Quaker and fire-worshipper, we get them all to help us in this ghastly maniacal hunt which is our doom and our suicide.
>
> The last phallic being of the white man. Hunted into the death of upper consciousness and the ideal will. Our blood-self subjected to our will . . .
>
> Hot-blooded sea-born Moby Dick. Hunted by mono-maniacs of the idea.

All this must seem like Lawrence swallowing American literature too quickly, digesting it ill, regurgitating gobbets of doubtful philosophy, but what counts is less the thought than the excitement. It is the excitement that survives a great number of contradictory ideas, and the excitement proceeds as much from the books considered as from the very notion of America which binds the work into a whole – a notion big and fantastic enough to admit any number of contradictions. And this brings us, or Lawrence, to Walt Whitman.

Whitman, whom Lawrence is encouraged to address with gross familiarity, is first of all an author of poems that are 'really huge fat tomb-plants, great rank graveyard growths. All that false exuberance. All those lists of things boiled in one pudding-cloth! No, no!' Too much all-embracing going on, thinks Lawrence, too much burbling of One Identity. And finally the chant of Death! Death! – 'the great merge into the womb', the ultimate Ex Pluribus Unum. But Walt, or Walter as he is occasionally genteelly called, does not know what his real message is. What it is, Lawrence asserts, is the Open Road – 'the leaving of the soul free unto herself, the leaving of his fate to her and to the loom of the open road. Which is the bravest doctrine man has ever proposed to himself.' And so Lawrence pushes Walt out of the way and tells America what the great grey poet really meant:

> The love of man and woman; a recognition of souls, and a communion of worship. The love of comrades: a re-cognition of souls, and a communion of worship. De-mocracy: a recognition of souls, all down the open road, and a great soul seen in its greatness, as it travels on foot among the rest, down the common way of the living ... Purified of MERGING, purified of MYSELF, the exultant message of American Democracy, of souls in the Open Road, full of glad recognition, full of fierce readiness, full of the joy of worship, when one soul sees a greater soul.

It is heady stuff, a series of kicks and lunges, it is meant to jolt Americans into listening to the articulate Americans (the greater souls) for their own good. It is also Lawrence yearning west-ward.

The major achievement of those bad years remains *Women in Love*. Martin Secker offered to publish it, and also *The Rainbow*, in March 1920: he was brave enough to do this despite the whines and growls of the dirty-minded. It is one of the ten great novels of the twentieth century and it now merits a chapter to itself.

8

Nakedness

The setting of *Women in Love* is Lawrence's native province, as in *The Rainbow*, but a brutal change has taken place in it between the two books. The countryside is recognisably the same, except that it holds a deeper ferocity than before, but the coalmining industry is no longer what it was when Lawrence's, or Paul Morel's, father worked in it. It has ceased to be primitive and loosely organised, a kind of neolithic continuation of a Silurian culture which dug out coal with its bare hands for iron-smelting. Where it was paternalistic and easygoing it has become impersonal, tyrannical and scientifically efficient. This is the work of Gerald Crich, son of a mine-owner who held to the old way and, unable to accommodate his thinking and his feeling to the brutality of change, is slowly dying. Gerald has 'got hold of everything' and initiated 'the great reform'.

> Expert engineers were introduced in every department. An enormous electric plant was installed, both for lighting and for haulage underground, and for power. The electricity was carried into every mine. New machinery was brought from America, such as the miners had never seen before, great iron men, as the cutting machines were called, and unusual appliances. The working of the pits was thoroughly changed, all the control was taken out of the hands of the miners, the butty system was abolished. Everything was run on the most accurate and delicate scientific method, educated and expert men were in control everywhere, the miners were reduced

to mere mechanical instruments. They had to work hard, much harder than before, the work was terrible and heart-breaking in its mechanicalness.

With the end of the butty system there is no longer room for Walter Morel, the easy elder brother foreman of the coalface. The miners who are left see 'the joy leave their lives' but they get a perverse satisfaction out of submitting to the machine. 'There was a new world, a new order, strict, terrible, inhuman, but satisfying in its very destructiveness.' It is the death of the organic, the cyclical but unpredictable, and the victory of the mechanical deterministic: now men know where they stand, and it is 'a sort of freedom'. It is also 'the first and finest state of chaos'.

Gerald Crich, the new kind of magnate, is clearly not based on John Middleton Murry, a small neurotic editor and critic, despite the identification assumed when the book first appeared. As with all Lawrence's characters, there is a tendency for the creator to draw the essence out of himself, impose appearance out of a mixture of fancy and real people, and introduce habits or actions observed among his friends and enemies. It is important to raise this matter now, since *Women in Love* is supposed to be full of real people who recognised themselves and tried to cause trouble, and its satirical intentions have been exalted above its fictional or poetic or mythopoeic ones. If we are to look for models for Gerald Crich and his family, we had best stay in the Eastwood district: there is a family living there today which believes itself to be the model and goes on bearing a grudge against the dead author. When, in 1984, I took a television team to the area to make a film on Lawrence, severe restrictions were enforced on how much of the family estate we could visit. This is worth mentioning as an instance of the unwillingness of some people to separate fiction from real life. It is an unwillingness that leads to libel actions, as most novelists know. Lawrence could have suffered from this more than he did, but it is best to believe in his fundamental innocence: he was trying to write novels.

The appearance of Gerald Crich is in accordance with his function as the freezer out of humanity in a great industrial organisation. He is not himself a machine but a part of nature, so he had better be ice. Gudrun Brangwen sees him and, somewhat perversely, falls.

There was something northern about him that magnetised her. In his clear northern flesh and his fair hair was a glisten like sunshine reflected through crystals of ice. And he looked so new, unbroached, pure as an arctic thing . . . His gleaming beauty, maleness, like a young, good-humoured, smiling wolf, did not blind her to the significant, sinister stillness in his bearing, the lurking danger of his unsubdued temper . . . 'Am I *really* singled out for him in some way, is there really some pale gold, arctic light that envelops only us two?' she asked herself.

There seems to be a hint here of the popular novel about the Napoleon of industry and the palpitant millgirl who wants to be crushed in his arms (enforced by the title of the book), but it is always unjust to drag things out of context. The context is the wedding between one of the Crich girls and a young naval officer, but it is not an Ethel M. Dell wedding. The bridegroom is late, and he runs to the altar. The bride runs too. Although Lawrence very clearly delineates what the company is wearing – indeed, with the exactitude of a fashion magazine – we have a strange impression that everybody is suddenly stripped naked and that a sort of mock-rape chase (as in Stravinsky's *Sacre du Printemps*) is proceeding.

And it is this stripping down which is of the essence of the book. The characters are, in their externals, drawn with a delirious sharpness, but they are not human beings as we expect to meet them either in real life or in fiction. They are close to animals in the discontinuousness of their emotions, with unpredictable shifts of feeling which are always intense; their unconscious minds are, as in surface mining, a little too close to the light; they are capable of great emotional and even physical violence; they all seem to have a skin missing. This is the peculiar quality of *Women in Love*, which could as well be called *Women in Hate*. Emotional responses to words or events are not classifiable according to the old melodramatic tradition: we can find no easy name for them. The dynamic of the characters goes beyond the covenant of the realistic novel, and we are inclined to think of Thomas Hardy and gales on Egdon Heath. But Lawrence has gone beyond Hardy: we are in the age of the depth psychologist now, though no more than in Joyce is there any hint that the author is impressed by psychoanalytical theory. The artist is alone with his intuitions and, as always with this artist, takes terrible chances.

Ursula and Gudrun Brangwen are not quite the girls we met

in *The Rainbow*. They are mature women now and (Gudrun
especially) of almost mythical beauty. Gudrun was nicknamed by
her schoolmates 'Good runner', but Ursula calls her 'Prune': there
has been a shift of stress. Ursula teaches in the local grammar
school, and her specialisation seems to be botany. Gudrun works
there too, but desultorily. Her line is drawing and idiosyncratic
woodcarving (she is her father's daugher), and she has had little
exhibitions in London. Both girls are dissatisfied with their life in
a kind of Eastwood and think of marriage. If Gerald Crich seems
destined for Gudrun, Ursula's man will be Rupert Birkin, a local
inspector of schools – clever, moody, self-destructive, capable of
great tenderness, damnably dogmatic but, in elevated company,
rather subdued. He is clearly Lawrence himself. Some of his
eventual quarrels with Ursula turn her into Frieda; Gudrun has
borrowed some of Katherine Mansfield's temperament and, in a
late scene, she performs a public act which Katherine Mansfield
was seen to perform. This, and his relationship with Birkin,
imposes on Gerald Crich a Middleton Murry role, but there is no
need to labour the *roman à clef* element.

One reader of the book before publication was prepared to
labour it, and this was Lady Ottoline Morrell, who saw herself in
Hermione Roddice – 'a woman of the new school, full of intel-
lectuality, and heavy, nerve-worn with consciousness', also horse-
faced. Her country house, Breadalby, is Garsington transported
to the Midlands, and one of her guests at a house-party is very
obviously Bertrand Russell – 'a learned, dry baronet of fifty,
who was always making witticisms and laughing at them heartily
in a harsh horse-laugh'. Hermione's intensity goes beyond that of
the foreground quartet. She is the enemy, but Lawrence is
prepared to put his own views into her mouth:

> 'Isn't the mind –' she said, with the convulsed movement of
> her body, 'isn't it our death? Doesn't it destroy all our spon-
> taneity, all our instincts? Are not the young people growing
> up to-day, really dead before they have a chance to live?'

This is so that Birkin, with a passion that is the very substance of
the book and needs no plot-machinery to generate it, can cry out
at her:

> 'You and spontaneity! You, the most deliberate thing that
> ever walked or crawled! You'd be verily deliberately spontan-

eous – that's you. Because you want to have everything in your own volition, your deliberate voluntary consciousness. You want it all in that loathsome little skull of yours, that ought to be cracked like a nut. For you'll be the same till it *is* cracked, like an insect in its skin. If one cracked your skull perhaps one might get a spontaneous, passionate woman out of you, with real sensuality. As it is, what you want is pornography – looking at yourself in mirrors, watching your naked animal actions in mirrors, so that you can have it all in your consciousness, make it all mental.'

This, by the way, takes place in Ursula's classroom, though the children have just left. They might as well have stayed to hear Lawrence, in the unlikely guise of a school inspector, curse 'sex in the head', part of their education. Needless to say, Hermione is desperately in love with Birkin; needless to say, she hates him.

At Breadalby Birkin copies the drawing of a goose given to Hermione by the Chinese Ambassador. She, and we, are given a little of the charade-playing know-all Lawrence. Talking of geese, he says:

'I know what centres they live from – what they perceive and feel – the hot, stinging centrality of a goose in the flux of cold water and mud – the curious bitter stinging heat of a goose's blood, entering their own blood like an inoculation of corruptive fire – fire of the cold-burning mud – the lotus mystery.'

The correct response to this should be 'Oh my God', but Hermione shudders and feels a sick convulsion coming on. Birkin is destroying her 'with some insidious occult potency'. Later 'a terrible voluptuous thrill' runs down her arms; she is going to know 'her voluptuous consummation'. She takes a heavy paperweight of lapis lazuli and strikes Birkin down. 'It was one convulsion of pure bliss for her, lit up by the crushed pain of her fingers.' Birkin, who as Lawrence has had a number of plates thrown at him, does not greatly resent this. He says: 'It isn't I who will die. You hear?' Then he takes his semi-consciousness away to run naked among the primroses and hyacinths and, drying himself of their wetness and hurting himself among birch and hazel, he is fulfilled and happy. Those of us who are looking for a plot will now see the way open for the love of Birkin and Ursula, but, to those unready for the Laurentian approach to human relationships, that sequence will seem a very extravagant road to it. But this violence, with its concomitant near-submissiveness (it would be too clinical to speak of masochism) is an acceptable mode of action among these highly civilised people.

And so is the brutality of Ursula's denunciations of Birkin, when their love affair is well under way and not far from marriage. She is talking of Hermione when she yells: 'In her soul she's a devilish unbeliever, common as dirt. That's what she is at the bottom. And all the rest is pretence – but you love it . . . Because of the dirt underneath. Do you think I don't know the foulness of your sex life – and hers? – I do. And it's that foulness you want, you liar. Then have it, have it.' There is a great deal more of this, with Birkin castigated as obscene and perverse and death-eating. But everything comes right later when she says: 'See what a flower I have found for you.' It is purple-red bell-heather, and he responds: 'Pretty!' Then it is love under the chill Midland stars all night. 'It was so magnificent, such an inheritance of a universe of dark reality, and they were afraid to seem to remember.'

Do people really behave like this? It is a question not to be asked. If they do, it is not within the extravagant drapes and swags of Laurentian language. The irrational passionate rhetoric his characters utter rubs on to the *récit* and enforces action that sometimes looks demented. It is, if you like, an idealised working-class spontaneity of emotion made highly articulate and applied to intellectuals who inhabit, as Lawrence did, a special fringe of the bourgeoisie. But strip off convention and good manners, liquidate the influence of the public schools, and people can become passionate animals, as discontinuous in their behaviour as dogs. The joint achievement of Joyce and Lawrence (neither of whom was much interested in what the other was doing) was to clean off the veneer.

Lawrence said airily to Jessie Chambers, when he was contemplating the writing of a novel, that it was all a matter of setting up electricity and magnetism with a couple of couples. He had not at that time envisaged a relationship between the male elements of the couples, but it is the component of *Women in Love* which makes the work startling and, on first publication, caused murmurs and cries which Martin Secker stoutly ignored. Lawrence's old Cornwall preoccupation with *Blutbrüderschaft* is dramatised when Birkin, still sick from that blow with the lapis lazuli, is visited by Gerald. They are to love each other, says Birkin, as something more than friends, but there is no flavour of the erotic in his proposal. He mentions what the old German knights used to do:

> 'Make a little wound in their arms, and rub each other's blood into the cut?' said Gerald.
>
> 'Yes – and swear to be true to each other, of one blood, all their lives. That is what we ought to do. No wounds, that is obsolete. But we ought to swear to love each other, you and I, implicitly, and perfectly, finally, without any possibility of going back on it.'

But Gerald, Nordic only in his iciness, says he will think about it. Birkin says: 'You must tell me what you think, later. You know what I mean? Not sloppy emotionalism. An impersonal union that leaves one free.' But he is disappointed in Gerald and a little contemptuous.

Gerald seems afraid to touch even Birkin's 'extended fine, living hand', but he will be drawn into a close physical contact later. It will be reached circuitously, through an invocation of natural forces that are rather terrifying. Gudrun gives Gerald's young sister Winifred drawing lessons, and it is proposed that they drag the girl's pet rabbit Bismarck out of his hutch and use him as a model. We have already met some of Lawrence's rabbits in *The White Peacock* (the Haggs, the farm of the Chambers family, writhed with them): there they were an emblem of quiet pullulent energy, 'the good animals' that human beings ought to be. Here the one buck, brilliantly presented, is a cosmic force:

> There was a long scraping sound as it was hauled forward, and in another instant it was in mid-air, lunging wildly, its body flying like a spring coiled and released, as it lashed out, suspended from the ears. Gudrun held the black-and-white tempest at arms' length, averting her face . . . Her heart was arrested with fury at the mindlessness and the bestial stupidity of this struggle, her wrists were badly scored by the claws of the beast, a heavy cruelty welled up in her.

Gerald observes the cruelty. He grasps the rabbit.

> The long, demon-like beast lashed out again, spread on the air as if it were flying, looking something like a dragon,

then closing up again, inconceivably powerful and explosive.
The man's body, strung to its efforts, vibrated strongly.
Then a sudden sharp, white-edged wrath came up in him.
Swift as lightning he drew back and brought his free hand
down like a hawk on the neck of the rabbit. Simultaneously,
there came the unearthly abhorrent scream of a rabbit in the
fear of death. It made one immense writhe, tore his wrists
and his sleeves in a final convulsion, all its belly flashed white
in a whirlwind of paws, and then he had slung it round and
had it under his arm, fast. It cowered and skulked. His face
was gleaming with a smile.

An icy smile, we presume. The industrial magnate has tamed
nature, at least temporarily, but he is shaken, he has 'qualms of
fear'. He and Gudrun are torn and bleeding, and here is an opportunity for their bloods to mingle: if it does not take place in a
kind of perversion of the *Blutbrüderschaft* ceremony, at least the
show of wild force – nature enacting her own ritual – draws
them together: 'They were implicated with each other in
abhorrent mysteries.' The nature of the love that is to develop
between them is already adumbrated here: it is to be destructive,
and Gerald will want to kill Gudrun like a rabbit – 'His blind
consciousness was gone into his wrists, into his hands. He was
one blind, incontinent desire to kill her' – before meeting an
appropriately icy death of his own.

Gerald has seen his blood drawn, but not in a brotherhood
ritual with Birkin. Birkin meanwhile yells at the moon-goddess –
Cybele, Syria Dea – and tries to destroy the moon ritually by
throwing stones at its reflection in Willey Water. Ursula sees
him.

  And his shadow on the border of the pond was watching
for a few moments, then he stooped and groped on the
ground. Then again there was a burst of sound, and a burst
of flying light, the moon had exploded on the water, and
flying asunder in flakes of white and dangerous fire. Rapidly,
like white fires, the fires all broken rose across the pond,
fleeing in clamorous confusion, battling with the flock of
dark waves that were forcing their way in . . . But at the
centre, the heart of all, was still a vivid, incandescent quivering of a white moon not quite destroyed, a white body of
fire writhing and striving and not even now broken open,

not yet violated. It seemed to be drawing itself together
with strange, violent pangs, in blind effort. It was getting
stronger, it was re-asserting itself, the inviolable moon. And
the rays were hastening in in thin lines of light, to return to
the strengthened moon, that shook upon the water in
triumphant reassumption.

There is a lot of Lawrence himself in this unwilling acknow-
ledgment of the lunar power (the moon theme is to return later,
in *Kangaroo*). The fascinated fear of this power justified Lawrence's rejection of the dusty science of the selenologists: he would
not have it that the moon was all dead dust and minerals; it had
to be a living body of fire if it could drive men lunatic. Here, in
this remarkable scene, the moon is the goddess one can resist only
ritually. She always wins. We modulate from the mythical to the
realistic, and now Birkin asks, with old-fashioned formality, for
Ursula's hand in marriage. Having stabilised (but this is a story in
which nothing is really stabilised) his relationship with a woman,
he can revert to his need for the completeness which only Gerald
can grant him.

The third of this central trio of astonishing scenes is entitled
'Gladiatorial'. Birkin visits Gerald and almost immediately
proposes a bout of 'Japanese wrestling'. ('A Jap lived in the same
house with me in Heidelberg, and he taught me a little. But I
was never much good at it.') They strip naked and start. Readers
in the twenties, and readers even more so now, had, have, to
expect the wrestling bout to exhibit sly, or covert, homosexual
tones, but these are carefully avoided. 'It was as if Birkin's whole
physical intelligence interpenetrated into Gerald's body, as if his
fine, sublimated energy entered into the flesh of the fuller man,
like some potency, casting a fine net, a prison, through the
muscles into the very depths of Gerald's physical being.' It is a
meshing of entities, not identities, of which the body is an es-
sential part, but if sex comes into it it is not the sex of the 'gay'
magazines. The enjoyment by a male of another male body is of a
different order:

> 'We are mentally, spiritually intimate, therefore we should
> be more or less physically intimate too – it is more whole.'
> 'Certainly it is,' said Gerald. Then he laughed pleasantly,
> adding: 'It's rather wonderful to me.' He stretched out his
> arms handsomely . . .

'I think also that you are beautiful,' said Birkin to Gerald,
'and that is enjoyable too. One should enjoy what is given.'
    'You think I am beautiful – how do you mean, physic-
ally?' asked Gerald, his eyes glistening.
    'Yes. You have a northern kind of beauty, like light re-
fracted from snow – and a beautiful, plastic form. Yes, that
is there to enjoy as well. We should enjoy everything.'

The wrestling has been a kind of blood-brotherhood ceremony,
though perhaps nothing has been certainly 'pledged'. Readers
who smell a kind of perversity in all this have to be reminded of
Lawrence's sun–moon philosophy, in which a female force rules
the night and a male force the day and a healthy organism lives
through the whole twenty-four hours. A term like *sex* has the
wrong denotations. If we are startled by this scene we are merely
experiencing the shock that it was Lawrence's lifelong mission to
impart – the shock of meeting truths which logic and science,
concerned with (in Lawrence's view) only partial truths, have
tried to drive out.
    Love in this novel is a complex affair, with strong elements of
resentment and destruction in it, and it is set against the finality
of death, which is all too simple. The young couple we meet in
the first chapter, running to their wedding, we meet again
drowned (Lawrence was drawing on an actual fatality in the area,
rather as Shakespeare was remembering the drowning for love of
Kate Hamnett in the Avon when presenting Ophelia's death). It
is typical of Lawrence that this drowning carries little resonance:
it is not a stone thrown into a pool which sends widening circles
into the plot. If it has any narrative function it is that of drawing
the downstage quartet together. There is another death, that of
Gerald's father, which serves to break his spirit and make him
seek life in Gudrun. But the significant death of the story is a
collective and permanent condition which is located in a mythical
place called London.
    It is here that Lawrence has his chance to punish the defecting
Philip Heseltine, who, with his 'beautiful, broken body', stands
less for destruction than negation – the denial of life which is the
true death. Heseltine saw his portrait here and tried to prosecute
the book through a certain Purity League; he accepted fifty
pounds and was quiet thereafter. The weak ineffectual Halliday
of *Women in Love* has his obverse in Aldous Huxley's Coleman in

Antic Hay. Coleman has Satanic energy, a beard, a cynical laugh:
he is the model, beard and all, which the mild and melancholy
Gumbril takes for his Rabelaisian transformation. Huxley had
met (at a Queen's Hall Promenade Concert) Heseltine in his Peter
Warlock guise, the rumbustious Elizabethan, and had been impressed by his vitality. It is the mortality of a character that had
not yet learned how to disguise itself which Lawrence gives us in
his London episodes. When war began he saw the life of the
capital going out like the lights of 'last night's Café Royal', and
it is the Café Royal, renamed the Pompadour, which is the setting
for very effective satire of the London art-crowd, the anti-
Laurentians or life-haters. In the Pompadour life is directly
imitated, or very nearly. Halliday reads out one of Birkin's letters
in a mock-parsonical voice, and Gudrun snatches it from him.
Cecil Grey, reading this scene, had no doubt that it was straight
reportage, even to the mock-parsonical voice which Heseltine used
to mock what he thought of as pretension. It turned out that
mockery had been reserved for Lawrence's book of poems
Amores, and that Katherine Mansfield and John Middleton Murry,
angry at the derision of genius, got the book away from him and
stormed out.

This scene, with Birkin's letter 'harrowing hell, harrowing the
Pompadour', is a farewell to the 'foul town' which Gudrun hopes
never to see again. The two couples, one married, the other in a
state of fiery pre-marital trial, go to the Tyrol. Ursula and Birkin,
like Lawrence and Frieda, have found their peace, or something
like it; Gerald and Gudrun move to a resolution which is more
imbecilic than tragic. They sleep together, but there is something
wrong:

> She went to his room, hotly, violently in love with him.
> He was so beautiful and inaccessible. He kissed her, he was a
> lover to her. And she had extreme pleasure of him. But he
> did not come to, he remained remote and candid, un-
> conscious. She wanted to speak to him. But this innocent,
> beautiful state of unconsciousness that had come upon him
> prevented her. She felt tormented and dark.

Torment becomes the theme. Gudrun becomes fascinated by a
German Jew named Loerke, an artist like herself: they converse
with 'a queer interchange of half-suggested ideas, looks, ex-
pressions and gestures, which were quite intolerable, though

incomprehensible, to Gerald. He had no terms in which to think of
their commerce, his terms were much too gross.' Gudrun, in
Gerald's inexpressive view, is closer to the *habitués* of the Pompadour than she would care to think. Gerald saw a piece of primitive art – of the kind which Loerke loves – in Halliday's apart-
ment, and he hated 'the sheer barbaric thing . . . he wanted to
keep certain illusions, certain ideas like clothing'. He hits out at
the detestable Loerke (whose creator makes no effort to show
him as likeable), he is murderous towards Gudrun, he is both the
rabbit Bismarck and its would-be killer. He is, of course, an icy
anti-life mine-owner who has to be punished more severely than
Sir Clifford Chatterley, but he had seemed, before coming to this
place of ice, capable of redemption into a more than lifesize
Middleton Murry. Still, the reader is on his side; it is Gudrun
who becomes detestable. Of Gerald she thinks:

> He should have been a cockerel, so he could strut before
> fifty females, all his subjects. But really, his Don Juan does *not*
> interest me. I could play Dona Juanita a million times better
> than he plays Juan . . . As for Loerke, there is a thousand
> times more in him than in Gerald. Gerald is so limited, there
> is a dead end to him. He would grind on at the old mills for
> ever. And really, there is no corn between the millstones
> any more . . .

There seems to be too much crude sexuality in her sneers for our
comfort. This is not the Gudrun we once knew. She goes off into
Germany to live her own life, having accepted Loerke's sneers
against England, and Gerald dies in the snow, under one of the
half-buried crucifixes which are the subject of the first essay in
Twilight in Italy. He feels he is being murdered:

> Lord Jesus, was it then bound to be – Lord Jesus! He could
> feel the blow descending . . . vaguely wandering forward,
> his hands lifted as if to feel what would happen, he was
> waiting for the moment when he would stop, when it would
> cease. It was not over yet . . . But he wandered uncon-
> sciously, till he slipped and fell down, and as he fell some-
> thing broke in his soul, and immediately he went to sleep.

    The conclusion of the story is subdued, muffled. After Gerald's
death and burial in England (Gudrun has buried herself in
Dresden), Ursula and Birkin are 'both very quiet'. She, he admits,

is 'all woman' to him, but he 'wanted eternal union with a man too: another kind of love'. She thinks, as Frieda undoubtedly did, that this is perverse: you cannot have two kinds of love. 'You can't have it, because it's false, impossible.' Rather tamely he says: 'I don't believe that.' It is an *una corda* chord, not very convincing. Reading the novel has been a disturbing experience, but now one feels let down. All novels are difficult to bring to a conclusion, but one has become used to the Laurentian noise and fire and expected a Mahlerian consummation. But perhaps this descent to the tone of muted realism is right. Lawrence, who, unlike Joyce, never planned, is not often wrong with his endings. He says his say and then shuts up. He has said a very strange and disturbing say.

Why, in my view, is *Women in Love* one of the ten great novels of the century? Chiefly because, through the dangerous guesswork of introspection, Lawrence has come to certain conclusions about human emotions and motivations which draw men and women closer to nature – the world of plants, animals, sun and moon – than the old fictional emphasis on man as a social animal would allow. From Richardson on, the novel in English had admitted human passions enough, but only as checked by Christian ethics and social conventions. The victim-hero of Lawrence's first novel was a casualty of class (like his shadow the gamekeeper), but one has the impression there, reading back after this fifth novel, of forces getting outside the grip of society, of nature reclaiming human beings as irrational complexes of blood and nerve. It does not seem to me that the sun–moon relationship Birkin has been seeking with Ursula and Gerald is, in the overall scope of the novel, of first importance (an eccentricity it is big enough to accommodate), but that men and women should be shown as acting intensely according to their instincts is in accord with a view of humanity we all wish, but are too timid, to feel in 'the first and finest state of chaos' which is the industrialised twentieth century. Lawrence's achievement is all the more re-markable in that his naked primitives are also civilised beings who accede to the demands of society. Schools and coalmines have to be run, but there is a real life running underneath which has a claim on the novelist as on the poet. It was certainly no easy achievement to bring to a highly social form like the novel the intensity of high poetry.

Our first reading of *Women in Love* may impress us with a

sense of formlessness, of episode following episode without generation of a movement that may lead to a conclusion. Later readings show that there is no excess, no irrelevance, no self-indulgence. There is relentless motion with no sense of contrivance. The jettisoning of the artificial plot which had sustained the nineteenth-century novel was the joint work of Joyce, Ford Madox Ford, Hemingway and Lawrence. *Ulysses*, *The Good Soldier*, *The Sun Also Rises* and *Women in Love* demonstrate that human reality can be shown in a heightened form without manipulation, and that if a novel cannot present life direct and dangerous it is probably not worth writing.

9
A Snake and Sardinia

The man who was best equipped to appreciate the power and originality of *Women in Love* responded badly. John Middleton Murry, having remarked that its characters leave the reader cold – 'We remain utterly indifferent to their destinies' – added of their creator: 'He would, if he could, put us all on the rack to make us confess his protozoic god: he is deliberately, incessantly, and passionately obscene in the exact sense of the word.' Lawrence read this in Sicily in September 1921, along with headlines in *John Bull*: 'A Book the Police Should Ban' and 'Loathsome Study of Sex Depravity Leading Youth to Unspeakable Disaster.' To which Lawrence replied: 'Canaille, canaglia, Schweinhunderei, stinkpots. Pfui! – pish, pshaw, prrr! They all stink in my nostrils.'

But, in terms of its fictional representation, he had not finished with this longing for *Blutbrüderschaft* with Murry, though now it was to be openly converted into a desire for the submission to his master of a reluctant disciple. This comes into *Aaron's Rod*, a novel he had begun in London in 1918 and, after an interval of neglect, took up again and completed in the spring of 1921. It is a loose improvisation of which not much need be said. Aaron is a flautist (another of Lawrence's musician-heroes) who leaves the mining Midlands to play in an opera orchestra in London, grows sick of England, and decides to go to Italy for no other reason than that Lawrence himself had left England for Italy. That Aaron is partially based on Murry is made clear by his relationship with a man named Lilley, who speaks Laurentially to him and asks for his 'submission':

'All men say they want a leader. Then let them in their souls *submit* to some greater soul than theirs ... You, Aaron, you too have the need to submit. You, too, have the need livingly to yield to a more heroic soul, to give yourself. You know you have. And you know it isn't love. It is life-submission. And you know it. But you kick against the pricks. And perhaps you'd rather die than yield. And so, die you must. It is your affair.'

And when Aaron rather naïvely asks to whom he must submit, Lilley says: 'Your soul will tell you.' There are also episodes – like the one in which a sick Aaron is tended by a solicitous Lilley – which clearly derive from the wartime days of turbulent friendship. But Aaron is also, in his role of the working-class artist, Lawrence himself, especially when he is in contact with certain wealthy and cultured expatriates based on people Lawrence actually met in Turin. These, recognising themselves in the novel, were to speak loudly of 'a breach of hospitality'. It was merely the working-class Lawrence responding characteristically to *rentier* wealth and patrician manners.

Lawrence's aim on his first post-war exilic journey was to go with Frieda down to the village of Picinisco, remote, set in the mountains in the old kingdom of Naples, picturesque, primitive, totally unsuitable for a tubercular who had enough to do with passionate writing and did not need to weary himself with hill-treks to fetch supplies and mail. But Frieda had difficulty in fighting her way through the new frontier-ridden Europe and he waited for her in Florence. There he met Norman Douglas, author of *South Wind,* and a man who was to be a peculiar plague – Maurice Magnus, 'very pink-faced and very clean, very natty, very alert, like a sparrow painted to resemble a tom-tit'. Lawrence had already had vague literary dealings with Douglas but now he met him as the great representative of Mediterranean hedonism. A genuine pagan and a pagan puritan now confronted each other.

One Douglas, James, had been instrumental in getting *The Rainbow* suppressed. This new Douglas, no relation, was a fellow-Scot who had reacted against the sour Calvinism which bans books but had perhaps reacted too far. Having read Norman Douglas's few works and followed his life in Mark Holloway's detailed biography, I have to confess to a repugnance to the witty

cynicisms and the chortling pederasty. He is not my cup of tea or
thimble of Sambuca. Probably I have myself over-reacted to such
stories as the one in which Douglas boasted of having sodomised
a postman rendered unconscious by a bicycle accident. Douglas
in a sense justified his hedonism by taking time off from it to
write books which extol it, but a life of wine, buggery and joyful
scandal should, I think, ultimately be rather dull. On the other
hand, it may have been good for Lawrence to have his puritanical
earnestness assailed after a bad time in which his nerves had been
strung to breaking and his response to his troubles had been a
kind of prophetic hysteria. Relax, let go, enjoy life. For that
matter, enjoy Florence.

Lawrence did enjoy Florence; whether Florence enjoyed
Lawrence we do not know. When Frieda at last arrived there at
four in the morning, the lively husband had to take the exhausted
wife on a moonlight drive to see the city. He had written in his
book on European history about the great scourge Savonarola, a
masculine force whipping the soft sybarites, and it was to what
he thought of as the masculine strength of the town that he responded. It seems to some of us a soft enough place with a
mediocre cuisine redeemed only by the size of its beefsteaks,
provincial, self-regarding, living on its past, and the aesthetes who
call themselves Anglo-Florentines affirm the heresy that art is
best when it is dead. Lawrence rejoiced in the male nude statues,
which he saw as embodying the self-assertiveness of unspoilt pre-
industrial man. That they might be homoerotic did not occur to
him. Anyway, he and Frieda did not have the money to stay
long. They took the train to Caserta and a coughing mountain
bus towards Picinisco, ending the journey with a baggage-laden
donkey over a dry torrent, rickety planks over frothing streams,
up unclimbable paths, to reach the farm they were renting. Stone
floors, chicken-droppings, intense cold and no domestic facilities,
and above all the snow peaks of the Matese, ice on the air, an
impossible place for a man with Lawrence's lungs with the winter
beginning. They saw the light just before Christmas and walked
five miles to the bus for Cassino, took the train to Naples, then
endured the stormy night passage to Capri. The spirit of Norman
Douglas was leading them there.

Compton Mackenzie found them a flat. Lawrence loved the
lemon-scented refuge but recognised that the depravity of
Tiberius, or the salacity of Suetonius, had left its mark on an

island all sodomy, lesbianism, scandal and cosmopolitan artiness. Now there was leisure to be preyed upon by Douglas's friend Maurice Magnus, whom, inexplicably, Lawrence contacted first, though surely knowing what was in store. In certain people, particularly artists, there is a kind of masochistic fascination for the well-dressed, well-spoken sponger, the insouciant eater of a hard-earned substance. Lawrence now found that money was coming in, though not much. His association with Mackenzie, at that time something of a best-seller, certainly led Douglas to believe that he was wealthy but, in the manner of the jumped-up working class, unhealthily frugal and even immorally avaricious. Douglas had already suffered from Magnus, a shameless and inveterate beggar, and did not see why Lawrence should not suffer as well. Magnus replied to Lawrence in the tone of one whom the world has treated harshly, but he did not at first indulge the blatancy of asking for cash. The intelligent Lawrence was supposed to divine an immediate need and, soft-hearted, shell out. He did so, to the tune of five pounds. Then, when Magnus wrote that he was so destitute that he had had to fall upon the charity of the Benedictines at Monte Cassino, Lawrence went to visit him there. This was to result in one of the most remarkable prose evocations ever written of the life of the ancient monastery, embodied in the introduction Lawrence eventually wrote for Magnus's *Memoirs*.

The Magnus saga continued, a sore tooth that had to be probed to confirm its soreness, when the Lawrences left Capri – 'stewpot of semi-literary cats' – for Sicily. On the lower slope of Mount Etna, outside Taormina, they found an old house called the Fontana Vecchia and stayed there, off and on, for the next two years. With Magnus occasionally appearing as a mixture of nuisance and comic relief, Lawrence got down to writing and wrote well, or at least hard.

He had left in Germany the unfinished draft of a novel to be called *The Lost Girl* and, with the end of the war, this material had got back to him. He refashioned and finished it at the Fontana Vecchia, having in mind only the near-cynical fabrication of a pot-boiler, consciously imitating the style of Arnold Bennett and damping the Laurentian fires. The book offended no one and it even won the James Tait Black prize for 1921 – a hundred pounds – thus confirming its acceptability by the British public. It is not a great novel. It has a facetious perkiness like *Mr Noon*, full of a 'dear reader' buttonholing technique, and it cannot be bothered with the kind of psychological penetration that makes *Women in Love* so uncomfortable a masterpiece. But, Lawrence being Lawrence, it cannot resist exact visual notation of the world, as in the description of James Houghton's clothing business in the town of Woodhouse, which shows a Lawrence expert in silks and poplins, showing off with gratuitous catalogues:

> The women would pinch the thick, exquisite old chenille fringe, delicate and faded, curious to feel its softness. But they wouldn't give threepence for it. Tapes, ribbons, braids, buttons, feathers, jabots, bustles, appliqués, fringes, jet-trimmings, bugle-trimmings, bundles of old coloured machine-lace, many bundles of strange cord, in all colours, for old-fashioned braid-patterning, ribbons with HMS *Birkenhead* for boys' sailor caps – everything that nobody wanted, did the women turn over and over, till they chanced on a find.

This is Lawrence his mother's boy, out with her on a Friday evening's shopping. It is not like Henry James.

James Houghton's 'Manchester House' decays, and Alvina the daughter, twenty-six years old, settles to being a drudge for her father, feeling 'panic, the terrible and deadly panic which overcomes so many unmarried women at about the age of thirty. She would not care about marriage, if even she had a lover.' But there is no lover, and Alvina's brown hair shows signs of grey. Then Houghton starts a picture palace, with the cocky Mr May as manager, and she has to accompany *The Silent Grip* and Miss Poppy Traherne ('a lady in unnumerable petticoats, who could whirl herself into anything you like, from an arum lily in green stockings to a rainbow and a Catherine wheel and a cup and saucer: marvellous, was Miss Poppy Traherne' – the tone is almost Wellsian) on the pianoforte. The takings are counted, and Lawrence reveals his concern with the magic of specie, a man who does not think in terms of cheques:

> There they were: burly dragoons of stout pennies, heavy and holding their ground, with a screen of halfpenny light infantry, officered by the immovable half-crown general, who in his turn was flanked by all his staff of florin colonels

and shilling captains, from whom lightly moved the nimble sixpenny lieutenants, all ignoring the wan, frail Joey of the threepenny bits.

Alvina finds herself involved in a kind of Crummles ambience of travelling performers, and then she meets Ciccio.

Ciccio, a southern Italian, prefigures Lawrence's preoccupation with Indians, for he acts one and affects Alvina adversely: 'Ciccio's . . . muscular slouch made her feel she would not trust him for one single moment. Awful things men were, savage, cruel, underneath their civilisation.' This sounds like a spinsterish summation of *Women in Love*. When her father dies, Alvina is adopted by the troupe which puts on – in music halls or between films – a Red Indian act. Lawrence is remembering his reading of Fenimore Cooper here, what with the cries of 'We have no law but Huron law' and 'We have no law-giver except Kishwegin'. Alvina becomes the 'the squaw Allaye' and thus anticipates what happens to Kate in *The Plumed Serpent*. And Ciccio reveals 'the lovely, rich darkness of his southern nature' in his love for her, which leads to marriage and Italy. The farewell to England is Lawrence's own:

> She caught Ciccio's arm, as the boat rolled gently. For there behind, behind all the sunshine, was England. England, beyond the water, rising with ash-grey, corpse-grey cliffs, and streaks of snow on the downs above. England, like a long, ash-grey coffin slowly submerging. She watched it, fascinated and terrified. It seemed to repudiate the sunshine, to remain unilluminated, long and ash-grey and dead, with streaks of snow like cerements. That was England! . . . Home!
>
> Her heart died within her. Never had she felt so utterly strange and far-off. Ciccio at her side was as nothing, as spell-bound she watched, away off, behind all the sunshine and the sea, the grey, snow-streaked substance of England slowly receding and sinking, submerging. She felt she could not believe it. It was like looking at something else. What? It was like a long, ash-grey coffin, winter, slowly submerging in the sea. England?

Yes, England. Note Lawrence's technique, or mannerism, of repetition. Having found certain *mots justes*, like 'ash-grey' and 'behind all the sunshine', he is not content to let the single sounding reverberate. There is a liturgical quality about the re-statement. It is there at the very end of the book, where Alvina, whom Ciccio calls Allaye as if they were still acting Indians, faces his going to the war and the possible fatherless condition of her unborn child. 'I'll come back,' he says. 'I'll come back, and we'll go to America.' And she says: 'You'll come back to me.' And he: 'I'll come back.'

A re-reading of *The Lost Girl* discloses the kind of fictional virtues we associate with Bennett and Wells – much detail of English provincial life, a plot that wishes to move but finds its feet clogged in a great deal of realistic observation, a humour that approaches the facetious, honest emotion hampered by the limitations of vocabulary of lower-middle-class characters. It is at the tail-end of the Edwardian tradition, of which Lawrence, even at its most original, never entirely abandoned the artless style of *récit*. It is only with Joyce's *Ulysses* that we see the break being effected, but the first chapter of that revolutionary work still pays a kind of lingering homage to the old way. It was not a bad way, cheerfully ignoring the big Flaubertian preoccupations – point of view, economy, the planting of symbols. It was the Dickensian way, finding its swansong as late as the 1960s with J. B. Priestley's *The Image Men*. It was very British.

Lawrence, happy in Sicily though still poor, met one snake and wrote an astonishing poem about it. Another snake, Magnus, now slithered in and asked for money. The asking was done in the gentlemanly, highly plausible manner of a man used to better things whom life had unaccountably let down. Magnus said he had been staying at a hotel in Anzio, had paid his bill with a cheque on his American bank, had been mortified to see it bounce – the fault of people he had trusted but who had proved unreliable in the refreshing of his funds. He had done the reasonable thing – left his bags at Monte Cassino and come straight to Taormina, disap-pointed and even hurt to find Lawrence temporarily absent. He was naturally staying in a hotel in the town suitable for a gentle-man but could not pay his bill. Would Lawrence pay it, grant him the hospitality of his villa until he could sell some articles to newspapers and, duly paid, go off to Alexandria? Or perhaps Lawrence would prefer the alternative of advancing him thirty-five pounds on the security of certain manuscripts of considerable literary potential? A final and minor request was that Lawrence should go to Monte Cassino and pick up Magnus's bags.

The Lawrence–Magnus relationship represents a very curious symbiosis. Why did Magnus, who knew people like Norman Douglas far better, pick on a comparative stranger to resolve his problems? Why did Lawrence, still poor, feel vaguely responsible for a man he hardly knew? Questions not easily answered. The letters show that he paid Magnus's hotel bill, gave him a hundred lire, and cashed him a cheque for seven guineas which he had earned through one of Lawrence's literary contacts. Magnus then went to Malta, and that seemed to be the end of him. But, by chance, Gilbert Cannan, a novelist acquaintance of Lawrence's, had come to Taormina, and his wife Mary was rather anxious to see Malta, though her husband was not. Would the Lawrences, at the expense of the Cannans, chaperone her thither? They agreed, and all three travelled to Syracuse to take ship. A seamen's strike delayed departure. Lawrence assumed that Magnus had taken an earlier sailing and was now installed in some such luxury hotel as the Phoenicia in Valletta. But no: Magnus, to whom the strike was a great bother, had been sitting it out in the best hotel in Syracuse; naturally, he could not pay his bill. Lawrence paid it for him and, from the second class of the ship, was able to observe Magnus lording it in first. He nodded at Lawrence in a princely manner as he disembarked, then proceeded to Mdina, where some Maltese to whom he had been recommended by monks of Monte Cassino found him a house, furniture, and a loan of sixty pounds. But the police nets of Europe were beginning to widen, and the bad cheque of Anzio caught up with him. He took poison like a gentleman, leaving instructions that he should be given a first-class burial. His manuscripts were impounded by his creditors, who trusted the new acquaintance Lawrence more than the old friend Douglas and begged him to sell them so that the debts could be settled. Lawrence did his best, but a letter written to the *New Statesman* states that the bulk of them were worthless.

The letter was written in reply to an insinuation of Norman Douglas's that Lawrence had been 'unkind' to Magnus and that he had made money out of his literary effects. As Lawrence points out, he had written a long introduction to Magnus's *Memoirs of the Foreign Legion*, a book no publisher was willing to accept. 'More than one publisher said "We will publish the Introduction alone, without the Magnus Memoirs." To which I said: "That's no good. The Introduction only exists for the Memoirs."' We can read that introduction, apart from the *Memoirs*, in the posthumous miscellany entitled *Phoenix*. We get the eerie impression that the Muse had driven Lawrence to a noxious association with a cad and sponger only that a remarkable piece of literature could be written. Magnus has been made immortal:

> M— was a fervent Catholic, taking the religion, alas, rather unctuously. He had entered the Church only a few years before. But he had a bishop for a god-father, and seemed to be very intimate with the upper clergy. He was very pleased and proud because he was a constant guest at the famous old monastery south of Rome. He talked of becoming a monk; a monk in that aristocratic and well-bred order. But he had not even begun his theological studies. And D— [Douglas] said he only chose the Benedictines because they lived better than any of the others.

And here is Lawrence seeing everything, making no notes, achieving something like total recall:

> We went up the narrow stair and into the long, old, naked white corridor, high and arched. Don Bernardo had got the key of my room: two keys, one for the dark ante-chamber, one for the bedroom. A charming and elegant bed-room, with an engraving of English landscape, and outside the net curtain a balcony looking down on the garden, a narrow strip beneath the walls, and, beyond, the clustered buildings of the farm, and the oak woods and arable fields of the hill summit: and beyond again, the gulf where the world's valley was, and all the mountains that stand in Italy on the plains as if God had just put them down ready made. The sun had already sunk, the snow on the mountains was full of a rosy glow, the valleys were full of shadow. One heard, far below, the trains shunting, the world clinking in the cold air.

Charles Ryder, in Evelyn Waugh's *Brideshead Revisited*, paints stately homes due for destruction and describes himself as bringing along his paints and easel a little while before the forces of demolition. It could be said of Lawrence that Magnus led him to the memorialisation of Monte Cassino twenty years before total war flattened it – plenty of time, perhaps, but not for Lawrence, who had only nine years to live.

This post-war period in the Sicilian sun was dedicated to

drinking in life and also, less in fiction than in poetry and one outstanding travel book, conveying the taste and colour of life with that daring in which Lawrence excelled. The outstanding travel book is *Sea and Sardinia*, the most charming work he ever wrote and by far the best introduction to his *oeuvre*. He and Frieda spent a mere week on a winter trip to an island where he thought he might find men untainted by industrialism and the desire to die. The real urge for going was the restlessness which was soon to take him round the world, combined with discontent with a Sicilian January ('it thunders and lightnings for twenty-four hours and hailstorms continually') and probably distaste for the other English-speaking exiles of Taormina. Properly, I should now let Lawrence take over totally, for *Sea and Sardinia*, besides being a small miracle of a book, is a wonderful self-portrait and it shows Lawrence at his most attractive. Frieda, called 'the queen-bee' or 'the q-b', is a little in the background, but one is aware of a strong personality holding itself humorously in, attractive too, more passively responsive than Lawrence to the sights and sounds of travel. By the standards of the seekers of genuine foreign adventure, this account of a week's trip (4–10 February 1921) to a cold island (did Lawrence honestly think he could get away from a bad winter by merely shifting from one Mediterranean zone to another?) is banal and lacking in surprising events, but its magic lies in what the power of poetic observation can do with the ordinary. A couple of sea-trips, bus-rides, train-journeys, a few nights in bad inns – these are enough.

To say that the book is 'poetical' is not the best tribute to it, if by the term we mean the carefully wrought Paterian or the turgid purple Ruskinian. But by now we expect Lawrence's poetry to be different from any other man's: it is not the result of the creative process, it is the creative process itself. We are always in the smithy, watching the verbal hammering. In his impatience to find the right phrase for his referent, Lawrence cannot be bothered to hide his false starts; nor can he trouble himself with well-balanced 'literary' sentences. When he finds the *mot juste* he does not let it go; he invites us to walk round it and appraise its justness. There is a sense of reading a private notebook; there is also a sense of hearing actual speech, complete with fractured syntax, repetition, slang, facetiousness, buttonholing, even bullying. We have, of course, met these properties before, in the novels, but there they are often irritating, while here they charm and disarm and serve an end of sharp immediacy and strong colour.

What particularly charms and disarms is Lawrence's ineradicable Englishness. You would not think that here was a man who had abandoned, and been abandoned by, his country. There is something very touching about the pawky patriotism with which, when Italians attack it, he defends England. Only America and England have done well out of the war, complain the Italians: here are Englishmen in Italy taking advantage of the *cambio* and exploiting us nice, good people, and so on. There was a time when Lawrence had been apt to coo over Italian peasants and artisans, in the manner of those British tourists who want to be considered *simpatici*. Not now. Lawrence never worries about being *simpatico* (was Dante *simpatico*?). He knows his own class, and he is not bemused by the Italian representatives of it. The miner's son packs bacon sandwiches ('good English bacon from Malta') and a thermosful of strong tea for the start of the journey. If the little Sicilian bank clerks stare at the rucksack on his shoulder, then to hell with them. And yet no English traveller in Italy ever understood the bank clerks and the carpenters and the roadmenders better.

It is the anonymous people in this Sardinian travel book who have become immortal for us in a way that the named personages of many a sterner work have not. Even the most horrible of them, like the innkeeper whose dirty waistcoat is a brazen insult, or the fat handsome woman in the train who looks at Lawrence, evidently wondering if he considers her a *bel pezzo*, inhabit the back quarters of our memories and become confused with people we have met in actuality, not in books. The sharpness of Lawrence's eye is incredible, and his judgments are madly sane. The Sicilians are 'so terribly physically all over one another. They pour themselves over the other like so much melted butter over parsnips. They catch each other under the chin, with a tender caress of the hand, and they smile with sunny melting tenderness into each other's faces.' So they do, but who but Lawrence would have thought in terms of buttered parsnips? And who but he would have tried to explain the gross tenderness in terms of living under a volcano? 'Naples and Catania alike, the men are hugely fat, with great macaroni paunches, they are expansive and in a perfect drip of casual affection and love ... They never leave off being amorously friendly with almost everybody, emitting a

relentless physical familiarity that is quite bewildering to one not
brought up near a volcano.' This is typical good bad Laurentian
logic, always more persuasive than other men's cautious rationa-
lity.

Look at this opening:

> Comes over one an absolute necessity to move. And what
> is more, to move in some particular direction. A double
> necessity then: to get on the move, and to know whither.
>
> Why can't one sit still? Here in Sicily it is so pleasant: the
> sunny Ionian sea, the changing jewel of Calabria, like a fire-
> opal moved in the light; Italy and the panorama of Christmas
> clouds, night with the dog-star laying a long, luminous
> gleam across the sea, as if baying at us, Orion marching
> above; how the dog-star Sirius looks at one, looks at one! he
> is the hound of heaven, green, glamorous and fierce! – and
> then, oh regal evening star, hung westward flaring over the
> jagged dark precipices of tall Sicily: then Etna, that wicked
> witch, resting her thick white snow under heaven, and
> slowly, slowly rolling her orange-coloured smoke . . . She
> seems rather low, under heaven. But as one knows her better,
> oh, awe and wizardry! . . . When I look at her, low, white,
> witch-like under heaven, slowly rolling her orange smoke
> and giving sometimes a breath of rose-red flame, then I must
> look away from earth, into the ether, into the low empyrean.
> And there, in that remote region, Etna is alone. If you would
> see her, you must slowly take off your eyes from the world
> and go a naked seer to the strange chamber of the empyrean.
> Pedestal of heaven!

And so on. Once having started, one feels like transcribing the
whole of that first, leave-taking, chapter. But one is ready to be
told that it is bad prose – that affected inversion at the beginning,
the 'oh' and the exclamation points, the very Laurentian repeti-
tions. Still, what magic. And this Etna rhapsody is a mere loos-
ening of the fingers before Lawrence sails into a more various
music. It is not all music. Here are Lawrence and Frieda in a
ghastly inn in Risveglio:

> The be-shawled appeared with a dish of kid. Needless to
> say, the *ignoranti* had kept all the best portions for themselves.
> What arrived was five pieces of cold roast, one for each of

us. Mine was a sort of large comb of ribs with a thin web of meat: perhaps an ounce. That was all we got, after watching the whole process. There was moreover a dish of strong boiled cauliflower, which one ate, with the coarse bread, out of sheer hunger. After this a bilious orange. Simply one is not *fed* nowadays.

This is a very reasonable Lawrence, wanting the plain rights of a miner's son at table, quite unlike the whining and grousing Norman Douglas exiled to wartime rationed London. Then comes the filthy bedroom, the absence of coffee the following morning, and the righteous Lawrence giving out at the landlord:

> 'Why,' say I, lapsing into the Italian rhetorical manner, 'why do you keep an inn? Why do you write the word Ristorante so large, when you have nothing to offer people, and don't intend to have anything? Why do you have the impudence to take in travellers? What does it mean, that this is an inn? What, say, what does it mean? Say then – what does it mean? What does it mean, your Ristorante Risveglio, written so large?'

And he picks up every farthing of the change. The queen-bee suggests a tip. Lawrence is speechless.

This, then, is no idyllic sojourn among noble peasants cut off from Europe's growing commercial corruption. Lawrence is always looking for unspoilt Sardinian yeomen with stocking-caps and yellow leggings, and he actually sees a few of them proudly walking, but he is not taken in by meanness, ill-humour and rapacity. He gives out as his mother did at bad scrag-end in the Friday market. One loves him for this. And for this indomitable eye:

> The costumes had changed again. There was again the scarlet, but no green. The green had given place to mauve and rose. The women in one cold, stony, rather humbled broken place were most brilliant. They had the geranium skirts, but their sleeveless boleros were made to curl out strangely from the waist, and they were edged with a puckered rose-pink, a broad edge, with lines of mauve and lavender. As they went up between the houses that were dark and grisly under the blank, cold sky, it is amazing how these women of vermilion and rose-pink seemed to melt

into an almost impossible blare of colour. What a risky blend of colours! Yet how superb it could look, that dangerous hard assurance of these women as they strode along so blaring. I would not like to tackle one of them.

'Risky' – a word for Lawrence himself. To risk a memory unaided by Samuel Butler's little notebook in the waistcoat pocket and to come up with such exactness of description – not just here but everywhere on that Sardinian trip – was Lawrence's peculiar daring. Part of the remarkable piquancy of the book lies in the wonderful open generosity of this eye that misses nothing and its contrast with the Lawrence who so easily gets fed up with everybody:

> 'Ah,' she said, 'we Italians, we are so nice, we are so good. Noi, siamo così buoni. We are so good-natured. But others, they are not buoni, they are not good-natured to us.' And she nodded her head. And truly, I did not feel at all good-natured towards her: which she knew. And as for the Italian good-nature, it forms a sound and unshakable basis nowadays for their extortion and self-justification and spite.

Lawrence had no illusions about people, but he went on hoping that somewhere decency, unspoilt nobility, fine bodies and unclouded instincts coexisted. It depended, he believed, on place, on the spirit of place.

That spirit, he said, is a strange thing. 'Our mechanical age tries to override it. But it does not succeed. In the end the strange, sinister spirit of the place, so diverse and adverse in differing places, will smash our mechanical oneness into smithereens, and all that we think the real thing will go off with a pop, and we shall be left staring.' He meant, of course, certain gods, unconquerable *numina*, which we oppose at our peril. His search for these in the last years of his life took him far away from Sardinia.

10
The Prophecy is in the Poetry

One of the major achievements of the post-war exile was a series of poems eventually published under the title *Birds, Beasts and Flowers*. We call them poems because of the intense sensibility they disclose and the emotive and descriptive daring of the language, but they could as well be fragments of essays, jottings in a notebook, digressions in a story or a novel. That charging of language with meaning which Ezra Pound saw as the essence of literature (meaning poetry) is characteristic of nearly everything Lawrence wrote, even the odd dashed-off letter, but it is not often meaning in the William Empson sense, where complexity resides in the word as a product of linguistic and cultural history. Lawrence never wrote anything as obscure as this (by Empson):

> Bubbles gleam brightest with least depth of lands
> But two is least can with full tension strain,
> Two molecules; one, and the film disbands.

The charging of words in Lawrence is an emotional matter, not a polysemic one. He himself is always so very much there, pontific, self-doubtful, humble, raging, letting the free-verse lines rush out – units drawn from his own speech-patterns – and impatiently spending words as freely as seed in the search for an essence. Take the first poem in the collection – 'Pomegranate'. It seems at first to be very little concerned with pomegranates:

> You tell me I am wrong.
> Who are you, who is anybody to tell me I am wrong?
> I am not wrong.

Then comes a reference to the rock of Syracuse, 'left bare by the viciousness of Greek women', and a nasty attack on Venice – 'Abhorrent, green, slippery city' – with pomegranates thrown in as distracted bestowals – 'Oh so red, and such a lot of them' – and finally the essence of the whole mixed irritable poetic statement is located in the fissure of the fruit – 'the gold-filmed skin, integument, shown ruptured' – and its metaphoric applicability to the breaking of the poet's heart, which the poet wants: 'It is so lovely, dawn kaleidoscopic within the crack'. Lawrence seems to make poetry out of not caring a damn what poetry is supposed to be. He was a great disappointment to the Georgians and the Imagists alike.

The poems are immensely entertaining, a quality which is not supposed to be the primary desideratum of poetry, which ought to enlighten more than divert, but Lawrence is enlightening enough about peaches – 'Why the groove?/Why the lovely, bivalve roundnesses?/Why the ripple down the sphere?/Why the suggestion of incision?' – as well as wayward ('Somebody's pound of flesh rendered up') and aggressive:

But it wasn't round and finished like a billiard ball.
And because I say so, you would like to throw something at me.
Here, you can have my peach stone.

'Medlars and sorb-apples' is about 'the distilled essence of hell' and 'the *ego sum* of Dionysos' and 'the intoxication of final loneliness' and the coming unacceptability of the wine of Marsala 'in the pussyfoot West'. Since the Italian *fica* is the vulva, Lawrence makes his verse-essay on figs a kind of rhapsody of the female mystery as well as an attack on female self-assertion. Women are ripe for bursting out, but 'ripe figs won't keep'. The fig-tree itself, especially when bare, has a different kind of secret: it is a 'wicked tree', putting out casual buds from its thigh, every twig 'the arch twig' with a demotic right to point to heaven:

Demos, Demos, Demos!
Demon, too,
Wicked fig-tree, equality puzzle, with your self-conscious
    secret fruits.

And the almond-trees of Taormina, equally bare, take in strange messages 'From heaven's wolfish, wandering electricity, that prowls so constantly round Etna'. Lawrence's botany and

dendrology are highly symbolic, but the meanings of the symbols
shift, grow confused, collapse; what we are always left with is
a tree or a flower as a kind of communication from the dark
gods, a message in difficult code which only Lawrence can
unscramble:

> *Jesus the god of flowers* —?
> Not he.
> *Or sun-bright Apollo, him so musical?*
> Him neither.
>
> *Who then?*
> *Say who.*
> Say it — and it is Pluto,
> Dis,
> The dark one.
> Proserpine's master.

This discovery of the reality of that Greek hell which is also the
creative unconscious must serve here facetious gibes about the
'women's rights' of Ceres and her daughter, overborne by the
'purple husband–tyranny' of Pluto (Lawrence himself lording it
over Ceres-haired Frieda), but we, who know Lawrence is going
to die and who have read his 'Bavarian Gentians', can anticipate
the consolation of the ancient vegetation myth to one whose
life's work celebrated the cycle of life. It was in the lands of the
Mediterranean that Lawrence first became fully conscious of the
magic of that cycle, not in an English spring. None of the trees
and flowers he celebrates so strangely had been known to grow
near the Congregationalist Chapel in Eastwood.

The four curious poems about the 'Evangelistic Beasts' that
preface the rhapsodies on totally unsymbolic animals show
Lawrence worrying about the Christ of the Congregationalist
Chapel and trying to break his hold over the lion, the bull, the
man and the eagle that have been tamed into the gospel-writers.
'Oh put them back, put them back in the four corners of the
heavens, where they belong, the Apocalyptic beasts.' Some slight
confusion there, but Lawrence always took confusion in his stride.
Take St Mark, whose leonine ferocity has been paradoxically
dulled by his being given wings: 'Ah, Lamb of God,/Would a
wingless lion lie down before Thee, as this winged lion lies?'
Take St Luke, the bull:

Since the Lamb bewitched him with that red-struck flag
His fortress is dismantled
His fires of wrath are banked down
His horns turn away from the enemy.

Take St John the eagle, whom Lawrence with no trouble converts
into a phoenix which is 'only known to us now as the badge of
an Insurance Company'. (The variety of registers is, as always,
remarkable, encompassing the low colloquial and the prophetic,
and everything in between.) All the great beasts have been
brought low by the gospel of the Lamb. Lawrence turns from
their defiled hides and clipped claws to the unemblematic realities
of mosquito, fish, bat, snake, tortoise. Having got symbolism out
of the way, he is free to concentrate on bestial essences. The fish,
for instance:

And the gold-and-green pure lacquer-mucus comes off in
    my hand,
And the red-gold mirror-eye stares and dies,
And the water-suave contour dims.

This magical poem was written in Zell-am-See. Frieda had gone
to Germany to visit her family, Lawrence followed, became
depressed because somehow left out of the boisterous Teutonic
reunion, and very amateurishly took to fishing in the lake. It was
the holding of a landed fish in his hand that bred wonder, an
awareness that his God was not that of water-creatures, and a
strange tingling glumness:

Cats, and the Neapolitans,
Sulphur sun-beasts,
Thirst for fish as for more-than-water;
Water-alive
To quench their over-sulphureous lusts.

But I, I only wonder
And don't know.
I don't know fishes.

In the beginning
Jesus was called The Fish. . . .
And in the end.

Jesus again, waiting to be sexually fulfilled in *The Man Who Died* and then sent away in a boat.

Bats were easier to deal with than fish, being merely disgusting ('Creatures that hang themselves up like an old rag, to sleep'), but, Lawrence being Lawrence, he had to look deeper into the 'wings like bits of umbrella' and establish a relationship. A bat got into his bedroom in Florence 'at mid-morning' and it tried to get out through the open window, but Lawrence saw that its reluctance to engage the daylight was like that of a man faced with 'the white-hot door of a blast furnace'. The bat gyrated

> Till he fell in a corner, palpitating, spent,
> And there, a clot, he squatted and looked at me.
> With sticking-out, bead-berry eyes, black,
> And improper derisive ears,
> And shut wings,
> And brown, furry body.

Free, the creature is imagined as chirping derisively at the poet when night falls:

> *There he sits, the long loud one!*
> *But I am greater than he . . .*
> *I escaped him. . . .*

This fanciful anthropomorphism, suitable for children's stories and poems about cats by maiden ladies, is not typical of Lawrence. He likes animals to maintain their otherness. He has a respect for their utter at-homeness in a world in which not even he could be fully at home, and this respect sometimes approaches worship. This is true of the attitude he shows towards the snake in his garden at Taormina, despite the voices of his human education and his Adamic fear. He throws a log at the snake and forces it into a convulsion of 'undignified haste' as it escapes. And then he regrets the act: 'how paltry, how vulgar'. For the snake is a king in exile, 'uncrowned in the underworld', a claimant to the throne of Dis. 'And so I missed my chance with one of the lords of life.' No other writer has this unpretentious sense of the sacredness of the world of beasts and reptiles, nor this willingness to give up his own raging ego (the curse he always carried with him) in an almost desperate desire for identification with pure being untortured by thought and feeling.

Faced with two very unpoetically titled works of this post-war

era, *Psycho-Analysis and the Unconscious* and *Fantasia of the Unconscious*, the naïve reader of Lawrence might be inclined to
think that he had the capacity to split himself into nature-poet
and psychologico-metaphysician, but he was always, to use a hard
word, a holistic writer. 'This pseudo-philosophy of mine,' he
writes in a preface to the second of the works,

> is deduced from the novels and poems, not the reverse. The
> novels and poems come unwatched out of one's pen. And
> then the absolute need which one has for some sort of satis-
> factory mental attitude towards oneself and things in general
> makes one try to abstract some definite conclusions from
> one's experiences as a writer and as a man. The novels and
> poems are pure passionate experience. These 'pollyanalytics'
> are inferences made afterwards, from the experience.

The eponym of H. G. Wells's *Christina Alberta's Father*, a retired
laundry manager, reads a 'nice, confusing book called *Fantasia of
the Unconscious*' before sleep and finds it full of nice things like
the lost Atlantis. In one sense it is a nice book for uninstructed
laundry managers, as it needs in the reader no preliminary
grounding in anything. It posits a willingness to be wholly persuaded by its author that science matters not at all, and that all
we need is a faith in the Laurentian solar plexus.

The first published of the duo, brief, little more than a
pamphlet, upset Freudians by attacking the Freudian concept of
the unconscious and its exclusive freight of suppressed incest.
Lawrence, in the view of those intellectuals who had read *Sons
and Lovers*, was the last person who ought to diminish Freud; and
as for denying the importance of sex, was not Lawrence supposed
to be the self-proclaimed secular sex-prophet? Lawrence in fact
had very reasonably joined those who admired Freud without
being able to accept the totality of his doctrine, which was too
narrow. There was more in the unconscious than the stuff of
sexual neurosis. The unconscious, according to Lawrence, was
the great source of creation, a limitless forest of green or fiery life
which was diminished by a negative appellation – *un*, indeed. Nor
did Lawrence much care for the doctrine, as much Jungian as
Freudian, of the unconscious as a general or collective possession.
Each individual soul was unique, a fresh creation, not easily ex-
plained in the simple arithmetic of the conjoined genes of the
parents. Lawrence comes curiously close here to a poet he never

knew – Gerard Manley Hopkins S.J., who proclaimed God's glory in the multiplicity of separate selfhoods and inscapes which pied or variegated the world. A poet has to rejoice in particularities. This, naturally, turned Lawrence against science, whose task is to propound general laws. To Lawrence, as to Hopkins, every daisy was different from every other daisy. As it was the special skill of the human brain to formulate life-denying generalities, it was only natural that Lawrence should turn against the brain and find the centres of thought and feeling in the body. He is very plausible about this, locating powerful *élans* below the navel and seeming to think little of the cerebral cortex which made him the genius he was and, for that matter, earned him his living.

Lawrence admits that he is:

> not a proper archaeologist nor an anthropologist nor an ethnologist. I am no 'scholar' of any sort. But I am very grateful to scholars for their sound work . . . from the Yoga and Plato and St John the Evangel and the early Greek philosophers like Herakleitos down to Frazer and his 'Golden Bough' and even Freud and Frobenius. Even then I only remember hints – and I proceed by intuition. This leaves you quite free to dismiss the whole wordy mass of revolting nonsense, without a qualm.

This is all very disarming, especially the tongue in the cheek when praising the 'sound work' of scholars (the Yoga? St John?) whom he reads only to reject or wilfully misinterpret. Having disclaimed scholarship, he proceeds, in the preface to the *Fantasia*, to summarise in terms far from tentative his conviction that there used to be a kind of ancient international knowledge when 'men wandered back and forth from Atlantis to the Polynesian Continent as men now sail from Europe to America. The interchange was complete, and knowledge, science was universal over the earth, cosmopolitan as it is today.' Certain talismanic names are invoked – 'Druids or Etruscans or Chaldeans or Amerindians . . .' who did not forget an ancient irrational science but 'taught the old wisdom, only in its half-forgotten, symbolic forms. More or less forgotten, as knowledge: remembered as ritual, gesture, and myth-story.'

This can be embarrassing to a certain kind of trained mind: it even sounds like burbling about the dimensions of the Great

Pyramid or the sanctity of Haile Selassie. But Lawrence is right in his insistence that there is a way of knowing the world not available to modern science, and that modern science, explaining essences, is not very efficient at relating essences to appearances. We are told, and can see demonstrated, that water is compounded of two gases, but abstract gaseousness does not accord with physical wetness. It is the old business of the noumenon and the phenomenon. Whatever the thing-in-itself happens to be, we live in a universe of phenomena, and the sun, seeming to rise in the east, has long irradiated our brains (or solar plexuses) and our very language with the need to accept an appearance as a reality. The Malays locate emotion in the liver and Europeans in the heart, and Tertullian the church father warned against dismissing the wisdom of popular tradition. Our bodies are intimately involved in both thought and emotion; what Lawrence was trying to do, in these two strange books as elsewhere, was to dethrone the central nervous system and its epiphenomenon the intellect and revive the ancient claims of the entire physical complex. This was a salutary thing to do.

It was, of course, a poetic thing to do. Baconian and Newtonian science have to be very wary of poetry, which does not proceed according to the method of unassailable first principles and the syllogistic arrival at a necessarily equally unassailable conclusion. But clearly poetry, even when in prose, springs from a desperate need to establish relationships between elements drawn from experience whose rationale is irrational. The evening *does* lie against the sky like a patient etherised upon a table. It is only because prose is the traditional medium of rational discourse that some of Lawrence's prose assertions occasionally sound absurd, and the intenseness appropriate to a poem appears shrill and hectoring:

> You've got first and foremost a solar plexus, dear reader; and the solar plexus is a great nerve centre which lies behind your stomach. I can't be accused of impropriety or untruth, because any book of science or medicine which deals with the nerve-system of the human body will show it to you quite plainly. So don't wriggle or try to look spiritual. Because, willy-nilly, you've got a solar plexus, dear reader, among other things . . . Now your solar plexus, most gentle of readers, is where you are. It is your first and greatest and

deepest centre of consciousness ... There you have the profound and pristine conscious awareness that you are you. Don't say you haven't. I know you have. You might as well try to deny the nose on your face.

It is a bullying tone, not very well mitigated by its facetiousness. But it frequently serves the blunt empirical sense of a Nottinghamshire boy who has seen the world and experienced the problems of living with other people:

> Wives, don't love your husbands any more: even if they cry for it, the great babies! Sing: 'I've had enough of that old sauce.' And leave off loving them or caring for them one single bit. Don't even hate or dislike them. Don't have any stew with them at all. Just boil the eggs and fill the salt-cellars and be quite nice, and in your own soul be alone and be still. Be alone, and be still, preserving all the human decencies, and abandoning the indecency of desires and benevolencies and devotions, those beastly poison-gas apples of the Sodom vine of love-will.

I feel uncomfortable, as do many people, with this Lawrence the Croydon teacher transformed into the prophet of polarities. Lawrence presumably wanted to impart discomfort.

Before leaving the Lawrence of the prophetic books, I had better anticipate and notice a work written late and published posthumously, a brief work whose title puts many off, implying as it does some ultimate sacred vision. Apocalypse, as Lawrence says, merely means Revelation, and he has some privy, sensible and quite unshrill revelations to impart about the possible true meaning of what – 'in day-school or Sunday-school, at home or in Band of Hope or Christian Endeavour' – the Eastwood lad considered the least attractive of the books of the Bible. What Lawrence's *Apocalypse* tells us in effect is that we are all part of the cosmos, a living thing which would communicate with us if only science and Christianity did not get in the way, and with which in turn we could ourselves communicate: 'We and the cosmos are one. The cosmos is a vast living body, of which we are still parts. The sun is a great heart whose tremors run through our smallest veins. The moon is a great gleaming nerve-centre from which we quiver forever.' Unfortunately, however, 'we have lost the cosmos. The sun strengthens us no more, neither

does the moon.' This can all be blamed on Plato and Aristotle
and St Thomas Aquinas.

For, says Lawrence, the Athenian and scholastic urge to get at
what was called the Truth resulted in intellectual abstractions, 'a
non-vital universe of forces and mechanistic order ... and the
long slow death of the human being set in. This slow death
produced science and machinery, but both are death products.'
Accepted, perhaps, but what has this to do with the purple language and strange images of St John of Patmos? Lawrence
believed – naturally without evidence – that the Book of Revelation uses a symbology derived from pre-Christian cosmogonies
in the service of destroying those ancient life-sustaining systems:
the Christian mystics had not been able to devise a new symbolic
language for themselves so, brutally, they used what already
existed but turned its meanings inside out. Moreover, the cosmic
power expressed in the symbology was being meanly reduced to
a frustrated desire for power of a different order. The words of
Revelation were, to the chapelgoers of Lawrence's youth, a
vehicle of class resentment: the rich would be brought low and
the common people inherit the earth. Babylon the Great must
crumble to dust and the snarling underdog feed in the ruins.

The anti-democratic – or anti-demos – bias of the book is in
accord with the philosophy of an individualist who saw political
levelling as an aspect of the generalising, reductive tendencies of a
civilisation based on reason. And yet the book, in its remarkably
cool and reasonable way, preaches no anarchy: man, it states, is
fulfilled in society, though not the mechanistic levelled one; there
is need for hierarchy, a fulfilment of the ruled in the glory of the
ruler. Dangerous words, perhaps. We have to remember that
Lawrence died three years before Hitler came to power. But the
political theme had best be ignored: this philosopher writer can
rarely be swallowed whole.

What ought to be savoured before swallowing is the final
manifesto, that of a dying man in whose rhetoric there is nothing
moribund. It is, of course, more than rhetoric:

> What man most passionately wants is his living wholeness
> and his living unison, not his own isolate salvation of his .
> 'soul'. Man wants his physical fulfilment first and foremost,
> since now, once and once only, he is in the flesh and potent.
> For man, the vast marvel is to be alive. For man, as for

flower and beast and bird, the supreme triumph is to be most vividly, most perfectly alive. Whatever the unborn and the dead may know, they cannot know the beauty, the marvel of being alive in the flesh. The dead may look after the afterwards. But the magnificent here and now of life in the flesh is ours, and ours only for a short time. We ought to dance with rapture that we should be alive and in the flesh, and part of the living, incarnate cosmos. I am part of the sun as my eye is part of me. That I am part of the earth my feet know perfectly, and my blood is part of the sea. My soul knows that I am part of the human race, my soul is an organic part of the great human soul, as my spirit is part of my nation.

Generous final words, for a man whose nation seemed to have spurned him. But Lawrence accepted the concept of belonging in a manner which his detractors have always been unwilling to understand. His grief was that cosmos and human society had alike been brought low. Where were the raging lions and the soaring eagles? Only in his poems.

11
Eastward

We are still in 1921, a year of unprecedented heat and drought which, on a purely meteorological level, is commemorated in Eliot's *The Waste Land*. It was a year in which Lawrence should have been content to stay put under Etna, going into the garden in pyjamas 'for the heat' and encountering lizards and black snakes, but his restlessness – partly an aspect of temperament, but perhaps mostly a symptom of the tubercular condition which he refused to recognise – drove him into European travel and dreams of world travel. He was also intensely irritable – what with the response to *Women in Love*, the fancied defection of his friends in England (but it was he who had done the casting off – even of old loyal supporters like Edward Garnett), and Frieda's going off alone to Germany to see her sick mother and renew family ties. The irritability is memorialised in the novella called *The Captain's Doll*, where a pair of invented characters soon turn into Lawrence and Frieda, with Lawrence raging at everything, even the mountains of Zell-am-See: 'I hate them, I hate them. I hate their snow and their *affectations*.' To which the Frieda-response is good-humoured exasperation. Things had come to their limit when Alps could take on Lady Ottoline postures, but Lawrence was bigger than his own violent moods, and the effect of all these fictionalised rages is nearly always the confirmation of female sanity and male, or at least Laurentian, dementia. It was a kind of dementia that forced him to drag Frieda from the cool of an Alpine lake down to Florence, in sweltering second-class compartments of trains that Mussolini had not yet taught to run on time, and then on to Rome and Naples and Capri.

Capri acquaintances who became friends were Earl H. Brewster and his wife. Brewster, seven years older than Lawrence and destined to survive him by twenty-seven years (Lawrence again promoting longevity in all he touched), was a painter from Chagrin Falls, Ohio, who had lived in the East and proposed living there again. He was a student of Oriental philosophy and religion, subjects which might have been expected to appeal to Lawrence the perennial searcher after pre-industrial wisdom but did not. The Brewsters remained good friends of Lawrence even when he satirised them in the story 'Things'. At that time they were preparing to go to Ceylon, and Lawrence wondered whether to go with them. He was still attracted to the idea of leaving Europe, in which he considered that his heart and soul had been broken (but surely the blame was only England's?), when a remarkable proposition reached him at the villa outside Taormina.

Sea and Sardinia had begun to appear as a serial in *The Dial*, a magazine of repute though limited circulation, in October 1921. A wealthy American lady read the first instalment and, rightly, was enchanted by it. She was Mrs Mabel Dodge Luhan (or Lujan), born Mabel Ganson in Buffalo, NY, a much-married woman – though only forty-two – who had been successively Mrs Evans, Mrs Dodge and Mrs Sterne. She had tasted the fashionable life and found it insufficiently seasoned, so she had moved to the small town of Taos in New Mexico, where she tried to build an artist's colony and protect the native Indians from the incursions of post-Columbian culture. What was needed, in her view, was a resident writer who could limn the peculiar qualities of Taos and pass a true and vivid record on to posterity. It was shrewd of her to pick on Lawrence, to whom she wrote proffering an invitation to live permanently there, rent-free, in one of the adobe houses she was building. Lawrence replied on Gunpowder Plot Day, 1921:

> Truly, the q-b and I would like to come to Taos – there are no little bees. I think it is quite feasible. I think I have enough dollars in America to get us there. Are you practical enough to tell me how much it would cost, per month, for the q-b and myself to keep house in Taos? We are *very* practical, do all our own work, even the washing, cooking, floor-cleaning and everything here in Taormina: because I loathe servants creeping around. They poison the atmo-

sphere. So I prefer to wash my own shirt, etc. And I *like*
doing things. – Secondly, is there a colony of rather dreadful
sub-arty people? – But even if there is, it couldn't be worse
than Florence. – Thirdly, are your Indians dying out, and is
it rather sad?

The world being round (a fact which Lawrence, according to
mood, might be prepared to deny), it was possible to sail west-
ward by going east. Lawrence and obedient Frieda sailed for
Colombo from Naples on 26 February 1922. The ship was the
Osterley, British, well-appointed, and Lawrence subdued his
puritanism in enjoyment of the ample food, the comfort, the
dancing and flirtation and shipboard games. In Frieda there was
nothing to subdue. Proud to be British on a British ship, he
became very empire-building British in Kandy, where the
Brewsters were temporarily living. He even developed the nostalgia of the expatriate – 'I really think that the most living clue
of life is in us Englishmen in England' – and that slight contempt
for the Eastern way of life (including Buddhism) which would
be proper for a working-class boy jumped up into a minor
colonial post. He wrote a long poem about elephants while in
Kandy, and it says more about the Laurentian concept of power
than about wicked-eyed pachyderms. For the Prince of Wales,
was visiting the island, and the ceremony of a Pera-hera was
arranged for him. Lawrence saw a 'pale fragment' of a prince to
whom elephants salaamed under the torches and reflected that his
motto was *Ich dien* – I serve. Supposing the elephants knew that
motto, along with 'the jungle men running with sweat, with the
strange dark laugh in their eyes, glancing up'? They were all
foiled, says Lawrence, for they had come to see royalty, and all
they found was 'a weary, diffident boy whose motto is *Ich dien*
. . . Drudge to the public.' What they had wanted was 'to hear
the repeated

> Royal summons: *Dient Ihr!*
> *Serve!*
> *Serve, vast mountainous blood, in submission and*
>   *splendour, serve royalty.*
> Instead of which, the silent, fatal emission from
>   that pale, shattered boy up there:
> *Ich dien.'*

It is the philosophy of the hierarchy coming out, getting ready for its fuller statement in *Apocalypse*. The British Empire, not yet democratised, could still accommodate an absolutist ruler, so long as he was forged on the Lawrence pattern or, better, was Lawrence himself. The pale, shattered boy was an affront. The imperial death-knell was to be sounded in George Orwell, who shot an elephant – a product of the fringe of the imperial administrative class – but the Nottinghamshire miner's son affirmed the empire as a kind of poem of the Laurentian power mystique. Unfortunately, the reality was too much for him, a tubercular man sweating in immense humid heat. Nor would Brewster, who had the nerve to learn Pali and proclaim the virtues of Buddhism, consent to be a blood-brother, meaning a Laurentian disciple. Lawrence had to move on, and he moved on to Australia, that most democratic of countries, where the princely servant of the people got the Aussie slow handclap.

The Lawrences had got to Colombo in March 1922. By the beginning of April Lawrence was ready to dismiss the East as 'silly' – 'I don't like it one bit. I don't like the silly dark people or their swarming billions or their hideous little Buddha temples, like decked up pigsties – nor anything.' That was to Mary Cannan. To Mabel Dodge Luhan he was more specific:

> Its boneless suavity, and the thick, choky feel of tropical forests, and the metallic sense of palms and the horrid noises of the birds and creatures, who hammer and clang and rattle and cackle and explode all the livelong day, and run little machines all the livelong night; and the scents that made me feel sick, the perpetual nauseous overtone of cocoanut and cocoanut fibre and oil, the sort of tropical sweetness which to me suggests an *Untergang* of blood, hot blood, and thin sweat: the undertaste of blood and sweat in the nauseous tropical fruits; the nasty faces and yellow robes of the Buddhist monks, the little vulgar dens of the temples: all this makes up Ceylon to me, and all this I cannot bear. *Je m'en vais. Me ne vo'.* I am going away. Moving on.

Now, all that Lawrence says of the East is, in a measure, true. But it is true only of the casual visit. Still, if one stays long, for years, as I did in Malaya, one loses the capacity to see, smell, hear, judge with the newcomer's unfair sharpness. The spirit of

place in Lawrence discloses itself in an instant and, since Lawrence
then has to move on in his restlessness, has no chance to be
muffled and settle into the background of daily life. What has
been said about Lawrence's next full-length fiction, with its
Australian setting, is that it pretends to a knowledge of the continent that, considering the brevity of his stay, was not available
to him. This is a complaint made mostly by native Australian
authors, who have not succeeded in producing a novel as good as
Kangaroo. Visitors like myself have found Lawrence's Australia
magical and authentic.

The Lawrences sailed to Fremantle on the *Orsova*. Sea air and
no nauseous tropical fruits raised his spirits. They stayed with
friends outside Perth, and it was in Western Australia that
Lawrence met a certain Maria Louisa Skinner, who had humble
literary ambitions and had already published *Letters of a V.A.D.*,
an account of her work as a nurse in the Voluntary Aid Department in Burma and India during the war. She, a spinster in
early middle age, was running a combined guesthouse and nursing
home in Darlington, and it was here, as guests, that the Lawrences
stayed for a time. Mollie Skinner showed Lawrence the draft of a
novel which he thought amateurish but promising. He was then
fired to an act of collaboration which resulted later in *The Boy in
the Bush*. That he was willing to share the title-page with another
author, and a very inconsiderable one, has embarrassed some
critics, who, having no evidence of how the workload was ap-
portioned, have thought it safer to ignore the novel altogether.
On the continent of Europe, publishers without shame issue the
work as Lawrence's own. Anglophonia is more scrupulous, but
Laurentians would dearly like to know precisely what is Miss
Skinner's part of the work, as the original draft seems to have
vanished.

As the noted Lawrence scholar Harry T. Moore points out,
Lawrence was never averse to collaboration. He had thought of
himself and Jessie Chambers as joint authors of both poetry and
fiction, he actually made use of a manuscript of his friend Helen
Corke when writing *The Trespasser*, and later, in New Mexico,
he was to propose a joint novel with Mrs Luhan, though Frieda,
for reasons to be considered in their place, frowned on the venture
and broke it up. Probably his wish to work on *The Boy in the
Bush* (a title that had already been used for an Australian novel
published in 1869 but better, he thought, than Mollie Skinner's

proposed *The House of Ellis*) had a good deal to do with the fascination of Western Australia. Miss Skinner knew the factual and historical truths of the region but he, Lawrence, believed he had captured its spirit on first acquaintance. You cannot make a novel out of pure spirit; he needed the flesh and bones of Skinner. The work comes somewhat later than his solo performance *Kangaroo*, but there are various reasons for considering it briefly now: it is built, in its Laurentian aspects, on his first contacts with Australia (*Kangaroo* is set in New South Wales: there had been time for a certain digestion of the continent and its inhabitants); it is certainly an ancillary work to *Kangaroo* and has to be viewed as a curtain-raiser to it; it is a book which, like *The Lost Girl*, one has to approach as a duty and be glad to get out of the way.

No: perhaps that is unfair. It is very far from being a mediocre novel; the trouble is that we wonder at the un-Laurentian nature of the theme (the décor is a different matter). It belongs to the genre known as the novel of apprenticeship, and Lawrence takes over from Mollie Skinner an apprentice who has little in common with himself: in other words, Lawrence has taught us to be interested in Laurentian man, and here is a mere boy outside the pale of Laurentian *Sturm und Drang*. 'He stepped ashore, looking like a lamb.' One of the most arresting of his openings, and the disparity between appearance and reality conveyed, with professional novelist's efficiency, in a few lines: 'Far be it from me to say he was the lamb he looked. Else why should he have been sent out of England? But a good-looking boy he was, with dark blue eyes and the complexion of a girl, and a bearing just a little too lamb-like to be convincing.' The boy is Jack Grant, not quite eighteen, son of an English army officer and a 'handsome, ripe Australian woman with warm colouring and soft flesh, absolutely kindly in a humorous, off-hand fashion, warm with a jolly sensuousness, and good in a wicked sort of way.' That, over a century after the setting of the novel, sounds like a sound Laurentian hitting off of the Australian feminine type: or is it Mollie Skinner's delineation? This looking for authentic Lawrence can become irritating, a test of one's literary perceptions cheekily and gratuitously imposed with no extra charge. Jack has not behaved well in England, and he has been sent to his mother's homeland for a year, there to learn the skills of the land, live with an Australian family, have a certain quality of unjustifiable superiority knocked off him. The story is simple enough. Jack lives with the Ellis family, learns to ride a horse (a little too quickly, say the Australian critics, but Lawrence seems to have transposed his own speedily won equestrian skill in Taos – where the book was written or rewritten – to his and Miss Skinner's hero), falls in love, fights a rival, hunts kangaroo, marries, becomes a father, becomes an Australian, stays.

This is undoubtedly Lawrence:

> It was spring in Western Australia, and a wonder of delicate blueness, of frail, unearthly beauty. The earth was full of weird flowers, star-shaped, needle-pointed, fringed, scarlet, white, blue, a whole world of strange flowers. Like being in a new Paradise from which man had not been cast out.
>
> The trees in the dawn, so ghostly still. The scent of blossoming eucalyptus trees; the scent of burning eucalyptus leaves and sticks in the camp fire. Trailing blossoms wet with dew; the scrub after the rain; the bitter-sweet fragrance of fresh-cut timber.
>
> And the sounds! Magpies calling, parrots chattering, strange birds flitting in the renewed stillness. Then kangaroos calling to one another out of the frail, paradisal distance. And the birr! of crickets in the heat of the day. And the sound of axes, the voices of men, the crash of falling timber. The strange slobbering talk of the blacks! The mysterious night coming round the camp fire.

But when we get authoritative descriptions of wattle, sandalwood, karri and jarrah, the technique of house-building, the whole world of the bush (which Lawrence never visited), then we know where the information is coming from. Lawrence just did not have the time to pick up all this outback lore.

One could say that there is too much of this outback lore, displayed with the fine prodigality of a writer who has stolen it from another writer (but that is what a good deal of fiction is all about: borrowing with no convention of printed acknowledgments). Still, we have to learn about Jack's apprenticeship, from bee-keeping to fist-fights. With love-making in the middle. This seems to be Lawrence:

> 'Kiss me!' she whispered, in the most secret whisper he had ever heard. 'Kiss me!'

He turned, in the same battle of unwillingness. But as if magnetised he put forward his face and kissed her on the mouth: the first kiss of his life. And she seemed to hold him. And the fierce, fiery pain of the pleasure that came with that kiss sent his soul rebelling in torment to hell. He had never wanted to be given up, to be broken by the black hands of this doom. But broken he was, and his soul seemed to be leaving him, in the pain and obsession of this desire, against which he struggled so fiercely.

It is Monica who asks for the kiss, and Monica he marries. She is one of the Ellis daughters, and the Ellises may be taken as an antipodean version of the Chambers family at the Haggs, with the young Lawrence cleansed by the outback and eventually submissive to a stronger Jessie. But the Ellises are wholly Mollie Skinner's work and so is the red Easu (strange spelling) who is the rival of Jack. The fight between them discloses that skill in depicting physical violence which Lawrence, who restricted himself to yelling and throwing plates, deployed as a catharsis, especially in the later novels. The fight in *Sons and Lovers* with Dawes is very small stuff compared to the bloody fisticuffs here:

> He sprang and dashed at his gasping, gulping adversary, whirling his arms like iron piston-rods. Jack dodged the propelled whirl, but stumbled over one of the big feet stuck out to trip him. Easu hit as he fell, and swung a crashing left-right about the sinking, unprotected head. And when Jack was down, kicked the prostrate body in an orgasm of fury . . . Easu, absolutely blind with rage and hate, stared hellish and unseeing . . . He was unconscious with fury, like some awful Thing, not a man.

In *Kangaroo* and *The Plumed Serpent* the violence is transferred to the political arena. Those who consider that, by 1922, Lawrence had become sexually impotent may ponder on that 'orgasm of fury' which sits so strangely in a novel set in 1882.

Lawrence had much writing of his own to do. Why did he think it worthwhile to take over Mollie Skinner's manuscript and produce this puzzling hybrid? It is not enough to say, as he did, that the novel as she wrote it was lacking in psychological truth, and that Jack's character needed fuller development. It seems to me that he was yielding to an urge that many English writers are aware of when they visit Australia: that here is a country which demands literary exploitation, and, in that philistine culture, there is no one to do it well (the standard of Australian writing in Lawrence's time was low: Banjo Patterson had a long time to wait to give place to Patrick White): the Pommy visitor will show these Aussies how to do it. *Kangaroo* is Lawrence's true Australian novel, but it is a novel about Frieda and himself, mere visitors. *The Boy in the Bush* is written, as it were, from the inside, and there is the name of an Australian lady on the title-page to prove it. It is a pledge of the fact that Lawrence took the beautiful exasperating continent, or what he saw of it, rather seriously.

One remarkable poem came out of the brief stay. Nobody has described a kangaroo as well as Lawrence, and nobody has, with the daring or cheeky reliance on intuition which he always displayed, divined so convincingly the relationship of the beast to the land:

> In the northern hemisphere
> Life seems to leap at the air, or skim under the wind
> Like stags on rocky ground, or pawing horses, or springy
>   scut-tailed rabbits.
> . . . But the yellow antipodal Kangaroo, when she sits up,
> Who can unseat her, like a liquid drop that is heavy, and
>   just touches earth.
> The downward drip
> The down-urge,
> So much denser than cold-blooded frogs.

And the huge 'plumb-weighted' creature, with her 'beautiful slender face', has eyes 'big and quiet and remote, having watched so many empty dawns in silent Australia'. That sounds true, we are convinced it is true, it has to be true. But Lawrence himself has not even seen that silent Australia; even now he is merely in Sydney Zoo, feeding the lovely mysterious marsupial peppermint drops.

The Lawrences stayed a mere fortnight in Western Australia; then they sailed by the RMS *Malwa* to Sydney. Sydney he admired – 'a great fine town, halflike London, halflike America' (which he had not yet seen), but it cost too much for them to stay there. (Stay? Were they not supposed to be on their way to New Mexico?) They rented a little house about fifty kilometres south of Sydney, on the coast, where Frieda could rhapsodise about *'Der grosse oder stille Ozean'*, like the heroine of Weber's *Oberon* (Lawrence is writing to the baroness his mother-in-law, which also explains the kilometres). The house had one of those depressingly facetious names dear to the Australian heart – not Avarest or Easystreet but Wyewurk. Lawrence found it too dirty to satisfy his puritan soul so he scrubbed until the jarra-wood floors shone. The town, Thirroul, was in a mining area with rich farmland about: Lawrence had travelled far to come home. He approved, despite his hierarchical ideas, the easy democracy of the people, but neither of them made any friends. They were totally alone in a region to which both he and Frieda responded as if it were an Eden. Lawrence fell in love with the Australian skies, landscape, seascape, but, like Jack in *The Boy in the Bush*, he found 'the fierce, fiery pain of the pleasure . . . sent his soul rebelling in torment to hell'. He would not yield. He stayed long enough to write, with immense dispatch, the strangest but in some ways most satisfying novel of his entire career, then he and Frieda were on their way – further east to reach the west. Let us now look at *Kangaroo*.

12

A Comical-Looking Bloke

Critical rejections of *Kangaroo* are based usually on the looseness of the book, its appearance of being an improvisation (which it is – thrown together in about five weeks), its carelessness of language as well as construction. It is crammed with impertinences which hold back the plot, it takes time off from narrative obligations to preach, it is a kind of literary ragbag. But the formlessness contributes to the impression of life, which bubbles and seethes throughout, and the flashbacks and polemics have the effect of confirming the authenticity of Lawrence's Australia. If he has the leisure to think about things other than Australia, which reminiscence of wartime Cornwall and pretty exact reproductions of rows with Frieda firmly suggest, then he is not being touristy: he has really settled in the wilful lavish continent. This is an artistic illusion – the Lawrences moved into Wyewurk at Thirroul on 28 May 1922, and they were out of the country by the end of July – but one that works or wyewurks. This is a real Australian novel in respect of its exact observation of the people and their country; the plot, which is concerned with politics and power and allegiance and betrayal, is a very European one grafted on to an antipodean stem. What Lawrence presents as possible Australian history – namely, the rise of a fascist party in the most democratic, and even near-anarchic, country in the world – is acceptable only in the terms of fantasy. But the characters involved in this impossible political movement are so credible that we are inclined to believe, and even to credit Lawrence with prophetic powers: this sort of thing has not yet happened, but some day it may.

The liveliness of the characters is all the more remarkable when we remember that Lawrence and Frieda had no social life at all during their stay in Thirroul. The Australians of his story apparently derive from shipboard acquaintances made when moving east and then south. The central character Ben Cooley, the 'Kangaroo' who is the leader of the authoritarian Diggers party, is said to be partly based on Dr David Eder, a pioneer of Freudian studies in England, who probably was mainly responsible for promoting *Sons and Lovers* as a kind of Freudian text. As a sympathiser with Lawrence's utopian projects, he offered the prophet and his pioneers some land in South America. He was a Jew, as is Ben Cooley, and Lawrence borrowed elements of his physical appearance. Libel-fearing since the publication of *Women in Love*, the author denied totally, however, that there was any real resemblance. It does not matter, but Kangaroo is so powerfully drawn that readers are tempted to look for a real-life counterpart. This often happens with novelists, and it is not the best tribute to their art.

Two very recognisable real-life personages are Frieda and her husband, who are seen through Australian eyes on the very first page. Frieda appears as 'a mature, handsome, fresh-faced woman, who might have been Russian'. Lawrence is 'a smallish man, pale-faced, with a dark beard' and an 'absent air of self-possession'. He is, considers a Sydney workman, 'a comical-looking bloke! Perhaps a Bolshy.' The red-bearded Lawrence, who was not all that smallish, is refashioned to become a European intellectual stereotype, importer of ideas to a country where ideas are bombs. He is an ideas man, a thinker, not a poet or novelist. His name is Richard Lovat Somers, and his wife is Harriet. In the endearing Lawrence manner these are introduced to us, and to a bungalow called Torestin, at leisure, with no intimation of a plot stirring. Probably Lawrence had no plot. It is enough for many pages merely to record food prices, flora, night sky:

> . . . Overhead the marvellous Southern Milky Way was tilting uncomfortably to the south, instead of crossing the zenith; the vast myriads of swarming stars that cluster all along the milky way, in the Southern sky, and the Milky Way itself leaning heavily to the south, so that you feel on one side if you look at it; the Southern sky at night, with that swarming Milky Way all bushy with stars, and yet with

black gaps, holes in the white star-road, while misty blotches
of star-mist float detached, like cloud-vapours, in the side
darkness, away from the road; the wonderful Southern night-sky, that makes a man feel so lonely, alien: with
Orion standing on his head in the west, and his sword-belt
upside down, and his Dog-star prancing in mid-heaven, high
above him; and with the Southern Cross insignificantly
mixed in with the other stars, democratically inconspicu-
ous . . .

That 'democratically' prepares us for the political theme of the
novel. Or, put it another way, for the theme of power; for it is
this theme which unifies the disparate constituents of the book. It
is the malignant power of the British state at war which justifies
the long chapter called 'Nightmare', with its total recall of
Lawrence's agony in Cornwall, and the chapter following –
'"Revenge!" Timotheus Cries' – which is about wresting some
kind of programme of living out of the 'accumulation of black
fury and fear, like frenzied lava quiescent in his soul'. And what
is the programme? Lawrence's reading for his history book is
evoked: 'When a man follows the true inspiration of a new, living
idea, he then is the willing man whom the Fates lead onwards:
like St Paul or Pope Hildebrand or Martin Luther or Cromwell.'
But when the idea is dead, the man who follows it is destroyed
by the fates – 'Like Kaiser Wilhelm or President Wilson'. Only
revenge seems to be the programme, vengeance on the destructive
past. So long as this is located in the individual soul, meaning the
soul of Lovat–Lawrence. The vengeful mob, which finds its
voice in fascism or communism, is different – 'the most terrifying
of all things'. Of all the Eight Beatitudes, only 'Blessed are the
pure in heart' has any validity, if 'the pure in heart are those
who quiver to the dark God, to the call of woman, and to the
call of men. The pure in heart are the listeners and the answerers.'
The place of the chapter of wartime reminiscence and the long
muddled meditation on the human or Laurentian soul and its
purpose do not really pull away from the narrative: they are
there to explain why Lovat–Lawrence is in Australia. The world
has to be turned upside down, and the author-narrator's blood
has to be jolted by the atmosphere of a Britain that is not quite
Britain.
    As for 'the call of woman', this is a trumpet-call to battle. Or

rather an invitation to storm, seasickness and possible shipwreck, for Lawrence presents the marital voyage of himself and Frieda in terms of who shall be captain of the good ship *Harriet and Lovat*. This is done whimsically and not without pawky humour:

> 'We will be perfect companions: you know how I love you,' said Harriet, of the good ship *Harriet and Lovat*.
> 'Never,' said Lovat, of the same ship. 'I will be lord and master, but, ah, such a wonderful lord and master that it will be your bliss to belong to me. Look, I have been sewing a new flag.'
> She didn't even look at the flag.
> 'You!' she exclaimed. 'You a lord and master! Why, don't you know that I love you as no man ever was loved? You a lord and master! Ph! you look it. Let me tell you I love you far, far more than ever you ought to be loved, and you should acknowledge it.'

Harriet does not like the design of the new flag, which is that of the Lawrence collected edition – a phoenix rising from its fiery nest. If he is the bird, Lovat says, Harriet is the nest, but she disdains the role of home-tender, fire-maker, mother. '"Mr Dionysus and Mr Hermes and Mr Thinks-himself-grand. I've got one thing to tell you. Without *me* you'd be nowhere, you'd be nothing, you'd not be *that*," and she snapped her fingers under his nose, a movement he particularly disliked.' Lovat now proposes a different flag and a new ship – the frigate *Hermes*, 'which name still contains the same reference, *her* and *me*, but which has a higher total significance.' To which Harriet's response is speechlessness followed by 'You're mad'.

At least Lovat–Lawrence recognises his madness. 'Him a lord and master! Why, he was not really lord of his own bread and butter; next year they might both be starving.' All too true, as is the admission that his utter dependence on her is the very reason for the pose of arrogant ascendancy:

> He *wanted* to be male and unique, like a freak of a phoenix. And then go prancing off into connections with men like Jack Callcott and Kangaroo, and saving the world. She could not stand these world saviours. And she, she must be safely there, as a nest for him, when he came home with his feathers

pecked. That was it. So that he could imagine himself absolutely and arrogantly It, he would turn himself into a nest,
and sit on her and overlook her, like the one and only
phoenix in the desert of the world, gurgling hymns of salvation.

That is well put, and it is put well by the man who would, we
would in our innocence presume, prefer not to put it at all. But
in this marital chapter, brought down from his high horse or nest
by the easygoing Australian ambience, Lawrence–Lovat is coming
to terms with the dynamic of marriage, which mirrors the
dynamic of his own soul. Energy goes into wanting rather than
doing. There is a dialectic, but it leads nowhere. It is the realisation
of this that determines Lovat's final negativity in the field of
imagined Australian politics.

The Jack Callcott of Harriet's inner monologue, or Lovat's
accurate divination of it, is a neighbour of the Somers. He and
his wife are very convincingly drawn; Victoria comes to tea 'in a
pale gauze dress of pale pink with little dabs of gold – a sort of
tea-party dress – and with her brown hair loosely knotted behind,
and with innocent sophistication pulled a bit untidy over her
womanly forehead, she looked winsome. Her colour was very
warm, and she was gawkily excited.' She is all Australian woman-
hood, attracted to the comical-looking bloke who breathes
European culture and mystery, and her provincialism draws
Lovat–Lawrence back to the cosy high teas of Eastwood, with
Harriet–Frieda transformed into a mother expert with roast pork
and brown crackling. Lawrence moves into the lower-middle-
class Australian world with perky confidence. It is Jack Callcott,
who has seen Europe in the war, who wants to move, politically
speaking, some way out of it. There is a conspiracy to impose a
kind of autocracy on Australia. Jack says;

> 'What's a man's life for, anyhow? Is it just to save up like
> rotten pears on a shelf, in the hopes that one day it'll rot
> into a pink canary or something of that? . . . What we want
> in Australia . . . isn't a statesman, not yet. It's a set of chaps
> with some guts in them, who'll obey orders when they find
> a man who'll give the orders.'

Jack recognises in Lovat a quality necessary to the new Australia: he is not a whingeing Pom but (a curious image when we

remember what Lawrence called Frieda) 'a sort of queen bee to a hive'. He represents the intellectual element which will temper the blind male energy of the movement. So we are led to Lovat's first meeting with Ben Cooley, an intellectual like himself but endowed with the positive convictions and the leader's charisma which Lovat finds lacking in himself. In a way Cooley is comical-looking, but the bizarreness of his appearance draws him into the mythical. He is the first Australian myth (if we except Ned Kelly, whose name chimes with his); called Kangaroo, he *is* a kangaroo:

> His face was long and lean and pendulous, with eyes set close together behind his pince-nez: and his body was stout but firm. He was a man of forty or so, hard to tell, swarthy, with short-cropped dark hair and a smallish head carried rather forward on his large but sensitive, almost shy body. He leaned forward in his walk, and seemed as if his hands didn't quite belong to him. But he shook hands with a firm grip. He was really tall, but his way of dropping his head, and his sloping shoulders, took away from his height. He seemed not much taller then Somers, towards whom he seemed to lean the sensitive tip of his long nose, hanging over him as he scrutinised him sharply through his eye-glasses, and approaching him with the front of his stomach.

Lovat is attracted to the marsupial belly and, since he is Lawrence, at the same time revolted. It is, says Cooley, 'a pouch to carry young Australia in'; it is a womb and not a womb; Lovat half-fears being put into it to become a sort of joey; he has broken free of mother England and faces the prospect of a bizarre filiality down under. What does Kangaroo want of Lovat? Friendship, allegiance, *Blutbrüderschaft*? The tables are in a sense turned: Kangaroo has taken over the Lawrence role and Lawrence is bewildered in the part of Murry. Kangaroo is all heart, he loves, he wants love; Lovat's name is comical-looking because it contains what its owner does not want to give.

Lawrence's political insights are sound. Somers has a kind of political authority: he has written a book on democracy, and Willie Struthers, the socialist leader, has read it. The two men meet, and Lovat discloses where Lawrence got his knowledge of post-war politics in action from: Italy, where 'the Fascisti, seeing the Socialists in a funk, got up and began to kick their behinds'. Will Australian socialism work? It all depends on trust, which means love. Love of comrades, which Australia calls mateship. The perverse Lovat–Lawrence reflects that 'love is the greatest thing between human beings, men and women, men and men, women and women, when it is love, when it happens. But when human love starts out to lock individuals together, it is just courting disaster.' So love is shown to be the theme of the novel, as well as power, but is there any real difference? There are three kinds of love at work – the one of vertical allegiance, which is for the Diggers; the egalitarian love of mates and workers; the love, sustaining and destructive, of marriage. 'But human love without the God-passion always kills the thing it loves.' Love needs an Absolute, and this is 'the great dark God who alone will sustain us in our loving one another. Till then, best not play with more fire.' Try telling that to the Diggers, or to Willie Struthers's party. Struthers has no use for 'the first, dark, ithyphallic God whom men had once known so tremendous'. In other words, politicians will not yield to the prophet Lawrence. The working man's son will not help the workers. Will he help Kangaroo?

Hardly. He cries:

> 'What's the good, men trying to be gods? You're a Jew, and you must be Jehovah or nothing. We're Christians, all little Christs walking without our crucifixes ... Struthers is the anti-Christ, preaching love alone. I'm tired, tired. I want to be a man, with the gods beyond me, greater than me. I want the great gods, and my own mere manliness.'

He looks at Cooley with hate, and this is reciprocated. Kangaroo speaks like a man, telling Lovat to get out of Australia, but he turns into a Thing, 'a great ugly idol that might strike. He felt the intense hatred of the man coming at him in cold waves ... He stood up in a kind of horror in front of the great, close-eyed, horrible thing that was now Kangaroo. Yes, a thing, not a whole man. A great Thing, a horror.' In fact, a parody of a dark god. But Lovat does not leave. There has to be, in the spirit of the popular novel or film, an immense physical climax, in which the destructive power of the political is shown, and Lovat–Lawrence has to preface it with his philosophy of the mob, which shows an acuteness worthy of Adolf Hilter. The dark god knocks at the door, but the mob hears nothing. 'The vast bulk of mankind has

always been, and always will be, helpless . . . The curious throbs
and pulses of the God-urge in man would go on for ever ignored,
if it were not for some few exquisitely sensitive and fearless souls
who struggle with all their might to make that strange translation
of the low, dark throbbing into open act or speech.'

There is a meeting of the Labour Party, and Willie Struthers
gives a very persuasive speech. This is in Sydney. Lovat has eaten
a custard apple and tasted in its soft, sweet creaminess the 'magic
like sleep . . . a vast, endless, sun-hot, afternoon sleep with the
world as a mirage' which enfolds the city. He has not yet recognised the latent violence. Struthers is orating about the 'marvellous "Empire" . . . with its out-of-date Lords and its fat-arsed
hypocritical upper classes' when the very Aussie counting-out of
the speaker begins. Lawrence has prepared us for this with Lovat's
earlier reading of the *Sydney Bulletin* (a newspaper Lawrence,
with memories of *John Bull* and other British periodicals that hated
him, greatly admired), in which the counting-out of the visiting
Prince of Wales – for a fancied pommy snootiness – is recorded.
Now the tolling bells of the voices of the Diggers start with
'*One!*' They reach '*Eight!*' and hell breaks loose. Lovat, typically,
is drawn two ways, ready for violent participation in the name of
some dark god or other. But then:

> 'I can't do anything. I can't be on either side. I've got to
> keep away from everything. If only one might die, and not
> have to wait and watch through all the human horror. They
> are my fellow-men, they are my fellow-men.'

It is the great Laurentian impasse. The violence is described with
large skill, in the tones of obsessive fascination. Kangaroo is struck
down: 'Bullets in my marsupial pouch.' They have to be there.
He is taken to hospital, there to die. Lovat goes to see him. In
their final meetings the whole strange issue of love and power is
summed up, in so far as anything is ever really summed up in
Lawrence.

Kangaroo, first as last, stands for love. It sounds, in its final statement, very much like the Australian mateship on which socialism
can be built, but Kangaroo means something more mystical:

> 'We've got to save the People, we've got to do it. And
> when shall we begin, friend, when shall we begin, you and
> I? Only when we dare to lead them . . . The love of man for

wife and children, the love of man for man, so that each
would lay down his life for the other, then the love of man
for beauty, for truth, for the Right. Isn't that so? Destroy no
love. Only open the field for further love.'

This is close enough to the Laurentian view, which has begun to
see the danger of the Marxist metaphysic: when men are thought
of as workers, they are mere abstractions; Kangaroo wants a
political doctrine of the whole man, which, of course, is a political
impossibility. He now, before he dies, wants the love of Lovat,
who remains, as in his relationship with Harriet, an 'obstinate
little devil and child', But, like Stephen Dedalus beside his
mother's deathbed, Lovat will not dissemble. 'I don't want to
love anybody. Truly. It simply makes me frantic and murderous
to have to feel loving any more.' He is coming closer to an
understanding of the dark gods. There is a God of love, true, but
he demands total allegiance. Lovat–Lawrence believes 'in the God
of fear, of darkness, of passion, and of silence, the God that made
a man realise his own sacred aloneness'. Kangaroo will acknowledge no such god, and so Lovat will not love him.

The tension of the situation is screwed to the limit. The dying
Kangaroo accuses Lovat of having killed him. He lies there like a
stricken animal, 'sulking to death'. Jack, who has come with
Lovat, is more reasonable than either of the others.

> Kangaroo turned his face and looked at Somers vindic-
> tively.
> 'That man's killed me,' he said in a distinct voice.
> 'No, I think you're wrong there, old man,' said Jack. 'Mr
> Somers had never done anything like that . . .'
> 'Leave me alone.' Then, in a fretful, vague voice, 'I
> wanted him to love me.'
> 'I'm sure he loves you, 'Roo – sure he does.'
> 'Ask him.'
> Jack looked at Richard and made him a sharp, angry sign
> with his brows, as if bidding him comply.
> 'You love our one-and-only Kangaroo all right, don't you,
> Mr Somers?' he said in a manly, take-it-for-granted voice.
> 'I have an immense regard for him,' muttered Richard.

We have to agree with Jack, who later says: 'If Old Harry himself
had lain there like that and asked me to say I loved him I'd have

done it. But I suppose some folks is stingy about sixpence, and others is stingy about saying two words that would give another poor devil his peace of mind.' Buck Mulligan, in a book published a year earlier, finds in Stephen Dedalus, who made a cognate refusal, something worse than stinginess. Stephen is 'sinister', and so is Lovat Somers.

Also totally perverse. He will not love Kangaroo, but he loves the marsupials in the zoo, to whom he gives, as in his poem, peppermint drops. He loves the whole country, with a kind of desperate hopeless love. If we want to blame his dementia on something, it had better be the Australian moon, as magical and terrifying here as it is in *Women in Love*. 'The night was full of moonlight as a mother-of-pearl. He imagined it had a warmth in it towards the moon, a moon-heat. The light on the waves was like liquid radium swinging and slipping. Like radium, the mystic virtue of vivid decomposition, liquid-rushing lucidity.' And so on. He has found a non-human god, 'without feet or knees or face'. Lovat has, in his rejection of the words of allegiance, de-humanised himself. 'The moon, the concave mother-of-pearl of night, the great radium-swinging, and his little self. The call and the answer, without intermediary. Non-human gods, non-human human beings.' Kangaroo dies and has a great funeral, and it is time for the Somers to leave Australia. Naturally, because he loves it so much. 'It's like wanting a woman . . . I want it.' But he 'won't give in, not yet. It's like giving in to a woman: I won't give in yet. I'll come back later.'

Lawrence never did, except in this strange and disturbing novel. No novel, not even by a native Australian, has caught so well the spirit of a place whose magic has been virtually denied by the inarticulate culture that has been dumped upon it. Jack Callcott speaks for Lawrence when he says that the land has never been loved, only ravished and used. But loving the land seems, to Lawrence, to mean not loving its inhabitants. He himself, in a sense, exploits it brutally, making it the background for the working out of a philosophy which, having begun by denying the importance of human identity, has ended by denying humanity itself. Or, to qualify that, the humanity which expresses itself in the basic human functions of community-making and forging political systems. Which, naturally, have everything to do with love, mutual need, the speaking of certain words. Humanity, says Lawrence, has to rejoin the cosmos.

One can see why Aldous Huxley, who comes into the Lawrence story as Lawrence approaches death, was drawn to a mind so unlike his own. Huxley was an intellectual, which Lawrence was not, but both wished to remove themselves from the queasy stickiness of human involvement on the level of identity. Lawrence may have yearned for blood-brotherhood, but this meant control of another, the quelling of that other's sense of identity. It was a strange item on the programme of progressive freedom from self, but we must never, as I have already probably said far too often, look for consistency in Lawrence. What Huxley thought was the Laurentian essence 'was an extraordinary sensitiveness to what Wordsworth called "unknown modes of being". He was always intensely aware of the mystery of the world, and the mystery was always for him a *numen*, divine. Lawrence could never forget ... the dark presence of the otherness that lies beyond the boundaries of man's conscious mind.' If Lawrence was religious, which he was, it was not in the sense of hungering after God's righteousness. 'There is a spiritual world, as Kierkegaard insists, beyond the ethical – rather, that makes for life, for divineness, for union with the mystery. Paradoxically, this something not ourselves is yet a something lodged within us; this quintessence of otherness is yet the quintessence of our proper being.'

Well, one can see why Kangaroo, who drips to the earth's centre with love and the desire to be loved, has to be rejected. Doctrinally, as it were. Lovat–Lawrence needs to keep himself clean. If Lawrence had been an inferior novelist, Kangaroo might have been a mere piece of animated pasteboard easily disposed of in the phoenix fire. But he is very much alive, like the continent he (a very European Jew thrust inside a marsupial) wishes to nurse in his pouch. There were, and still are, readers who scold the living or dead Lawrence for his prissy treachery. It is a backhanded tribute to very considerable art.

13
Quetzalcoatl

On 31 August 1922, Lawrence was writing from RMS *Tahiti* to his old companion of the Malta trip, Mary Cannan:

> Well here we are after 21 days on board this ship – everybody getting very nervy and on edge. We were a day at Rarotonga and two days at Tahiti: very pretty to look at, but I didn't want to stay, not one bit. Papeete is a poor sort of place, mostly Chinese, natives in European clothes, and fat. We motored out – again beautiful to look at, but I never want to *stay* in the tropics. There is a sort of sickliness about them, smell of cocoa-nut oil and sort of palm-tree, reptile nausea. But lovely flowers, especially Rarotonga. These are supposed to be the earthly paradises. You can have 'em.

There was no pleasing Lawrence. Once the noble savage put on European clothes he became corrupted by industrialism. And his view of God's nature was highly selective. He was not yet ready to acknowledge that the sickliness he found in the tropics was really in himself. 'At Tahiti we took on a crowd of cinema people who have been making a film *Captain Blackbird* ... So undistinguished, so common.' This crowd ('rather like successful shop-girls') stimulated the puritan in him. They rollicked and probably got drunk, and Lawrence took the pulpit and denounced excess. He might have denounced, while he was at it, his own excess of bile. Touching at Wellington, he remembered that Katherine Mansfield was a New Zealander and broke a silence of two and a half years by sending her a postcard. His last communication had been a letter 'so monstrously, so inhumanly cruel', according to Murry, that the irate husband swore he would beat up the sender if he ever met him again. Meanwhile, Katherine Mansfield, dying of the disease that was to kill Lawrence, was beyond reconciliation.

On 4 September he was writing to Mrs Luhan, whom he addressed as Mabel Dodge, that he and Frieda were at the Palace Hotel, San Francisco, with less than twenty dollars in his pocket (he had overspent on the trip, but the days of true penury were over: there was money for him in New York). From then on Mrs Luhan was to pay his expenses. 'So American!' he wrote to his mother-in-law (in German). 'All is comfortable, comfortable, comfortable – I really hate this mechanical comfort.' As I say, there was no pleasing him. On 18 September he wrote to Koteliansky from Taos, New Mexico, that he was settled into 'a new and charming adobe house' which Mrs Luhan, who has now become Mabel Sterne, has had built for him 'because she wants me to *write* this country up. God knows if I shall. America is more or less as I expected: shove or be shoved. But still it has a bigness, a sense of space, and a certain sense of rough freedom, which I like. I dread the petty-fogging narrowness of England.' It was in Taos that he was to write the final chapter of *Kangaroo*, crammed with nostalgia for a land he had forced himself to leave. But he was prepared to accept Taos.

Taos was linked to Santa Fé by a very rough road, virtually cut off from American modernity, close to the Rockies, with a view of the sage-brush desert and an Indian *pueblo* three miles away. The unspoilt pre-industrial Apaches revolted the Eastwood puritan in Lawrence by refusing to wash and emitting 'an unbearable sulphur-human smell', but they were acceptable at a decent distance, performing their ceremonies and dancing 'with their buttocks stuck out a little, faces all inwards, shouting open-mouthed to the drum, and half laughing, half mocking, half devilment, half fun'. Lawrence was not in Fenimore Cooper country, but he had made a kind of general literary preparation for his contact with Indians. Yet he joined the cowboys, learning to ride and never, apparently, sustaining a tumble. He remained a paleface.

Lawrence was sent away on a five-day motor trip so that he could see an Apache fiesta. This was Mrs Luhan's idea, and it was fulfilled a little too soon after the Lawrences' arrival (it had been a time of tiring travel); the idea apparently was that Mrs Luhan should get Frieda to herself and pump her about her husband: after all, she had committed herself to accepting on her territory a man she had heard strange things about (she had had a letter from England saying that 'His vituperation is magnificent. He spares none. He has quarrelled with everyone' but adding 'And yet he is the gentlest, kindest person . . . that anyone could be on this earth'). Lawrence resented Frieda's artless 'giving of the show away', especially to another woman, most especially to an American woman, a modern, free, unsubmissive and reputedly bossy creature. What show she gave away is less important, however, than the triangular situation he should have foreseen. Mrs Luhan, multiply married, was capable of a polyandry that could, if he let her, engulf Lawrence. Frieda saw this early. Lawrence saw the tension between the two women but saw also the problem of living under the eye of a *padrona* on whom he was, in some material measure, dependent. He should have foreseen the dangers of patronage: he lacked that Jesuit man-of-the-world insouciance which enabled Joyce to get on with the writing of *Finnegans Wake* and his heavy drinking and other extravagances without caring too much whether his own patron, Harriet Shaw Weaver, approved or not. But Joyce was neither a puritan nor innocent.

The Lawrences moved out of Taos to a mountain slope called the Lobo, about seventeen miles away. There they rented a couple of adobe cabins from a local rancher; later Mrs Luhan was to donate property to the Lawrences in this territory (which, a hundred and seventy acres of it, she owned) – the Kiowa ranch, their first and only piece of real estate. The life was rough, the winter cold, the work – log-felling included – too heavy for a man who was sick but would not admit it. Two Danish painters appeared, Merrild and Gòtzsche, and Lawrence gave them the use of one of the two cabins rent free in exchange for their help with the all too primitive chores. It was no life for a writer, and Lawrence did not write much. Eight thousand feet up in the Rockies he and Frieda lived through months of bitter weather, and one has to ask why Lawrence did this to himself; Frieda was tough and easy-going enough to sustain any amount of privation. The masochist in him was balanced by the sadist: it was in this fastness that his strange power-hunger took an intolerable form. If he could not subdue Frieda (and how hopeless such an aspiration

was he had recently enough expressed fully in *Kangaroo*) he would
lord it over a female animal that could not fight back. The story
of the bitch Bibbles does not make pleasant reading.

He wrote a poem about her, one of his best.

Believe in the One Identity, don't you,
You little Walt-Whitmanesque bitch?
First time I lost you in Taos plaza,
And found you after endless chasing,
Came upon you prancing round the corner in exuberant,
    bibbling affection
After the black-green skirts of a yellow-green old Mexican
    woman
Who hated you, and kept looking round at you and cursing
    you in a mutter,
While you pranced and bounced with love of her, you
    indiscriminating animal,
All your wrinkled *miserere* Chinese black little face beaming
And your black little body bouncing and wriggling
With indiscriminate love, Bibbles;
I had a moment's pure detestation of you.

Like Kangaroo, Bibbles cries out for love, but, unlike Kangaroo,
not just Lovat–Lawrence's love, anybody's, and this detestable
unselectivity is the fabric of her whole nature:

Everybody so dear, and yourself so ultra-beloved
That have to run out at last and eat filth,
Gobble up filth, you horror, swallow utter abomination and
    fresh-dropped dung.

She must, Lawrence cries, learn 'Fidelity! Loyalty! Attachment!,
as must, or should, Frieda. But these are abstractions 'to your
nasty little belly. You must always be a-waggle with LOVE.'
Nemesis arrives when Bibbles is on heat and the ranch-dogs come
sniffing:

You loved 'em all so much before, didn't you, loved 'em indis-
    criminate.
You don't love 'em now.
They want something of you, so you squeak and come
    pelting indoors . . .

All right, my little bitch.
You learn loyalty rather than loving,
And I'll protect you.

What the poem does not record is the unreasonableness of
Lawrence's demand for loyalty at a time when Bibbles is totally
in the grip of nature (or the cosmos, to which man ought to
yield himself). To tie her up or shut her in was not to engage her
free will, which should see the point of her master's demands.
Bibbles ran away into the pinewoods with one of the ranch-
dogs, came back and was viciously whipped, so rightly ran away
again. With her season over, she came fawning to the two Danes,
who took her in. Lawrence came, saw her, went mad with rage,
and, if the Danes had not intervened, would certainly have killed
her. He himself was in danger of being struck down by his tenants
and helpers, and, according to the Laurentian ethos, he should
have thrown them out or at least libelled them in his fiction. It
was a choice between abasing himself to them or going back into
the ambience of the *padrona*: this latter (submitting to another
bitch) he could not do, so he submitted an apology to the Danes
(on behalf of the other bitch) in the form of an ovenload of
loaves and cakes.

The murderousness he had exhibited to a mere animal was, in
a way, a kind of compliment: he had elevated her to human
status. The murderousness towards genuine human beings,
though it was all talk, disturbed the Danes, as it disturbs us, since
it seems premonitory of a breakdown. He was not writing anything substantial and, during his tree-felling, baking, cooking,
sweeping, laundering chores, seems to have been brooding unhealthily on the breakdown of all things that the war had presaged. It
was back to the '"Revenge!" Timotheus cries' of *Kangaroo*, revenge on the whole rotten world, it's already decaying, chop it
up and throw it on the fire. The first person he wanted to murder
was Mrs Mabel Luhan.

He needed to write a novel, and the need was partially fulfilled
by his working on *The Boy in the Bush*. But Mexico, not New
Mexico, was obviously demanding to be put into a substantial
work of wholly original fiction, and Lawrence, with obedient or
obedient-seeming Frieda (she too was sick of the long Lobo
winter) left in March 1923 for Mexico City. There was plenty of
the murderous chopping-up spirit there, but Lawrence did not

wish to participate. 'Here in Mexico,' he wrote to his mother-in-law from the Hotel Monte Carlo on 27 April,

> there's . . . Bolshevism and Fascism and revolutions and all the rest of it. But I don't care. I don't listen. And the Indians remain outside. Revolutions come and revolutions go but they remain the same. They haven't the machinery of our consciousness, they are like black water, over which go our dirty motorboats, with stink and noise − the water gets a little dirty but does not really change.

He had his eyes on the Indians, or rather the Indian gods. But his eye also on Mexico itself. To see it better, he and Frieda got away from the huge metropolis and settled, on 2 May, in a house on Lake Chapala. Here he began to write *The Plumed Serpent*.

This is the least liked of all Lawrence's novels, and one can see why. It totally lacks humour, and it pontificates in an area of no vital interest to readers with no knowledge of the ancient Aztec gods and what they could mean to a revitalised or Laurentianised Mexico. The difficulty of pronouncing their names may have something to do with it also − Itzapapalotl, Huitzilopochtli and Quetzalcoatl, this last the great plumed serpent himself. Those final liquids are only the Aztec definite article, as in *chocolatl* and *tomatl*, but they sing sinisterly. Lawrence had been prepared to find the old brutal religion of the Mexicans still alive, having in New Mexico witnessed the blood-drawing flagellations of the *penitentes* − a pagan rite thinly disguised as Christian sorrow for Christian sins. What he found in true Mexico was merely the history of the old cults, where the virgin goddess later transformed into the Virgin Mary brought forth from her womb not a redeemer but a knife for cutting out the heart of the victim sacrificed to the god of the sun. All this shedding of blood to feed the sun was too primitive for the son of the Congregationalist Chapel, but he convinced himself, in one part of his brain, that a return to that faith would be better for the Mexicans than the milk-and-water importation of gentle Jesus, which they had never really learned to understand. At least, that is what *The Plumed Serpent* is about.

We meet Frieda in the novel, disguised as the Irishwoman Kate, but we wonder at the absence of Lawrence. Lawrence is to appear, however, in the improbable disguise of a Mexican general who believes himself to be a reincarnation of an Aztec deity. At the

same time Kate is there not merely to submit to a man changed
into a god, but to voice the very European objections of the
puritan Lawrence to the things that Lawrence—Quetzalcoatl is
supposed bloodthirstily to embrace. For instance, Kate's attitude
to bullfighting and to its Mexico City *aficionados*:

> There was no glamour, no charm. A few commonplace
> people in an expanse of concrete were the elect, and below,
> four grotesque and effeminate-looking fellows in tight,
> ornate clothes were the heroes. With their rather fat pos-
> teriors and their squiffs of pigtails and their clean-shaven
> faces, they looked like eunuchs, or women in tight pants,
> these precious toreadors.

And the fight itself disgusts her:

> The shock almost overpowered her. She had come for a
> gallant show. This she had paid to see. Human cowardice
> and beastliness, a smell of blood, a nauseous whiff of bursten
> bowels! She turned her face away.
> When she looked again, it was to see the horse feebly and
> dazedly walking out of the ring, with a great ball of its own
> entrails hanging out of its abdomen and swinging reddish
> against its own legs as it automatically moved.

This is the phase of the bullfight which Ernest Hemingway, with
the great purple tragic epiphany of the moment of truth still to
come, deemed comic. Kate yells at the bull to run at the men,
not the cloaks. This is Lawrence rejecting the ancient Mithraic
cult of the taurine sun-sacrifice like the decent animal-loving
Englishman he is. Tauromachy sounds fine in poetry; the actuality
is a dirty dago business.

Leaving the plaza, Kate is not too eager to re-engage the city
either.

> She was afraid more of the repulsiveness than of anything.
> She had been in many cities of the world, but Mexico had
> an underlying ugliness, a sort of squalid evil, which made
> Naples seem debonair in comparison. She was afraid, she
> dreaded the thought that anything might really touch her in
> this town, and give her the contagion of its crawling sort of
> evil. But she knew that the one thing she must do was to
> keep her head.

Then General Viedma, or Don Cipriano, appears to help her keep it. He is Mexican enough, but he speaks the English of Oxford, where he met – so bland a coincidence outside a bullring – the brother of Kate's dead husband. Thus Kate is brought into casual contact with the potential leaders of the cult of the Plumed Serpent. Don Cipriano and his friend Ramón Carrasco are to revivify the ancient faith and, with Laurentian improbability, make a political movement out of it. The Mexicans need a new saviour; indeed, according to one of Kate's informants, they need a miracle. They sleep on the bare cold ground, less sensible than dogs, and they wake to burn their stomachs with chilli and find a cognate innutritive excitement in sex. They have nothing else; they must await a revelation superior to the epiphany of coition, which, with fine Laurentian inconsistency, is their 'moment of supreme hopelessness', when they throw themselves 'down the pit of despair'. And, like Lawrence, Kate both recognises the death-urge of Mexico, which she and he identify with the whole American continent, and, rejecting the deadness of Europe, thinks perhaps Mexico is the only place where the 'unknown gods' will come back and, redeeming it, also 'put the magic back into her life, . . . save her from the dry-rot of the world's sterility'. She moves from the city to that same Lake Chapala where she is being written about, and there enters the real Mexico, brilliantly rendered as we expect, along with its denizens. The boatmen who take her across the lake, for instance:

> In the great seething light of the lake, with the terrible blue-ribbed mountains of Mexico beyond, she seemed swallowed by some grisly skeleton, in the cage of his death-anatomy. She was afraid, mystically, of the man crouching there in the bows with his smooth thighs and supple loins like a snake, and his black eyes watching. A half-being, with a will to disintegration and death. And the tall man behind her at the tiller, he had the curious smoke-grey phosphorus eyes under black lashes, sometimes met among the Indians. Handsome, he was, and quiet and seemingly self-contained. But with that peculiar devilish half-smile lurking under his face, the half-jeering look of a part-thing, which knows its power to destroy the purer thing.

Not content with describing a real Mexico and planning a

fantastic programme for its regeneration, Lawrence goes to the trouble of composing a Quetzalcoatl liturgy, complete with hymns. The hymns are chanted, printed, the revived religion spreads. Jesus is gently sent back into the shadows and Quetzalcoatl comes into the sun. But the priests inevitably oppose the spread of the cult and forbid the people to read the liturgy. Naturally, as it is written by Lawrence, this liturgy is brilliantly poetic and, if we are willing to dissolve reason, highly convincing, much more, say, than the Book of Mormon. But neither the rhetoric nor the reasoning of the Quetzalcoatlites convinces the Bishop of the West. He is not big, or Laurentian, enough to comprehend the new theology. Ramón says:

'I come to ask you for peace. Tell the Archbishop what I say. Let him tell the Cardinals and the Pope, that the time has come for a Catholic Church of the Earth, the Catholic Church of all the Sons of Men. The Saviours are more than one, and let us pray they will still be increased. But God is one God, and the Saviours are the Sons of the One God. Let the Tree of its Church spread its branches over all the earth, and shelter the prophets in its shade, as they sit and speak their knowledge of the beyond.'

And the Bishop of the West feebly replies, in the manner of priests, that he is not a clever man and that he lives by faith. He symbolises the emptiness of the religion of the *gringo*. The Church now has to have its worn-out icons removed that the Plumed Serpent may enter. In a terrifying and convincing scene (and a highly cinematic one) Kate sees an actual church, the one at Sayula, ceremonially reconsecrated to the new religion, with a priest who has unfrocked or refrocked himself intoning:

'Jesus, the Son of God, bids you farewell.
Mary, the Mother of God, bids you farewell.
For the last time they bless you, as they leave you.
Answer *Adiós!*
Say *Adiós!* my children.'

Across the lake the crucified Christ, his mother, all the saints are borne to their burning. The priest casts off his old vestments and indues the white cotton and *serape* of the men of Quetzalcoatl. Mexico is ready for its redemption.

So, in *Kangaroo*, is Australia. The two novels touch in sequences

of bloodshed which Lawrence clearly enjoyed writing. Ramón
and Cipriano have their political enemies, and they strike.

> Kate could not believe that the black, ghastly face with the
> sightless eyes and biting mouth was conscious. Ramón had
> him clasped round the body. The bandit's revolver fell, and
> the fellow's loose black hand scrabbled on the concrete,
> feeling for it. Blood was flowing over his teeth. Yet some
> blind super-consciousness seemed to possess him, as if he
> were a devil, not a man.

Ramón has been struck down but lives; it might just as well have
been Cipriano. The reader often has difficulty in distinguishing
between them, and apparently so has Lawrence, who seems to
have distributed his new mythical persona among the two of
them. It is Ramón who identifies himself with Quetzalcoatl and
Cipriano with the god Huitzilopochtli, but Kate is destined to
join the Aztec pantheon by marrying Cipriano. She is to be the
First Woman of Itzapapalotl, says Ramón, 'just for the sound of
the name'. And, rhyming as in a comic opera, Kate responds by
saying, 'I should die of shame.' She does not show this good Irish
sense for long.

She is 'legally married' to Cipriano, though we are not told
whether under Mexican state law or the law of the new paganism.
Anyway, she is to sail off for Europe after a month, and Huitzilopochtli agrees. The account of the consummation of the marriage is interesting, and one wonders how far it reflects Lawrence's
own sexual practice. The union is phallic, all male thrust and
puritanical rejection of what is termed 'frictional voluptuousness'.

> She realised, almost with wonder, the death in her of the
> Aphrodite of the foam: the seething, frictional, ecstatic
> Aphrodite. By a swift dark instinct, Cipriano drew away
> from this in her . . . And she, as she lay, would realise the
> worthlessness of this foam effervescence, its strange ex-
> ternality to her. It seemed to come upon her from without,
> not from within. And succeeding the first moment of dis-
> appointment, when this sort of 'satisfaction' was denied her,
> came the knowledge that she did not really want it, that it
> was really nauseous to her.

The wish-fulfilment of male fantasy, in which the man's satisfaction promotes the woman's. Kate's decision to go home wavers: the great godlike potency of the male has captivated her. At the end of the novel she says to Cipriano: 'You don't want me to go, do you?' And he replies: '*Te quiero mucho! Mucho te quiero! Mucho! Mucho!*', which is rather feebly translated as 'I like you very much! Very much!' But Kate is aware of his 'soft, wet, hot blood', shivers, and says: 'You won't let me go!' Thus the story ends, and there is no less convincing end in the entire Lawrence canon. But Lawrence has lost interest, having done the thing he set out to do – namely, convert the whole of Mexico to the cult of Quetzalcoatl; Frieda–Kate's submission may now be taken for granted.

> It was a wild moment. In Zacatecas General Narciso Beltran had declared against Montes and for the Church. But Cipriano with his Huitzilopochtli soldiers had attacked with such swiftness and ferocity, Beltran was taken and shot, his army disappeared.
>
> Then Montes declared the old Church illegal in Mexico, and caused a law to be passed, making the religion of Quetzalcoatl the national religion of the Republic. All churches were closed. All priests were compelled to take an oath of allegiance to the Republic, or condemned to exile. The armies of Huitzilopochtli and the white and blue *serapes* of Quetzalcoatl appeared in all the towns and villages of the Republic. Ramón laboured ceaselessly. Cipriano appeared in unexpected flashes, in unexpected places. He managed to rouse the most discontented States, Vera Cruz, Tamaulipas, Yucatan, to a sort of religious frenzy. Strange baptisms took place in the sea, and a scarlet and black tower of Huitzilopochtli rose along the shores . . . The Archbishop was deported, no more priests were seen in the streets. Only the white and blue and earth-coloured *serapes* of Quetzalcoatl, and the scarlet and black of Huitzilopochtli, were seen in the streets. There was a great sense of release, almost of exuberance.

Lawrence is playing a game not uncommon among English writers. It began with Swift and reached its consummation with Orwell. He is imagining a country with a social and political system built according to the specifications of a mad idea. The Laurentian idea falls between the stools of Swiftian satire and

Orwellian prophecy: it is not funny and it is not possible. How the new faith is to regenerate the political and economic life of the state we are not told, nor is Lawrence greatly interested. He could always reinterpret politics in terms of religion, but economics was a science and therefore could not be felt in the solar plexus. One shudders with relief that Lawrence did not try to remake Australia out of the animistic beliefs of the bushmen. He did not go into the bush, and the abos did not attract him. It was enough to present the possibility of a fascist takeover in a land not much given to deferring to authority and then, through an accident of violence, to cancel it. In writing *Kangaroo* Lawrence still had a sense of proportion and humour had not yet deserted him.

Nineteen Eighty-Four was a metaphysical game to Orwell, and *The Plumed Serpent* a politico-religious game to Lawrence. It is probably not in order to speculate how far the killing tubercle was, with both men approaching middle age and death, responsible for their respective fantasies. But it would be profitable for devisers of courses in utopian fiction to consider Lawrence, on the strength of two late novels, as eligible for inclusion in a very British canon. A new edition of *The Plumed Serpent* ought to have, as frontispiece, that design which Hobbes prefixed to his *Leviathan*: a great kingly head crammed with little people. A flying snake could replace the crown and the head should be recognisably Lawrence's.

The Plumed Serpent, like other books of Lawrence's, was composed at two different times: the beginning is demonstrably different from the end. The interruption to the work was partly due to Frieda's growing tired of the burning heat of Mexico and sick of 'hearts still quivering held to the sun for the sun to drink'. She wanted to go home, to her children in England and her family in Germany. And she was probably not happy with the Quetzalcoatl postures of her husband, who wanted her to be Kate and submit to dark frictionless embraces. If Lawrence would not take her back to Europe she would go alone. And she did.

14
A Spot of Red

The contest of wills came to its climax. Lawrence at first seemed to submit to Frieda, perhaps being surprised into a temporary reasonableness by the strength of her determination to go away. Certainly he travelled with her by ship from Vera Cruz to New Orleans and then on by train to New York. It was August, and the transatlantic liners were fully booked by American tourists eager to escape Prohibition. When Frieda succeeded in getting a passage, Lawrence decided he was not going with her, and it was on the quay with the liner hooting that they had a quarrel so violent that Frieda believed that this was the end of their marriage. She boarded the ship, leaving the Plumed Serpent bedraggled and morose, unwaving among the wavers. She had done the right thing: it would have been fatal, in the obstinate and demanding state that her husband was in, to show a willingness to obey. It would be a question now of how long either could subsist without the other.

Lawrence virtually declared himself the loser from the very start of the separation. He went west, by way of Buffalo and Chicago, to Los Angeles, where, he knew, his two Danish friends were staying. The quarrel over the bitch Bibbles had healed; they were disposed to be helpful, even solicitous: they saw that he was not looking well. They met him at the station and drove him to the Miramar Hotel in Santa Monica. Lawrence, who had sold nothing to the film moguls and saw no future in the art of the cinema, thus got to Hollywood very prematurely. It is a pity he did not write a short story about the celluloid capital nor even commemorate it (as Aldous Huxley was to do, in a rather Laurentian manner) in one of his travel essays. He was restless and lonely and without occupation; a less puritanical man would have taken to drink. He took instead to wearing himself out with aimless travel, bruised by jolting over bad roads in decrepit buses and on muleback, back in the Mexico he had only recently left. Without Frieda Mexico was a changed country. Without Frieda Lawrence was a changed man. The Danes believed he was going mad. On 20 November 1923, writing to Mabel Dodge Luhan from the Hotel Monte Carlo in Mexico City, he shows himself ready to give in: 'I am just packing, to leave in the morning . . . I don't want to go to England – but suppose it is the next move in the battle which never ends and in which I never win.' The nature of the battle is not specified. He invokes Quetzalcoatl, but the snake must learn biblical cunning and subdue the will to strike: 'Leave the world to me. And know that with the world I must go as the serpent – if I am open they will destroy me. The serpent of the Sun.' Who are 'they'? He sailed for England.

The estrangement between himself and Mabel Luhan was a thing of the past, though not a very distant past. Perhaps she, with her history of dissolved marriages, believed that he was now permanently free of Frieda, who had legitimately opposed her possessiveness. On 27 December he was writing amiably to 'dear Mabel' as his only apparent ally ('I am glad to know you are with me') in the fight against everything, chiefly the horror of England ('I feel the English much more my enemies than the Americans. I would really rather be in America'). He does not mention Frieda in this letter. Frieda had apparently been getting on well enough without him, rejoicing in her grown children, friendly with Middleton Murry, basking in the vicarious warmth of her husband's fame. She believed that she and Lawrence could settle in London, becoming part of its highly provincial literary life. *The Plumed Serpent* had not yet been finished and she knew what, if he ever finished it, would be its consummation. It was one thing to be Kate sickened by the New Mexico bullfights, quite another to be Kate yielding to the dark gods. The book would seem to its readers a celebration of Laurentian victory over the subdued spouse, and that would be a betrayal of the historical truth. Frieda had won; Lawrence had come to her defeated but, naturally, unwilling to concede defeat. There was a sufficiency of physical threats, loud scoldings in the dialect of

Eastwood, teapots and plates and cups smashed with a poker. If Lawrence wanted submission, he knew where he thought he could get it. Dear Mabel had, with woman's cunning, promised it. In the humourless phase into which Lawrence had moved it is instructive to read the following, sent on 9 January 1924:

> Dear Mabel: You certainly are an egoist, and your letters are egoistic, as you say. Soon you must learn to forget yourself. You must learn *not to care*, not to think, and simply to laugh. *Poco a poco* . . .
>
> I find that here in London they all *instinctively* hate me: much more so than in America. But that too, in the end, only makes me laugh. My gods, like the Great God Pan, have a bit of a natural grin on their face. *Nous nous entendons* . . . You are one of the very few people in the world at the moment who are capable of this: this fierce recklessness, based on trust, like the recklessness of Pan; trusting deep down to the springs of nature, the sources: and then the laughter.

He was planning to return to New Mexico, to a submissive Mabel. While his hand was in, he might as well revive the old dream of the society of friends, Rananim, plenty of scope for demanding submission there, and so arranged a dinner party for such friends as were willing to throw everything over and reify the dream. His guests were Mary Cannan, Dorothy Brett, Murry, Koteliansky, and Catherine and Donald Carswell. Donald Carswell was a London barrister presumably willing to give up his practice to follow Lawrence; his wife Lawrence had known since 1914 and never seriously alienated. She was to write useful books on Robert Burns and Giovanni Boccaccio and, in 1932, one of the best of the Lawrence biographies, *The Savage Pilgrimage*. Dorothy Brett was the daughter of Viscount Esher and the sister of the notorious Ranee of Sarawak (one of whose tricks was to stand on a billiard table, lift her skirt to the limit, and say: 'Come on, boys, pot the red'). She had first met the Lawrences in 1915 and remained faithful to both till the end. Her story is told in a biography by Sean Hignett – *Brett: From Bloomsbury to Mexico* (1985).

That title indicates that she joined Rananim. Nobody else did. The restaurant that Lawrence had chosen for the sacramental dinner was inauspicious – the Café Royal, scene of Philip

Heseltine's various betrayals, the Pompadour of *Women in Love*. We do not know what was eaten on this occasion, but we do know that Lawrence drank claret and too much port and vomited over the tablecloth. Koteliansky had just made a speech about Lawrence's greatness, and Murry had given him a Judas kiss, promising not to promise not to betray the master. Frieda was not amused, and left it to Dorothy Brett and Catherine Carswell to clean up the vomit and to Murry and Koteliansky to put the messiah, who had passed out, into a taxi.

On 5 March 1924, Frieda and Lawrence and Brett (as she was always unceremoniously known, except when Lawrence – secretly proud that he, a miner's son, had trapped an aristocrat into discipleship – referred to her as the Hon. Dorothy Brett) boarded the *Aquitania* and set sail for America. Although Lawrence referred to Brett as 'a little simple but harmless', the lady was not without character nor, for that matter, talent. She had studied at the Slade and, apart from the prospective excitements of Rananim, foresaw useful subjects for her painting in the harsh Mexican light. What Francis King, the literary critic, has called her 'unrealistically elongated Mexican peasants' were to fetch good prices, but her less considered sketches, mere improvisations, show her real strength. She was no beauty – thin, small-headed, with a receding chin – and was so deaf that she had to use an ear trumpet (like Evelyn Waugh, she used it selectively). She is the only woman in the history of the married Lawrence with whom the master considered going to bed (the anecdote goes that he actually got there and desisted, saying 'Your pubes are wrong'). She certainly slept with Middleton Murry, even when Katherine Mansfield was alive. She wrote a letter to the dead wronged wife, saying: 'Dearest Tig, For the first time in my life I slept with a man and that man was yours.' In Mexico she carried a dagger, and the natives considered her dangerous. There is danger and danger.

The three went, via New York and Chicago, to Taos. Mabel Luhan considered Brett a kind of 'holy Russian idiot' but later discovered she was really a lady, which the Baroness Frieda was not. Lawrence did not find Mabel all that prepared to be submissive, and, like distant Mexican thunder, a row promised to erupt. With huge generosity Mabel now donated to the Lawrences the entire hundred and seventy acres of land she owned on the Lobo. Strictly, it was Frieda who received the gift, since

Lawrence, who had been yearning for years for a farm in the Rockies, perversely refused it. But he did not reject the work entailed in rebuilding, with Indian help, the decayed adobe shacks on the estate, digging an irrigation ditch to fetch water from the Gallina Canyon, planting vegetables and flowers (his little English garden is still there, or was a few years ago), milking, cooking, baking, reverting to the handyman his father had been. He was totally happy, though he was doing his frail lungs no good, labouring under that burning sun eight thousand feet above sea-level. And, being totally happy, he was also totally unhappy, or enraged, or suffused with hate. If Lawrence meant nothing else to the world, he would still be a perfect working model of human inconsistency, demonstrating the folly of trying to reduce man's sensibility to a set of scientific laws.

The novella *St Mawr* belongs to this period – a wedge driven between the two parts of *The Plumed Serpent*. It is a brilliant piece of fiction, though it has the Laurentian tendency to split open like a fruit into two segments. The second segment of the work glorifies, with little attempt at fictional invention, Lawrence's own Kiowa Ranch and the land beyond:

> The desert swept its great fawn-coloured circle around, away beyond and below like a beach, with a long mountainside of pure blue shadow closing in the near corner, and strange, bluish hummocks of mountains rising like wet rock from a vast strand, away in the middle distance, and beyond, in the farthest distance, pale blue crests of mountains looking over the horizon from the west, as if peering in from another world altogether.

The only fictive element is the owner of the ranch, a woman from New England, who, 'with her tense, fierce soul and her egoistic passion of service', appears justified in responding to the New Mexican scene with a passion almost hysterical. Lawrence is not there: he has reserved for himself a role which fades out as soon as the road runs to Kiowa Ranch. For he is not to be a wandering man of letters or a Mexican general but a horse. He is the stallion St Mawr, pretending to be tamed but really vindictive and unpredictable, kicking a man in the face, deliberately falling and almost crushing his rider to death, but God's own work, savage and beautiful – 'like a marigold, with a pure golden sheen, a shimmer of green-gold lacquer upon a burning red-orange'. He is to be seen in Rotten Row, 'pulling at the bit and wheeling sideways up against the railing, to the terror of the children and the onlookers, who squealed and jumped back suddenly, sending the nerves of the stallion into a rush like rockets'. Policemen come along, the authorities get to know about St Mawr, he is banned from polite society. The situation presages what is to happen to the author of *Lady Chatterley's Lover* and the painter of certain neo-pagan fleshly pictures.

It was while Lawrence was reading *St Mawr* aloud to Frieda and Brett, rejoicing in the fierce destructiveness of the stallion (*mawr* is Welsh for big), that he suddenly spat blood. He did not, like John Keats, say calmly 'That is my death-warrant'; he refused to see a doctor, he poulticed his chest in the manner of his mother, he denied totally that he had a tubercular condition. 'Nothing wrong; the lungs are strong. It is just a touch of bronchial trouble – the tubes are sore.' This, though a lie, justified his wanting to go south for the winter. He wrote to Murry on 3 October 1924:

> The country here is very lovely at the moment. Aspens high on the mountains like a fleece of gold. *Ubi est ille Jason?* The scrub oak is dark red, and the wild birds are coming down to the desert . . . It is time to go south, where there is no autumn, where the cold doesn't crouch over one like a snow-leopard waiting to pounce. The heart of the North is dead, and the fingers of cold are corpse fingers.

His father had died on 10 September, the day before Lawrence's birthday. Death was in his mind, but not his own. The real justification for returning to real Mexico was the need to complete *The Plumed Serpent* in the appropriate territory. Mexico City was more appalling than before, and the train journey to it made uneasy by the endemic anarchic condition of the country (bandits aboard, some of them disguised as soldiers). The whole of Rananim made the trip, and Brett gushed over the wild unwashed masculinity of the Indians. The British vice-consul in Mexico City found a little house for the Lawrences in the town of Oaxaca, well south, but nothing for Brett, who had to go to a hotel. The only trouble with Oaxaca was that it was in the malarial zone.

Lawrence finished *The Plumed Serpent* and wrote the sketches of local life which make up *Mornings in Mexico*. Here is a relaxed and likeable Lawrence who has got the apocalyptical temporarily

out of his system. He is quietly informative about the Dance of
the Sprouting Corn and the Hopi Snake Dance and, with the
unique insight that he never lost, the character of the Indian, in
thrall to the great white monkey:

> But the great white monkey has got hold of the keys of the
> world, and the black-eyed Mexican has to serve the great
> white monkey, in order to live. He has to learn the tricks of
> the white monkey-show: time of the day, coin of money,
> machines that start at a second, work that is meaningless and
> yet is paid for with exactitude, in exact coin. A whole exist-
> ence of monkey-tricks and monkey-virtues. The strange
> monkey-virtue of charity, the white monkeys nosing round
> to *help*, to *save!* Could any trick be more unnatural? Yet it is
> one of the tricks of the great white monkey.

Well, Lawrence recognised his own monkeydom and accepted
that he could not escape from the monkey-puzzle of his own
civilisation. He remains a *gringo*, separated from the Mexican by
certain Protestant monkey-virtues he could never renounce, like
the capacity for hard work and a passion for cleanliness. But he
and the Mexican peasant meet in a very basic region, where the
demands of a revolution and the demands of a European war-
machine excite a common terror. Lawrence's *mozo* Rosalino
refused to join the army; he said:

> *No quiero!* He is one of those, like myself, who have a horror
> of serving in a mass of men, or even of being mixed up
> with a mass of men. He obstinately refused. Whereupon the
> recruiting soldiers beat him with the butts of their rifles till
> he lay unconscious, apparently dead ... But in the city, the
> winning side seized Aurelio, since he was the *cousin* of the
> delinquent. ... A friendly servant gave the message Aurelio
> had left: '*Adios ... Me llevan.*' Oh, fatal words: '*Me llevan.*'
> They are taking me off ... Not to be *caught!* Not to be
> *caught!* It must have been the prevailing motive of Indian-
> Mexico life since long before Montezuma marched his prison-
> ers to sacrifice.

With the theological politics of *The Plumed Serpent* out of his
system, Lawrence was preparing to take up the implied stance of
Lady Chatterley's Lover: that we are impotent to change the evil
imposed by the mass or by the authoritarian state, and that

salvation lies only in the cultivation of the personal life. Others had found this resigned solution before him, but Lawrence was to give it a new slant, that of personal tenderness. First, though, he had to recover personal tenderness in his own life; with his mad desire for submission it had been absent for too long. The recovery was made in desperate circumstances.

He had, in seriousness or the near-serious speculations of his art, tried to invoke the dark gods. Now, in the tranquillity of Oaxaca, they appeared, but not as he had expected them. In his private theology they had stood for power, but he had assumed this power to be beneficent. Now he discovered that it was malignant. He went down with malaria and also with diarrhoea and dysentery and, to compound his agony, an earthquake struck Oaxaca. He had trusted too much in beneficent nature, eating fruits and vegetables that carried infection, and in the etymology of *malaria*, which he was prepared to believe was really only 'bad air'. Their house shook with earth-tremors while Lawrence lay impotent in bed and Frieda, sick with terror, under it. When the quake subsided, Lawrence was moved to the one Oaxaca hotel, where he accepted that he was very sick, and where, according to her memoirs, Frieda wept hysterically, realising that 'He will never be quite well again, he is ill, he is doomed. All my love, all my strength will never make him whole again.' And Lawrence, the old fight gone out of him, the foolish talk of submission in ashes, said: 'If I die, nothing has mattered but you, nothing at all.'

He was moved to a hotel in Mexico City, and there, in the presence of both himself and Frieda, a local doctor made the pronouncement that could never again be refuted with talk of 'inflamed bronchials'. Lawrence had tuberculosis, and, so Frieda was told in private, he had a year or two to live at the most. He must go home, which meant back to the ranch, but now they were made to realise how much 'home' was a place on alien territory. At the Mexican border the immigration authorities, with their endemic fear of the pollution of the United States by sick or dirty foreigners, made great difficulties about letting him in. What was he to do? Go back to a wrecked house in Oaxaca? The doctor in Mexico City had pronounced him much too weak to make the sea voyage to England, where the cold spring of 1925 was waiting to inflame tubercles which, in a warmer zone, had a chance of healing. It was only by the kindly intervention of the United States Embassy in Mexico City that the pedantry of the immigration officers was overridden. But

Lawrence had a visa for six months only and, in his state of health, it was unlikely to be renewed.

He recovered enough strength and energy to enjoy his last summer at the ranch. Indeed, his recovery seemed miraculous: he was soon leaping into the saddle of his horse, cooking, baking, gardening, digging his irrigation ditch. And that thinking sensibility, which he would have scorned to limit to his cerebral cortex, was working as busily as ever, pondering the mystery of his black cow, Susan – her 'queer, jerky cowy gladness', her 'cowy peace' – and, in the remarkable essay entitled 'Reflections on the Death of a Porcupine', ruminating, long before Sartre, on the categories of being and existing. A stray dog had porcupine quills in his nose and was in agony. With patient care Lawrence removed them, and then the dog thought he had at last found a loving master. But Lawrence could not commit himself to the ownership of a dog, threw a stick at him which caught the sore nose, and in anguish and remorse heard the dog's desperate departing howl.

There is no need to labour Lawrence's sense of the unity of the living world, but the onslaught of the dark gods of Oaxaca had taught him that it was partly sustained by destruction. There were creatures around the ranch that had to be destroyed because of their own destructiveness, and among these were the huge porcupines, big as bears. For the first time in his life Lawrence took a gun to one of them, failed to kill, found the barrel empty, then finished him off with a cedar pole. He had to justify the act by reference to the economy of a ranch, but his one experience of slaughter led him to a philosophical zone, where he tried to distinguish between the unique importance of any living form to itself and its relative importance in the whole scheme of being. There is a conflict between the two approaches to life – 'a tangle of existence and being, a tangle which man has never been able to get out of, except by sacrificing the one to the other.' But, he says, 'sacrifice is useless'. We can only sustain our own (Laurentian) vitality by drawing on the vitality of other beings, recognising the need 'to consume and *consummate* the lower cycles of existence, into a new thing'. He may say that sacrifice is useless, but the porcupine has been sacrificed in the name of 'conquest, conquered and conqueror, for ever'. And he ends, having come a long way from that rifle-shot and cedar stick, with an attack on modern man:

We have tried to build walls round the kingdom of
heaven: but it's no good. It's only the cabbage rotting
inside.

Our last wall is the golden wall of money. This is a fatal
wall. It cuts us off from life, from vitality, from the alive
sun and the alive earth, as *nothing* can. Nothing, not even
the most fanatical dogmas of an iron-bound religion, can
insulate us from the inrush of life and inspiration, as money
can.

We are losing vitality: losing it rapidly. Unless we seize
the torch of inspiration, and drop our moneybags, the
moneyless will be kindled by the flame of flames, and they
will consume us like old rags.

We are losing vitality, owing to money and money-
standards. The torch in the hands of the moneyless will set
our house on fire, and burn us to death, like sheep in a
flaming corral.

All this from brooding on the shooting of a porcupine.

The United States visa was due to expire at the end of September 1925. Lawrence looked his last on a loveliness he deluded
himself he would one day see again, but in one layer of his being
he accepted the truth. On 15 September he and Frieda were at 71
Washington Place, New York, waiting to board the SS *Resolute*.
Brett, who was to follow later, was still in New Mexico. He
wrote to her saying: 'Of course one is a fool to leave the ranch,
but perhaps Europe will be good for us, for the winter' – Laurentian nonsense. They sailed, and Lawrence disapproved of the
Atlantic – 'a dismal kind of ocean: it always affects me as the
grave of Atlantis' – while getting ready to disapprove of England. He had completed his circling of the globe and, in early
October, felt not like one who had come home but 'queer and
foreign'. The eternal foreigner, he felt less foreign in Europe, and
it was to Europe he went for the last phase of his strange career.
But in Europe he would have his eye very much on England.

15
Life in Death

In the autumn of 1925 Lawrence and Frieda were in Baden-Baden, then they settled in the Villa Bernardo, Spotorno, for the winter. Italy was Lawrence's true home, the Mediterranean his only sea, the gods of vine and olive the only ones that did not let him down. The vicious deities of Mexico, which had delivered an earthquake and stricken him with malaria and dysentery, possessed his nerves for one last brief phase of vindictive enmity, when he attacked Frieda and her children, calling on his sister Ada to abet him in his rages, and using Brett, who had dutifully followed him, as a sounding-board for his howls and curses. But Brett was soon to be banished, and Lawrence and Frieda entered the last and more or less tranquil passage of their marriage either alone or in the congenial company of people like the Brewsters, who were back from Ceylon and resettled in Capri, and Aldous Huxley and his wife. He had first known Maria Huxley, who was Belgian, in the old Garsington days; Aldous he had met briefly during the war and almost persuaded him to join Rananim. In the very last days of his life Lawrence was to find comfort in the devotion of the Huxleys. But he still had five years of creative rage ahead of him, tempered by interludes of repose and resignation. Early in 1926 he wrote to Murry:

> *Ach! du lieber Augustin, Augustin, Augustin* – I don't care a straw who publishes me and who doesn't, nor where nor how, nor when nor why. I'll contrive, if I can, to get enough money to live on. But I don't take myself seriously, except

between 8.0 and 10.0 a.m., and at the stroke of midnight. At other seasons, my say, like any butterfly, may settle where it likes: on the lily of the field or the horsetod in the road: or nowhere. It has departed from me . . . No, no! I'm forty, and I want, in a good sense, to enjoy my life. Saying my say and seeing other people sup it up doesn't amount to a hill o' beans, as far as I go. I want to waste no time over it . . . The Mediterranean is glittering blue today. Bah, that one should be a mountain of mere words! Heave-O! my boy! get out of it!

Easier said than done. Lawrence could no more have stopped being a mountain of words than he could have ceased breathing, though breathing was to be increasingly hard. The urge to move about the world was still there: he wanted to sail round the isles of Greece; he even started to learn Russian, so that the Leninist utopia could relocate itself in the loins; but the strength was no longer in him. He yearned, naturally enough, to be back at the ranch, but by June 1926 Brett had taken over the tasks of running it ('by now you are in your breeches and feeling like a real *ranchero!*') and, with all her alleged empty-headedness, Brett was reliable. He wrote to her in July:

> For some things, I wish I was really there. I would love to see the flowers, and ride up the raspberry canyon, and go along the ditch with a shovel. Then something else, I can't find out what it is, but it is something at the pit of my stomach, holds me away, at least for the moment. It is something connected with America itself, the whole business — yet of course I feel the tree in front of the house is my tree. And even the little aspens by the gate, I feel I have to keep my eye on them.

There were a lot of things he felt he had to keep his eye on, including England, which was soon to receive, in *Lady Chatterley's Lover*, a lesson in regeneration it was to reject sternly. In 1927 his eye was mostly a visionary channel for the generation of a final allegiance. He had travelled the world looking for a people unspoilt by the commercial and industrial heresy of the West, but he had not found it. He had hated the tropics, been indifferent to the bushmen, seen the Mexicans corrupted by the great white monkey. Now it was on his true home territory of Italy that he found, or thought he found, a race blessed through its harmony with the cosmos, its laws built in the loins and the solar plexus – in a word, a Laurentian race. With Earl Brewster he visited the ancient towns of the Etruscans.

The book that came out of this trip – *Etruscan Places* (published in 1932) – was intended to be a much bigger book than it is. As early as 1930 Lawrence had been interested in the Etruscans, and he had read the classic works – D. Randall-MacIver's *Villanovans and Early Etruscans*, Pericle Ducati's *Etruria Antica*, and the great survey by the Englishman, and hence a potential competitor, George Dennis. He recognised that he could not rival these works on the level of observation and scholarship. And, of course, his eye was not wholly innocent: he needed the Etruscans more than they needed him; their posthumous task was to confirm the Laurentian mystique of phallism. But he brought to the book qualities at least as acceptable as exact scholarship – a sense of immediacy which brings not only the Etruscans back to life but also the Italy of the 1920s, when there were no *autostrade* or Agip motels and the trains did not run on time, if at all. The inn food was usually filthy – stewed-out meat fibres, the skimmed meat fat used to warm over tired spinach – and the beds were dirty and verminous. *Etruscan Places* is perhaps the last travel-book in the old laborious tradition – the eye slowly taking it all in, the aching feet imposing the leisure to observe the common people in the inn kitchen. A sick man easily tired, Lawrence would not nevertheless have taken kindly, I feel, to the delights of modern Italian travel – the abstract motor roads, the despair at not being able to find a parking-place in Spoleto – and he would have raged at the smog over Ravenna. He would have seen all this as the ultimate victory of Rome, that depersonalising force which destroyed the Etruscans and threw up monsters like Caligula and Mussolini. The theme of his book is the murder of a civilisation which, being based on the natural instincts and at one with the cosmos, inevitably had to be wiped out by the gods of vicious puritanism and cerebral abstraction.

The Etruscans, as everyone knows, were the people who occupied the middle of Italy in early Roman days, and whom the Romans, in their usual neighbourly fashion, wiped out entirely in order to make room for Rome with a very big R. They couldn't have wiped them all out, there were too many of them. But they did wipe out the Etruscan existence as a nation and a people. However, this seems to be the inevitable result of expansion with a big E, which is the sole *raison d'être* of people like the Romans.

People 'like the Romans' include the British, imperialists who would be happy to wipe out the neo-Etruscan Lawrence, and the Prussians. Prussianism, suggests Lawrence, was so strongly embedded in the soul of the great scientific historian Mommsen that he could not disguise his antipathy to the Etruscans. 'The Prussian in him was enthralled by the Prussian in the all-conquering Romans. So being a great scientific historian, he almost denies the very existence of the Etruscan people.' So, according to Lawrence, does everybody else. The Etruscans, where they are noticed at all, 'are put down as a feeble Graeco-Roman imitation'. They failed to leave a literature behind them, or even a language. They were not self-regarding enough to wish to push their image to the limits of time. They got on with life. This, naturally, endears them to Lawrence.

A love of life is, to the great abstract imperialists, accounted vicious. 'The Etruscans were vicious! The only vicious people on the face of the earth presumably. You and I, dear reader, we are two unsullied snowflakes, aren't we? We have every right to judge.' All that is left of Etruria is its tombs, and there is a certain appropriateness in Lawrence's seeking life underground, where there are not only bones but germinating seeds. To the Etruscans the dead were alive. They built a living city on a hill and, opposite on another hill, the necropolis, 'the near-at-hand city of their dear dead'. A part of him was already coming to terms with death, and he would be happy to spend it with the Etruscans. In their tombs they find 'a pleasant continuance of life, with jewels and wine and flutes playing for the dance. It was neither an ecstasy of bliss, a heaven, nor a purgatory of torment. It was just a natural continuance of the fullness of life. Everything was in terms of life, of living.' And the symbol of life is the phallus or lingam, with its female counterpart the *arx*, which Lawrence at once translates into Noah's Ark and the ark of the covenant – 'the womb – in which lies the mystery of eternal life, the manna and the mysteries'. These life-emblems Lawrence sought in the tombs and, when they had not been removed by the scavengers of purity and abstraction, saw in them the outward sign of the Etruscan consciousness, which, 'the whole Etruscan pulse and rhythm', must be wiped out.

Now we see again, under the blue heavens, where the larks are singing in the hot April sky, why the Romans called the Etruscans vicious. Even in their palmy days the Romans were not exactly saints. But they thought they ought to be. They hated the phallus and the ark, because they wanted empire and dominion and, above all, riches: social gain. You cannot dance gaily to the double flute and at the same time conquer nations or rake in large sums of money. *Delenda est Carthago*. To the greedy man, everybody that is in the way of his greed is vice incarnate.

The search for ancient Etruria took Lawrence and Brewster to Cerveteri, Tarquinia, Vulci, finally Volterra. Throughout the journey the living world is closely observed, as well as the dead one that goes on glorifying life. Lawrence sees a shepherd who looks like a faun and starts lamenting the disappearance of the 'faun-face', crushed, like so much of the Italian past, into the mud of the Great War. 'They can't survive, the faun-faced men, with their pure outlines and their strange non-moral calm. Only the deflowered faces survive.' He meditates on the asphodel, rejecting equally the romantic view of it as a tall and mysterious lily and its reduction to a daffodil:

However, trust an Englishman and a modern for wanting to turn the tall, proud, sparky, dare-devil asphodel into the modest daffodil! I believe we don't like the asphodel because we don't like anything proud and sparky. The myrtle opens her blossoms in just the same way as the asphodel, explosively, throwing out the sparks of her stamens. And it was just this that the Greeks *saw*. They were that way themselves.

Lawrence seems to be discursive, but he is never really off the point about life. That astonishing sensibility darted, sparked, exploded, and always came up with some new and astonishing variation on his fundamental theme. In Volterra he saw the funerary urns of the northern Etruscans, cursed the museums for meddling with them and, indeed, with everything else – 'It is sickening! Why must all experience be systematised? Why must even the vanished Etruscans be reduced to a system? . . . You break all the eggs, and produce an omelette which is neither Etruscan nor Roman nor Italian nor Hittite, not anything else, but just a systematised mess' – and then brooded on the bleak fortress of the city jail, where an old man languished for killing his wife, who had nagged at him continually for playing the piano. 'So the nagging of thirty years silenced, he got thirty years in prison, and *still* is not allowed to play the piano. It is curious.' But there were some men who escaped from that prison by moulding effigies of themselves out of bread, laying these sheeted on their cots while they made their getaway. Eggs, tombs, escape, eternal life in death. The fragments were waiting to be assembled into something new and strange. Brewster pointed to an Easter display in a Volterra shop window – a chicken escaping from its shell – and hardly had to mention the Christian allegory. Lawrence was ready to write the strange novella called *The Man Who Died*.

Lawrence's setting is Jerusalem under a Roman procurator: he sails into that alien territory and time with his usual confidence. A Judaean peasant has a fine gamecock and is fearful of its flying away. He ties it by the leg to a post, and the rooster grows subdued, but the life within him is 'grimly unbroken'. One morning he wakes, leaps forward on his wings, the cord snaps. He flutters to the top of a wall and crows earsplittingly to the world. At that same moment a man in a tomb wakes from a long sleep and breaks his own cord, the bandages that hold him to death. He feebly pushes open the stone door of his grave and faces 'the animal onrush of light'. He is neither alive nor dead, knowing no Easter triumph of resurrection. He has been taken down from the cross too soon; unless he hides, he will be crucified again. He finds a refuge with the peasant, his first act being to recapture the escaped cock and restore him to the arms of his master. For days he lies recovering strength, watching the newly tethered cock while it watches him.

> The man lay still, with eyes that had died now wide open and darkly still, seeing the everlasting resoluteness of life. And the cock, with the flat, brilliant glance, glanced back at him, with a bird's half-seeing look. And always the man who had died saw not the bird alone, but the short, sharp wave of life of which the bird was the crest. He watched the queer, beaky motion of the creature as it gobbled into itself

the scraps of food: its glancing of the eye of life, ever alert and watchful, over-weening and cautious, and the voice of its life, crowing triumph and assertion, yet strangled by a cord of circumstance ... And the destiny of life seemed more fierce and compulsive to him even than the destiny of death. The doom of death was a shadow compared to the raging destiny of life, the determined surge of life.

Christ (we may name him if Lawrence does not) identifies himself with this cock, recognising that the life of the flesh is all that matters, and the life of the spirit a chimera. Mary Magdalene (Gallicised by Lawrence into Madeleine) sees only bitterness in this reality, wishing to believe that the Saviour is indeed risen, but not as man – 'as pure God, who should not be touched by the flesh, and who should be rapt away into Heaven'. But for Christ the true significance of his death lies in its annihilation of the trivial life of his identity. He blesses the tethered cock, pure life untormented by the claims of the spirit, and Lawrence's language becomes ironically biblical:

> And the man smiled and held the bird dear, and he said to it:
> 'Surely thou art risen to the Father, among birds.'
> And the young cock, answering, crowed.

The risen Christ enters upon life with a new vocation, that of a physician, healer of the body not the non-existent soul. His peasant host gives him the cock, which he carries with him as a kind of living trumpet of life and virtue. But he permits the bird to fight another cock, common, less beautiful, and kill him. 'Thou at least hast found thy kingdom, and the females to thy body. Thy aloneness can take on splendour, polished by the lure of thy hens.' So, without his trumpet, Christ faces the life of the city and rejects it: it is crammed with 'compulsion' which violates the human right to aloneness, and, in a revival of his waking nausea, he sees that his own mission of the compulsion to love was fundamentally sinful. He sees fear of death, which is really fear of the life-cycle, and mad assertion of the ego (he is leaping out of Jerusalem into Vienna), so he rejects the city and moves on.

The scene changes to a temple of Isis by the seashore. A priestess of the goddess, aristocratic like Frieda, 'yellow and white and alone like a winter narcissus', watches a boy cover a girl as a cock covers a hen and turns away uninterested: they are only slaves and she is of good family and once knew Mark Antony, who had been drawn into the Egyptian life-cycle only to be killed by the linear vengeance of Rome. She identifies herself with Isis Bereaved, Isis in Search; she must reassemble the scattered fragments of dead Osiris into a living body and offer herself to the fecundating power of the god of the cycle. Then she sees Christ the wanderer who (and Lawrence gives back his own favourite Latin tag to him) has not yet 'accepted the irrevocable *noli me tangere* which separates the re-born from the vulgar'. He is willing to be touched, and the priestess sees in his unhealed body the lineaments of Osiris. But the touch must be the giving touch of life and not the possessive fingering of the egoistic and fearful. Christ is ready for the love of the body, remembering that all he has previously given is the corpse of love: 'This is my body – take and eat – my corpse –' He is now anointed once more by a woman, but not a prostitute like Mary Magdalene, who may be said to be as corpse-like in her approach to love as was the master himself; the priestess heals his wounds with oil and, after coition, sees them blossom into living suns. So now a Christ truly arisen can join the current of life symbolised by the sea, no longer in need of identification with that rampant rooster (the slave who has covered his girl in rooster fashion cowers at Christ's approach). He has not merely discovered physical love but has filled Isis with the seed of Osiris.

> The man who had died rowed slowly on, with the current, and laughed to himself: 'I have sowed the seed of my life and my resurrection, and put my touch forever upon the choice woman of this day, and I carry her perfume in my flesh like essence of roses. She is dear to me in the middle of my being. But the gold and flowing serpent is coiling up again, to sleep at the root of my tree.
>
> 'So let the boat carry me. To-morrow is another day.'

That last phrase, appropriated by Scarlett O'Hara, is taken to be a blessing on procrastination. Here in Lawrence it means not merely acceptance of the quotidian but a calm joy in yielding to the solar cycle. In preaching a tangential life, a straight line shooting up to a fleshless heaven, Jesus Christ sinned against the sun and the self-renewing cosmos. (Robert Graves, in his *King Jesus*, seems to have borrowed this thesis from Lawrence.) Christianity, implies Lawrence, has been a dangerous deviation, but, with Laurentian help, even the devotees of the Congregationalist Chapel may be led back to the light.

The Man Who Died may be taken as a codicil to *The Plumed Serpent* and the musings on the Etruscans (it is certainly appropriate that it sprang like a chicken out of the shell of northern Etruria). If the Christian God is to be rejected in favour of the great dark and solar forces, this is to be done with charity and a kind of regret: Christ is too gentle to be the enemy. There is the remnant of a boyhood devotion to the religion of Lawrence's mother and probably the author knew he was slapping her in the face (Jesus sleeping with a pagan priestess: what horror). It is curious that the story did not provoke general outrage, but it has to be conceded that Lawrence was cunning in not letting in the sacred name. And the whole work is so masterly a piece of prose poetry that it has the capacity to disarm even the faithful.

It is amusing, and moving, to read the article 'Hymns in a Man's Life', written in that closing phase when Lawrence was supposed to be taking things easy, like the Man Who Died himself, but was actually proving himself to be an efficient popular journalist. In this brief appreciation of the Nonconformist hymnody Lawrence equates the religious sense (which he considered he possessed in abundance) with the sixth sense or sense of wonder – 'the *natural* religious sense'. You do not, he says, have to accept Christianity as dogma, and such items in the orthodox Christography as the miracle of the loaves and the fishes do not need to be explicated in terms of historical truth. It is the wonder that matters. He is grateful for the wonder which was awakened by:

> Sun of my soul, thou Saviour dear,
> It is not night if Thou be near

which penetrated him with the mystery of twilight. He did not wish to locate 'Canaan's pleasant land': the wonder of the name was enough. The thing to do was not to *think* too much; otherwise the whole structure which sustained the mystery would collapse. The interesting thing about Lawrence and Christianity is his pride in being a particular kind of Protestant: his Congregationalists were 'the oldest Nonconformists, descendants of the Oliver Cromwell Independents. They still had the Puritan tradition of no ritual. But they avoided the personal emotionalism which one found among the Methodists when I was a boy'. The apparent inconsistency of Lawrence's being both a puritan and a pagan has worried many of his readers, but friends like Aldous Huxley (who was something of the same mixture) understood the need for such a duality, with its dialectic creating the true human dynamic. William Blake equated 'Enough' and 'Too Much', but excess, to Lawrence, was dissolution of the human entity, just as consistency was the food of the devouring ego. His puritanism also gave him the strength to fight for his paganism.

Thirty-six years ago, even Sunday School teachers still believed in the fight for life and the fun of it. 'Hold the fort, for I am coming.' It was far, far from any militarism or gun-fighting. But it was the battle-cry of a stout soul, and a fine thing too.

Stand up, stand up for Jesus,
Ye soldiers of the Lord.

Jesus standing for the Etruscan gods or Quetzalcoatl or Lawrence or sex. Life, anyway.

16
A Woman's Love

Lawrence had revisited his native Midlands on his return from
New Mexico to Europe in 1925. He paid another visit in 1926.
On both occasions he was appalled by the ugliness and de-
gradation wrought by the forces of industrialism:

> The car ploughed uphill through the long squalid straggle
> of Tevershall, the blackened brick dwellings, the black slate
> roofs glistening their sharp edges, the mud black with coal-
> dust, the pavements wet and black. It was as if dismalness
> had soaked through and through everything. The utter
> negation of natural beauty, the utter negation of the gladness
> of life, the utter absence of the instinct for shapely beauty
> which every bird and beast has, the utter death of the human
> intuitive faculty was appalling. The stacks of soap in the
> grocers' shops, the rhubarb and lemons in the greengrocers!
> the awful hats in the milliners! all went by, ugly, ugly, ugly,
> followed by the plaster-and-gilt horror of the cinema with
> its wet picture announcements: *A Woman's Love!*

This comes from *Lady Chatterley's Lover*, and there is a great
deal more of it. The puritan in Lawrence should have been glad
about the stacks of soap and ordered a consignment for the
Mexican peasants, and what is particularly horrible about rhu-
barb and lemons, splashes of colour in the black and grey? Perhaps the real key to the horror is the film entitled *A Woman's
Love*, with its suggestion of the cheap commercialisation of
human passion, vapid and innutritious balm for 'the weird,

distorted, smallish beings like men' who dwell in the heart of the nightmare.

Ruskin had preached against the nightmare, and in vain. Lawrence, whose multifarious roots are partly in Ruskin, had learned through his own life how powerless a man of words was to destroy or even indent a malignant system. The evil was there, and neither Kangaroo nor Quetzalcoatl could do much about it. Lawrence saw more and more clearly as he grew older (older? He never had the chance to grow old) that change had to come from within, not in the Christian world of the spirit but in the wells of 'phallic tenderness' which had to be cleared of their mud and restored to a pagan limpidity. There is perhaps no logic in this, which may be considered a doctrine of escape, an extrapolation of his own success in getting away from the squalor of his boyhood by marrying Frieda and plunging into the land of the grape and olive and the smiling priapic statues. Whatever casual readers or smuthounds expect from *Lady Chatterley's Lover*, the Laurentian message is clear: put your marital house in order and some of its radiance may burn out the ugliness and degradation of industrial slavery. Or if it will not, at least put your marital house in order.

It may seem strange that a novel which appears to glorify adultery between a gamekeeper and a titled lady should be interpreted as a celebration of marriage, but that is what it is. Frieda, writing about the book in 1944, said:

> Only an Englishman or a New Zealander could have written it. It is the last word in Puritanism. Other races have marriage too, but the Mediterraneans seem to have Homer's ancient pattern still of the faithful Penelope at home, but the man wanders off after Circes and Calypsos – to come home again to his Penelope when he has wandered enough; she is always there for him. The French have '*l'amour*', the Americans their easy and quick divorces and so on, but only the English have this special brand of marriage. It is not the bonds of interests, or comradeship or even children, but the God-given unity of marriage. England's greatness was largely based on her profound conception of marriage, and that is part of Puritanism.

Put it another way, *Lady Chatterley's Lover* is about a man and woman staying together. A loveless marriage may be disrupted, as Frieda's was, by the urgency of genuine love, but there is only room in life for one such urgency. There is no third union. At the end of the novel Mellors and Connie Chatterley look forward to marriage after the mess of two divorces, but the state has properly nothing to do with benefit of clergy or registrar: it is love, love, tenderness, phallic peace and the rest of the Laurentian shibboleths.

The novel was begun at Scandicci in October 1926, when Lawrence had the horror of industrial England fresh in his head. By the following February he had finished it, or rather the first of its versions (published eventually as *The First Lady Chatterley*). There were to be three altogether, the third being the one the world knows best, though there are critics who say the best is the first. It was during his work on the second version, in the summer of 1927, that Lawrence suffered the worst lung haemorrhage he had ever known. Over-exertion in the intense heat had much to do with it, but, as was his habit, he blamed it on the place where he was living, conceived a restless desire to travel and, by the end of January 1928, was out of an Italy he ungratefully termed 'stupid' and considered had 'sort of gone all dead', and, with the Huxleys, was at snowy Les Diablerets in Switzerland. The perpetual changing of abode was to continue until his death in Vence in the south of France. On the move, he completed his third version of *Lady Chatterley's Lover* and elected for trouble he foresaw clearly, but perhaps not clearly enough, by deciding to publish it.

Taking so much trouble over this book, he evidently considered that it, or its message, was vitally important: not since *Women in Love* had he refashioned a work of fiction so conscientiously. Unkind critics have imputed very impure motives to his wishing to write it at all. He was, after *The Plumed Serpent*, somewhat out of the light: 'Fame is the spur,' wrote Milton candidly, and authors are, unless they have something of the saint in them, and not always then, terrible examples of inflamed ego: they want to be noticed and will accept even martyrdom, so long as it is in public. Lawrence, it is alleged, envied James Joyce, who was causing worldwide scandal with *Ulysses*, allegedly a book crammed with sex and swear-words. Lawrence could do as well as Joyce, probably better, since he knew all the obscenities of the Eastwood miners and was experienced in erotic writing. He was to sustain this unseemly capacity for envy when Huxley's

Point Counter Point came out. It was a best-seller despite its 'denial of life' and it contained, in Mark Rampion, a rather inadequate portrait of Lawrence. Lawrence, anyway, proposed offending everybody with an acceptance of life and a select battery of ancient honest words.

In *Lady Chatterley's Lover* we meet the ancient honest word *fuck*. Lawrence believed that it could be cleansed of its centuries of accumulated filth and stalk nakedly through his pages like Connie and Mellors themselves, standing for an act of love which had been too long swaddled in euphemisms. There are many people who cherish the fallacy of a golden age of Anglo-Saxon candour in which lovers invited each other to fuck or be fucked, like the characters of Ms Jackie Collins or Ms Erica Jong. This was never so. The word has always been taboo. You will find no Anglo-Saxon document which contains it. True, it is old, cognate with the German *ficken*, but it stands for a brutal act unsuitable for the marriage bed. It connotes impersonality and aggression. When Dr Johnson said that drinking and fucking were the only things worth doing (disingenuously, one supposes) he was referring to getting drunk and going to brothels. A man can fuck a whore but, unless his wife is a whore, he cannot fuck his wife. Mellors does not fuck Connie, nor do he and she fuck a flame into being. They make love. This is not a euphemism. On the other hand, *fuck* is a genuine dysphemism. Joyce exploited it correctly in *Ulysses*, where it is an item in an explosion of obscenity and a carefully laid verbal climax. Molly Bloom refers to herself as being fucked by Blazes Boylan, but in a phase of resentment towards a husband who has ceased to make love to her. The 1961 lifting of the ban on *Lady Chatterley's Lover* seemed to rehabilitate the word as a legitimate item in the vocabulary of love, but there is no love in it. Lawrence made an aesthetic rather than a moral *gaffe*, and his error has been perpetuated in a great deal of the fiction which acknowledges him as the pioneer of sexual frankness.

Sexual frankness does not require the vocabulary of the Eastwood streets and, even with *fuck* replaced by the less inaccurate *love*, the scenes of erotic fulfilment in *Lady Chatterley's Lover* had to give grave offence. To some extent they still do, though they embarrass rather than shock. We know what goes on in the act of love, and those of us who are writers despair of ever finding verbal equivalents for the pain and pleasure of excitation fulfilled in what Rabelais's translator Urquhart called 'venerean ecstasy'. A mechanical description of the act tells us nothing, any more than a scientifically accurate account of mastication will convey the flavour of roast duck. (To talk of a fuck is to talk of a rapid release analogous to defecation.) Lawrence also embarrasses in other ways. We can read with a certain profit such Oriental manuals of amation as *Pokam* and the *Kama-Sutra*, since we are being instructed in valuable techniques of pleasure, but no man or woman who prizes the act of love can ever consider Lawrence's descriptions of it adequate, despite the ritual inflorations and the breasts that swing like bells. As in *The Plumed Serpent*, where Kate's satisfaction is an adjunct of her dark god's, Connie is not permitted the 'frictional' climax every woman has a right to expect; one sometimes wonders whether Lawrence's demand for domination over Frieda might not have gone as far as clitoridectomy, if he had had a sharp enough knife handy. Connie is not even permitted kisses on the mouth, since Mellors does not care for them. Somewhere back in Mellors's previous life is an estranged wife who seems to have been 'demanding'. Connie demands nothing but tenderness (*Tenderness* was one of Lawrence's proposed titles), and she seems to get this mostly from immediate penetration, the phallus entering like a deep thrust of peace.

One of Lawrence's aims in the book is to put down the flaming egos of unregenerate humanity, to muffle identity and exalt entity. The cock of *The Man Who Died* blazes with life untainted by the unhealthy aspirations of self, which is an all too human invention. The cock of the gamekeeper Mellors becomes as much a character in the story as the Judaean rooster, so does the vagina of Connie Chatterley. Another proposed title – subsequently attached to the second version of the novel – was *John Thomas and Lady Jane*, which names their respective sexual organs with what many consider to be an unholy facetiousness. Lawrence, of course, was right to endow the male organ with a life of its own, engorging and detumescing according to its own autonomous rhythms. Alberto Moravia wrote a novel called *Lui*, granting a separate existence to 'him', but both he and Lawrence have behind them a long demotic mythology of phallic personification. I remember in my army days being totally stripped for medical inspection and the recruit in front of me being rebuked for having an impertinent erection. 'I can't help it, sergeant,' he said. 'It's the

doctor here what he's taken a fancy to.' John Thomas takes more
than a fancy to Lady Jane, but the appellations are too fancy to
be acceptable. Is Lady Jane so called because she belongs to the
wife of a baronet? If we are getting down to elements why debase
them with a mocking aristocratic reference? We could accept
John Thomas if we were not already aware of our own john
thomases from the days of first drawing them out in the school
urinal. The facetiousness will not do.

Some critics and, more especially, litigants have seen in Connie
and Mellors little more than animated pudenda, their personalities
mere sketchy extensions of their erotic life or half-life. Connie,
whose full name is Constance, is one fidelity replaced by another;
Mellors is song and honey. Some have called the one a neurotic
idiot and the other a ram. It is hard to take Connie as seriously as
Gudrun or Ursula or even Kate: she is all passivity. Mellors is less
attractive than Lawrence's first gamekeeper in *The White Peacock*.
He exhibits his creator's own desire to have the best of both
worlds – the coarse mouther of dialect which justifies base Anglo-
Saxonisms, the speaker of 'good English' (there is snobbery for
you) when the mood takes him. There is something of Lawrence's
father in him perhaps, as also a little of Lawrence's mother – the
quiet reader of elevating books while the shepherd's pie browns
in the dutch oven. Putting erotic tenderness in the foreground,
Lawrence denies these two the right to live like normal people –
getting on with the ordinary tasks of life and enjoying sex off
duty.

Lawrence's apologia for his novel – *Apropos of Lady Chatterley's
Lover* – is in some ways more entertaining than the book itself; it
is certainly more humorous. He does not recommend that every
sexually dissatisfied lady should run off with a randy gamekeeper,
but he does locate 'the old blood-warmth of oneness and togetherness' in the lower social orders (which, like Lawrence himself,
Mellors is only too ready to spring out of into a kind of neo-
aristocracy when he feels like it). He has a paragraph in which he
slams the Janeites with the casual brutality at which he was so
adept:

> In the old England, the curious blood-connexion held the
> classes together. The squires might be arrogant, violent,
> bullying and unjust, yet in some ways they were *at one* with
> the people, part of the same blood-stream. We feel it in

Defoe or Fielding. And then, in the mean Jane Austen, it is gone. Already this old maid typifies 'personality' instead of character, the sharp knowing in apartness instead of knowing in togetherness, and she is, to my feeling, thoroughly unpleasant, English in the bad, mean, snobbish sense of the word, just as Fielding is English in the good, generous sense.

He then has something to say about Sir Clifford Chatterley whom, bizarrely, we have to relate to the Jane Austen tradition of pure 'personality'. Sir Clifford, crippled below the waist in the cause of fighting for king and country, betrayed by his wife and cuckolded by his gamekeeper, is punished as Gerald Crich was for being all iced inhuman industrialism. He has built a world in which a cinema debases a woman's love, his name connotes emptiness of discourse, he is one of the damned. If Gerald merely has to die in the snow, the poor baronet has to revert to a childhood in which he cries for kisses from his nurse and then emerges from infantile helplessness into a more than Crichian state of power-consciousness and chilled efficiency. Lawrence admits that Connie's desertion of a cripple severely limits our sympathy for her, but he does not care much. Denying, in the very first words of the book, that the modern age can admit tragedy, he gives us, in Sir Clifford Chatterley, something very like a tragic hero. Mellors and Connie come rather close to comedy. External nature remains blessedly immune from the human betrayals and illicit ecstasies and, as always in Lawrence, is wonderfully presented.

Both Lawrence's British and American publishers, Secker and Knopf, were brisk in rejecting his final novel, which had to wait for the dawn of the permissive age, thirty years after the author's death, to appear in an unexpurgated form in the Britain he had long wished to regenerate. In the case *Regina versus Penguin Books* Mr Griffith-Jones, counsel for the prosecution, put the case not merely for a literature of traditional reticence but for a set of social attitudes which, in 1961, already belonged to a museum. He asked the jury whether any of them would be willing to allow his wife, or his servants, to read *Lady Chatterley's Lover*. The assumption that servants still existed, that wives could do nothing without permission from their husbands, and that books were costly items in the breadwinner's budget, was effectively exploded by working-class Laurentians like Professor Richard Hoggart. It was a paperback firm that had been proceeded against, paperback books were cheap in those days, and the moment of victory was celebrated on television with images of the lower orders lining up outside bookshops to buy their copies of a book that had been part of the mythology of suppression but was now there in all its flowery nakedness, cheaply to instruct, divert, disappoint. Relief among those of us who had always denounced censorship, and not only of Lawrence, derived more from our now being able to say openly that *Lady Chatterley's Lover* was not a great book, rather than from the new liberalism of the law. For it had always been necessary previously to assert that an outstanding work of literature had been put in chains; now we could at last be honest.

Lawrence was back in Italy in the spring of 1928, and an old Florentine friend, Giuseppe ('Pino') Orioli, undertook to print *Lady Chatterley's Lover* and distribute it. He was both a publisher and a bookseller, had first met the Lawrences in Cornwall during the war, and had published a number of Italian books that the incredibly energetic Lawrence had edited or translated. He had close relations with the Anglo-Florentines. One of these was Reginald Turner, the illegitimate son of a British newspaper proprietor, who left his considerable wealth to Orioli. Turner, a friend of Oscar Wilde's and later of Norman Douglas's, is briefly lampooned in *Aaron's Rod* as Algy Constable; Orioli thus got his reward for being a good Laurentian in a rather roundabout way. After a sacramental lunch in Florence, Lawrence and Orioli took the typescript of the novel to the printers, who knew no English. The monoglottism of Joyce's Dijon printers of *Ulysses* had proved to be no great disadvantage (subsequent Anglo-American editions have contained as many errors as the pioneer one); the typos in the Orioli *Lady Chatterley's Lover* owe more to Maria Huxley's slapdash typing than to the inefficiency of the master printer Franceschini and his assistants (some of whom, according to Lawrence, were literally illiterate). The edition they produced is as handsome as the 1922 *Ulysses*. In the July of 1928 copies started going out to subscribers in Britain, and the protectors of public purity began to take action.

Neither Lawrence nor Orioli could be attacked frontally, in the British courts. Customs and postal officials bypassed legal procedure and, on an assumption of obscenity that was not permitted argument, confiscated copies of the book. The police were active too, under the Home Secretary Joynson-Hicks, popularly known as 'Jix', a grim high-collared relic of the Victorian age who needed the excoriating pen of a Dickens but got his due in newspaper cartoons. Scared booksellers began returning copies which Richard Aldington undertook to redistribute. Suppression in both Britain and America led, as always, to profitable piracy. Lawrence could not legally oppose this, as he had not been able to secure international copyright. He wrote about the problem in his *Apropos of Lady Chatterley's Lover*:

> Owing to the existence of various pirated editions . . . I brought out in 1929 a cheap popular edition, produced in France and offered to the public at sixty francs, hoping at least to meet the European demand. The pirates, in the United States certainly, were prompt and busy. The first stolen edition was being sold in New York almost within a month of the arrival in America of the first genuine copies from Florence. It was a facsimile of the original, produced by the photographic method, and was sold, even by reliable booksellers, to the unsuspecting public as if it were the original first edition. The price was usually fifteen dollars, whereas the price of the original was ten dollars: and the purchaser was left in fond ignorance of the fraud.
>
> This gallant attempt was followed by others. I am told there was still another facsimile edition produced in New York or Philadelphia: and I myself possess a filthy-looking book bound in a dull orange cloth, with green label, smearily produced by photography, and containing my signature forged by the little boy of the piratical family. It was when this edition appeared in London, from New York, towards the end of 1928, and was offered to the public at thirty shillings, that I put out from Florence my little second edition of two hundred copies, which I offered at a guinea. I had wanted to save it for a year or more, but had to launch it against the dirty orange pirate. But the number was too small. The orange pirate persisted.

And so the story goes on – money in the book for everybody except its author, and for him vilification, invitations to write for the popular press as a notorious dirty writer, and a new, but fortunately small, pulmonary haemorrhage.

1928 was a bad year, and Lawrence may be considered to have brought it all on himself. *The Man Who Died*, under its original title of *The Escaped Cock*, had been published in the American periodical *The Forum* and had provoked six months of shocked and vituperative letters in its columns, but it had not actually been banned. Britain would not publish it at all until 1931, when it was presumed that Lawrence had already been cast out from the presence of his Redeemer: there was little point in giving him further hell. 1928 was the year in which a serious writer and a dying man was treated as a public enemy. His scabrous reputation was to be further enhanced that autumn by an exhibition of his pictures at Dorothy Warren's art gallery in London, but it was considered wise to postpone this until the following summer.

In January 1929, two registered packages sent by Lawrence from abroad were seized by British postal officials and opened. The first contained the manuscript of *Pansies*, the collection of versified *'pensées'* which Lawrence had been writing to relieve moral congestion; the other held his introduction to the volume of reproductions of some of his paintings which P. R. Stephenson intended to publish. Stephenson was an Australian who, with his compatriot Jack Lindsay, operated the Fanfrolico Press in London and was to put out in 1930 Lawrence's *Apropos*. He, and the British postal officials, did Lawrence a lucrative service. The officials said they were looking for pornography and they alleged they had found some in *Pansies*. The Home Secretary was questioned about this confiscation in the House of Commons, but magisterially justified censorship before publication on the grounds of his usual concern with keeping Britain pure. The obscenity found in *Pansies* was excised, a purified version published, and Stephenson made a tasteful little book out of the cut bits, selling it very profitably to subscribers and handing over five hundred pounds to the impure author. There is nothing like the official imputation of dirt for the selling of books, but those days seem to be over.

Stephenson's book of reproductions came out simultaneously with the opening of the exhibition of the originals at the Warren Galleries. For a mere amateur who had never exhibited before, Lawrence's success was remarkable: twelve thousand people paid to see his pictures. Then, enraged, authority stepped in, egged on by the yellow press, and the police marched into the gallery to confiscate thirteen of Lawrence's canvases, four copies of the book of reproductions, and a volume of drawings by William Blake. Dorothy Warren, with her husband Philip Trotter, was summoned to appear before a magistrate named Mead: it was proposed that both pictures and books should be destroyed, and Mrs Trotter was to show cause, if any, why not. The Muskett who had fired at *The Rainbow* emerged to adjudge Lawrence's pictures 'gross, coarse, hideous, unlovely and obscene'. 'Obscene' remains the most ambiguous term in the whole legal vocabulary: if sex and nudity are made attractive, they are obscene; if they are made repulsive, they are also (though probably less) obscene. Mrs Trotter, or Dorothy Warren, was the niece of Philip and Ottoline Morrell and had known Lawrence in the old Garsington days. She defended him vigorously, and the names of William Orpen and Augustus John, who said they admired the paintings, were invoked. But aesthetic judgments have never mitigated moral decisions in English courts of law. The effect of the well-publicised legal proceedings, which were a mere brandishing of the fist of the establishment in the face of the absent Lawrence, was, naturally, to make the exhibition more popular than ever. Lawrence was in danger of becoming a martyr-hero for art.

My personal view of the pictures of Lawrence that I have seen is very favourable, but I am no Orpen or John. The colours are bright, the subjects life-enhancing, the flesh-tones unconvincing, the anatomy vile. But the Slade had taught Brett anatomy, and Lawrence was as much against the Slade as any other monument of orthodoxy. Lawrence's best paintings are those done by Mark Rampion in *Point Counter Point*, where Huxley has imposed a trained technique on an artist who is as much a professional preacher through paint and line as a verbal polemicist. This is the kind of thing that Lawrence should have done:

It was a smallish painting, in oils. Low down in the left-hand corner of the canvas, set in a kind of recess between a foreground of dark rocks and tree trunks and a background of precipitous crags, and arched over by a mass of foliage, two figures, a man and a woman, lay embraced. Two naked bodies, the woman's white, the man's a red brown. These two bodies were the source of the whole illumination of the picture. The rocks and tree trunks in the foreground were silhouetted against the light that issued from them. The precipice behind them was golden with the same light. It touched the lower surface of the leaves above, throwing shadows up into a thickening darkness of greenery. It streamed out of the recess in which they lay, diagonally into and across the picture, illuminating and, one felt, creating by its radiance an astounding flora of gigantic roses and zinnias and tulips, with horses and leopards and little antelopes coming and going between the huge flowers, and beyond, a green landscape deepening, plane by plane, into blue, with a glimpse of the sea between the hills and over it the shapes of huge, heroic clouds in the blue sky.

Burlap, who is, as we know, based on John Middleton Murry, does not like the painting much. 'The thing's not gentle-Jesusish enough for you,' cries Rampion. 'Love, *physical* love, as the source of light and life and beauty – Oh, no, no, no!' It is the sort of message that Lawrence at least wanted to convey in his grotesque nudes. But the time was growing short for the conveying of messages of any kind except ones of resentment. This is from *Nettles*:

Give me a sponge and some clear, clean water
and leave me alone awhile
with my thirteen sorry pictures that have just been rescued
from durance vile.

Leave me alone now, for my soul is burning
as it feels the slimy taint
of all those nasty police-eyes like snail-tracks smearing
the gentle souls that figure in the paint.

Ah, my nice pictures, they are fouled, they are dirtied
not by time, but by unclean breath and eyes
of all the sordid people that have stared at them uncleanly
looking dirt on them, and breathing on them lies.

Ah my nice pictures, let me sponge you very gently
to sponge away the slime
that ancient eyes have left on you, where obscene eyes
                    have crawled
leaving nasty films upon you every time.

Ah the clean waters of the sky, ah! can you wash
away the evil starings and the breath
of the foul ones from my pictures? Oh purify
them now from all this touch of tainted death.

It is a weary kind of resentment, and the weariness was closing in. In Baden-Baden in the autumn of 1929 he wrote about Bavarian gentians, 'black lamps from the halls of Dis, burning dark blue', torches which would lead him to the underworld. And then he turned from Pluto and Proserpina to the myths of the Egyptians, telling himself to build his ship of death.

> And everything is gone, the body is gone
> completely under, gone, entirely gone.
> The upper darkness is heavy as the lower,
> between them the little ship
> is gone
> she is gone.
>
> It is the end, it is oblivion.

But, in an afterword, he wrote:

> So build your ship of death, and let the soul drift
> to dark oblivion.
> Maybe life is still our portion
> After the bitter passage of oblivion.

Not the gentle-Jesus heaven, but the life the Etruscans asserted even in death. Yet it is difficult to assert life when one is dying.

17
Death in Vence

Lawrence's last days are best seen from the angle of Aldous and Maria Huxley. The rapport between two authors so apparently different continues to puzzle some people. Lawrence, as we know, was opposed to 'science', and Huxley was the grandson of a scientific giant, as well as the brother of another scientist of deserved eminence. He himself had been intended to follow a scientific career, while Julian was to have been the man of letters, and Aldous is perhaps the only literary man of the century to have assimilated, as a scientific amateur with a professional brother to call upon, enough of the specialist disciplines to bring a new intellectual rigour to the novel. The piquancy of *Point Counter Point* lies in the ironic juxtaposition of the ordinary empirical approach to life and its reduction to physics, chemistry, biology, physiology, demography and endocrinology. Huxley was fascinated by the tragedy and comedy implicit in the dual approach ('born unto one law, to another bound ... Passion and reason, self-division's cause'), whereas Lawrence was a bigoted monist. Huxley recognised in the other man a set of instinctual passions which he regretted he did not himself have: he wanted them, but he was temperamentally given to a certain emotional coolness. Lawrence gave him *in excelsis* one half of the human picture; he could supply the other half himself. More than anybody, perhaps, he saw, with a kind of scientific objectivity, the uniqueness of Lawrence: 'He is one of the very few people I feel real respect and admiration for. He is something superior and different in kind.' He could put up with the fury and the working-class aggressiveness: 'Sometimes he would get sort of cross. But he could be very amusing. Entertaining. I mean he was happy. Happiness is the greatest virtue, he would say. And he *was* happy.' That is Huxley recollecting to a tape recorder in late life. 'He would get sort of cross' is delightful. Huxley rarely got cross; he was calm and always charming. Lawrence could not make him quarrel. Nor Maria, who had a love amounting to worship of the master. Lawrence reciprocated with an almost fatherly affection; he remembered a bewildered young Belgian girl from the old days at Garsington:

> 'I'm a bit worried about your health, so please be a good child and *really* take care for a while – don't bother about *anything* else. Now do as you're bidden, and don't go squiffing about any more, but keep still and warm and well fed . . .

This solicitousness from a dying man is touching, but not untypical of Lawrence in his attitude to Maria and, with certain reservations, Maria's husband.

Maria's husband, when he had seen Lawrence's condition in the harsh winter of 1929, reported his concern to his brother Julian:

> . . . no energy . . . It's pathetic to see the way he just sits and does nothing. He hasn't written a line or painted a stroke for the last 3 months. Just lack of vital strength. He still talks a good deal and can get amused and excited into a semblance of health for an hour or two at the time. But it is only a semblance . . . He has gone to Germany now – or is just going: for he has been in Florence these last days – of all places in this weather! We have given up trying to persuade him to be reasonable. He doesn't want to be and nobody can persuade him to be – except possibly Frieda. But Frieda is worse than he is. We've told her that she's a fool and a criminal; but it has no more effect than telling an elephant.

These are hard words from the usually mild Aldous, and we have to take them seriously. We can so easily hypnotise ourselves into a view of Frieda as a shining Brünnhilde, strong-minded, self-willed but loyal and, above all an intelligent helpmeet for an intelligent man, that it comes as a shock to learn that some could regard her as a fool and even worse. Lawrence's foolishness in refusing to see a doctor was of a different order. His illness,

Huxley thought, was 'unnecessary, the result simply of the man's strange obstinacy against professional medicine'. But later, editing Lawrence's letters, he picked on a phrase he used in writing to Lady Ottoline – 'What is the matter with us is primarily chagrin. Then the microbes pounce . . .' – and remembered it. He was prepared to believe that tuberculosis was 'a disease of chagrin', but Huxley was in a phase of his life when he would talk to a man's cancer and tell it to go away and assert that bad eyesight was a disease of the spirit. Why should Lawrence die of chagrin? He had written well and much, and he was gaining an appreciative audience, though not in his native country; he had fulfilled magnificently his vocation as a writer. But he had failed to change the world, and he died too young to realise that that was no man's job. There was certainly chagrin there, but it was not lethal. Lawrence died of his own wilful neglect, abetted by a wife who showed 'submissiveness' at the wrong time.

On medical urging, he submitted to being moved from Bandol – where he had rented a coy and chichi villa intended as a nest for some long-gone illicit love affair – to a sanatorium at Vence. Lawrence would not admit it was really a hospital; he pretended it was a kind of hotel run by people in white coats. He wrote to Maria:

> They examined me with X-rays and all that. It is as I say – the lung has moved very little since Mexico, in five years. But the broncs are awful, and they have inflamed my lower man, the *centre* and the liver. I suppose that's why I've gone so thin – I daren't tell you my weight . . . It's dull here – only French people convalescing and nothing in my line. But I'm feeling more chirpy, and shall try to get *on my legs*. It would be fun to see you, end of this month. When I hope I can walk a bit. I wish we could have somewhere to have a good time like Diablerets. Or I wish I could sail away to somewhere really thrilling – perhaps we shall go to the ranch . . .

He always had the ranch on his mind – his own, or Frieda's, property, cut off from him by the flaming sword of US immigration regulations. He wrote that hopeful letter on 7 February. On 21 February he wrote for the last time to Maria:

> . . . I am rather worse here – such bad nights, and cough, and heart, and pain decidedly worse here – and miserable.

Seems to me like *grippe*, but they say not. It's not a good place – shan't stay long – I'm better in a house – I'm miserable.

His last letter of all was mailed four days later to Earl Brewster. Visitors tried to make him less miserable but they did not succeed. Jo Davidson came to model his head in clay, with, thought Lawrence, mediocre results. H. G. Wells called in from Grasse, where he was maintaining the love-nest Lou Pidou with Odette Keun – 'a common temporary soul'. The Aga Khan was better: 'a bit of real religion in the middle of his fat face'. The Huxleys, he reports, are in Cannes: 'Queer – something gone out of them – they'll have to be left now to the world – finished, in some spiritual way'. Not aware of this spiteful devaluation of two of the noblest souls of the century, the spiritually finished ones arrived in Vence on 25 February to find Lawrence 'terribly changed. He gave one the impression that he was living by sheer force of will and by nothing else. But the dissolution of the body was breaking down the will.' Lawrence perversely, or perhaps with a right instinct not to die an institutionalised death, insisted on leaving the sanatorium (which was, proleptically and indiscreetly, named Ad Astra). Frieda rented the Villa Robermond in Vence – now called the Villa Aurelia – and in a decrepit taxi Lawrence was jolted there and put to bed. He was, of course, exhausted.

The poet Robert Nichols and his wife were living in Villefranche. They were friends of the Huxleys, who had been visiting them. Nichols was not quite a friend of Lawrence, and his memoir of Lawrence's relationship with Philip Heseltine, contributed to Cecil Gray's *Peter Warlock*, is less than charitable. He had first met Lawrence in 1915 through Heseltine and briefly renewed the acquaintanceship in the Balearic Islands in 1929. In a long letter to Dr Henry Head, the neurologist, Nichols was to give an account of Lawrence's death and burial, but it concentrates more on the suffering of Maria Huxley than that of the dying man and his prospective widow. Nichols was devoted to Maria: 'Little Maria is much upset over Lawrence. She loves him very much. I am very sorry for her. Her face is worn and peaked over D.H.L.' When Nichols saw Maria and Frieda together he thought: 'This woman is a lot worthier of Lawrence than Frieda.' This evaluation apparently was made on the strength of Frieda's having got 'the kitchen into a hell of an unwholesome mess' after less than a day in the villa: 'Little Maria, though nearly a wreck, spent the morning scrubbing it out.' Frieda did not take any of the right hygienic precautions: she burned no clothes, she kept no special cup for her sick husband. 'She is one of life's natural "squatters", a gypsy and totally unpractical.' Aldous and Maria did all the work; Frieda's unworking presence was enough for Lawrence. And yet Lawrence said: 'I like them but don't love them anymore.'

He said this to Frieda's daughter Barbara, a tall and handsome young woman of twenty-six whose studies at the Slade School of Art did not endear her to the primitive painter Lawrence. Barbara reported to Nichols that Lawrence found the Huxleys too intellectual, 'not his sort', lacking in human warmth, which was totally untrue, but Nichols, with the ready British appeal to class, considered that Lawrence was dying as a son of Eastwood, going back to 'his miner's world', with the 'pronounced mother-complex' coming out. And yet Lawrence cried: 'Maria, Maria, don't let me die', and Maria held him in her arms. 'I am bound to add,' writes Nichols, 'as a statement of mere fact that I am afraid Frieda Lawrence was worse than useless as regards D.H.L.'s health'. We have it on the testimony of Aldous Huxley that, a day or two before he died, Lawrence said to his wife: 'Frieda, you have killed me.' Nichols says:

> Aldous would not repeat such a terrible saying unless he felt it to be true. And he said, 'I like Frieda in many ways but she is incurably and incredibly stupid – the most maddening woman I think I ever came across. Nevertheless she was the only sort of woman with whom D.H.L. could live.'

That was true. If Maria Huxley had married him she would have been as admirable a wife as she was to Aldous, solicitous, efficient, clean in the Belgian manner, above all loving. But she would have brought order into his life, and Lawrence needed chaos. Above all he needed the dialectical conflict which he interpreted as a battle of wills. He was content to be the housewife himself. Frieda's aristocratic squalor and amoral hedonism were the foil to his ingrained puritanism.

After pain eased by morphia, delirium in which he split into two and looked down upon himself from the corner of the ceiling, and the comforting grip of Frieda on his ankle – 'It felt

so full of life, all my days I shall hold his ankle in my hand' –
Lawrence settled to sleep and died quietly. That was on 2 March
1930. He was buried in Vence. There were flowers on his coffin
– freesias, violets, mimosa, primroses – but 'Maria wouldn't put
any on. She stood like one about whom the heavens had fallen'.
Frieda said 'Goodbye, Lorenzo' and no more, but she achieved a
kind of eloquence in the mosaic of the phoenix she had put up on
the head of his grave, made out of coloured pebbles from the
beach at Bandol. Lawrence's body was exhumed a year or so
later and taken to Taos for reburial, where, wrote Richard
Aldington in 1950,

> it lies in a memorial chapel on the slope of the Rockies just
> behind his ranch and almost shadowed by the great pine
> tree. It is a 'peaceful oblivious place' such as he desired, where
> in the hot months the bees hum in the many flowers, a jay
> calls harshly, the wind hisses softly through the pine-needles,
> and in the afternoons there come the crash and roar of
> thunder. In winter it is covered with silent snow, with some-
> times the scream of an eagle, and in the hard frost under the
> near sparkling stars the distant howling of coyotes.

Neither Eastwood nor Westminster Abbey has questioned the
propriety of the most English of our writers being interred in
American soil. Exile was a kind of affront to England in his life;
its perpetuation in death remains a reproach. Much of Lawrence's
work has achieved classic status, but its message continues to dis-
concert. The British expect comfort from their writers, and Lawrence offers very little.

Emma Maria Frieda Johanna, Baroness von Richthofen,
quondam Mrs Ernest Weekley, subsequently Mrs David Herbert
Lawrence, went to live on the estate in New Mexico which,
thanks to American generosity, she legally owned. In 1950, when
she was seventy-one, she contracted a companionate marriage
with Major Angelo Ravagli in New Mexico. She died on her
seventy-seventh birthday, 11 August 1956. In 1934 she had published a very candid and often moving account of her life with
Lawrence under the title *Not I, But the Wind* – a citation from
the sequence of her husband's poems called *Look! We Have Come
Through*. Her title is appropriate. Lawrence was a meteorological
phenomenon: 'Sometimes I hated him and held him off as if he
were the devil himself. At other times I took him as you take the

weather. Here's a spring day, glorious sunshine, what a joy!' Or again: 'What does it amount to that he hit out at me in a rage, when I exasperated him, or mostly when the life around him drove him to the end of his patience? I didn't care very much. I hit back or waited till the storm subsided. We fought our battles outright to the bitter end. Then there was peace, such peace.' Wind, storms, sun. As the reality of life with Lorenzo receded, the great writer became in her eyes a great saint, having undergone a great martyrdom. Handyman that he was, he may be considered to have forged his own gridiron and lit his own fire.

Anyone wishing to contact the ghost of Lawrence in Taos will find his books and books about him in the shop, as well as a display of some of his paintings at La Fonda, on the Taos plaza (the mildly erotic ones may be viewed only on request). The Lawrence Ranch is still there, the log cabin in which he lived with Frieda intact, and the small chapel where his remains are interred is kept in order for tourists. Brett's home has been turned into a restaurant called Whitey's. Telephone 505–776–2200 for reservations. The rack of lamb and the Provimi veal are to be recommended. Dinner for two costs, with wine, between fifty and sixty dollars.

18
On the Side of Life

Lawrence died midway between his forty-fourth and forty-fifth birthdays. Too young? An absurd question, but only if we consider that life is a quantifiable substance and that we all have a right to it. We all have a right to be born, perhaps, though this is being increasingly denied, but the other right seems to me to be debatable. We take what we can, and we do not complain if we can get no more. With artists, however, there is the tradition of regret at death cutting short genius not wholly fulfilled. Some words written by the music critic Ernest Newman in the *Sunday Times* of 12 June 1927 are worth considering in this connection. He regrets, like everybody else, the early deaths of composers like Mozart, Schubert, Purcell and Pergolesi, but is prepared to maintain the 'paradoxical proposition' that the composers who died too young were Wagner, at the age of seventy, Beethoven, at fifty-seven, Brahms, at sixty-four, Puccini, at sixty-six, and Verdi, at eighty-eight. These composers were still developing, while those struck down in their youth had developed to the limit of their capacity, and the untimeliness was only apparent: they had died on time. Newman speculates 'on the probable position of Mozart about 1830 had he survived Beethoven, as he could quite easily have done without being a very old man'.

Where would he have stood as regards his own work in the years that saw the Eroica, the No. 5, the No. 9, the Mass in D, and the last piano sonatas and quartets of Beethoven? Would he have been able to hold his own against these, to

grow as Beethoven grew, to transform himself from the
purest type of the eighteenth-century composer to the type
that alone could express the needs of the early nineteenth; or
would he have found himself superseded?

Speculations like this are admissible, in literature as in music.
They are profitless but, since human beings must speculate as
fish must swim, they have to be made. I personally have no
difficulty in imagining a Mozart who took in his stride the
spirit of the Revolution, the *Hammerklavier*, horns with valves,
and the need to shout his ego through an expansion of sym-
phonic form. But it is easier to see him as having done enough,
fulfilled the needs of the eighteenth century, and, after a brief
life granted a fourth dimension of hard work, which is a kind
of tangential prolongation, yielding to sickness or the fictitious
stroke of Salieri. I wrote a novel entitled *Abba Abba*, in which
I presented John Keats dying in Rome after the realisation that
there was a new style to develop, closer to the scabrous realism
of the Roman dialect poet Belli than to a romanticism he had
already outgrown. Yeats got the Nobel Prize for being one
kind of poet; then he became another. Dead at fifty-nine, Joyce
had nothing further to do. What can we speculate about
Lawrence?

Aldous Huxley thought that, if Lawrence had lived to a
reasonable age, he might have accepted the need to admit
the rational, to yield to the dualistic philosophy which was
Huxley's own:

> I don't think he could have *remained* where he was, because I
> mean there was a certain ambivalence even in a book like
> *The Plumed Serpent* where he is inviting us to go back to the
> dark gods and the dark blood and so on; but in the next
> breath he's saying how awful the Mexicans are because they
> are so slow and unintelligent and so on. It's a *very* odd book.
> You get these tirades against the Mexicans, almost in the
> terms of an English colonel talking about the natives; in the
> next breath you get these tremendous invitations to sink
> yourself in the dark blood. So there was even then a kind of
> ambivalence. I think he would even then have come round
> to what seems to me a more balanced view − I mean this
> *whole* thing that we have to make the *best* of both
> worlds . . .

The point is that you *must have both*. The blood and the flesh are there – and in certain respects they are wiser than the intellect. I mean if we interfere with the blood and the flesh with our conscious minds we get psychosomatic trouble. But on the other hand, we have to do a lot of things with the conscious mind. I mean why *can't* we do *both* – we *have* to do both. This is the whole art of life: making the best of all the worlds. Here again is one of those fatal examples of trying to make everything conform to the standard of only *one* world. Seeing that we are amphibians – it's *no good*.

(That is Huxley talking to his interviewer, John Chandos, thirty years after Lawrence's death.) The novels, stories and essays that Lawrence might have written had he lived to seventy, armed with the amphibian wisdom, we can envisage only as being rather like Huxley's own, though rather more fiery, bad-tempered, and, it must be admitted, better written. But it is difficult to imagine Lawrence as an ageing writer, probably because, even as a writer in early middle age or late youth, he had already done his best work.

There are some who consider *Sons and Lovers* to be his masterpiece. I, though preserving a soft spot for *Kangaroo*, am inclined to agree with those critics who, agreeing with Lawrence himself, rate *Women in Love* as the peak of his achievement. Professor J. I. M. Stewart, committing the judgment to the volume on the modern period which he contributed to the great *Cambridge History of English Literature*, asserts that *Women in Love* is the definitive fictional eye-opener of our century, placing the book above Joyce's *Ulysses*. After this work, despite the brilliance of such novelle as *St Mawr*, there is a decline in force and originality and speculation about possible recovery and renewal is out of order. The truly great Lawrence died long before he was forty-four. This, anyway, is the view held by many.

Another view, and one towards which my own career as a writer bids me incline, is that it is wrong to judge Lawrence on single works and obligatory to swallow, or reject, his entire output as one massive literary utterance. Lawrence himself, self-contradictory as always, wanted his books to be read but was also prepared to regard them as leaves of the tree of life that grew within him – leaves that could dry up and blow away on the wind, leaving the sap alive and the capacity for renewal untouched. The essence of his literary career was continuity, unimpeded flow, not, as with Joyce, the erection of isolated masterpieces (and not too many of those) separated from each other by prolonged silence. A more banal interpretation of the flow is to state that he was a professional writer.

The term 'professional' is not easily acceptable to those who consider Lawrence to be a St John the Baptist or a Jesus Christ or both. The messiah bears a message and a hope; the professional merely gets on with the job for money. Lawrence wrote for money because there was no other way of earning it; only writers like E. M. Forster, with his small legacy, or Joyce, with his patroness Harriet Shaw Weaver, or T. S. Eliot, who considered himself to be a publisher who occasionally wrote poems, are above the commercial grind. The astonishing thing about Lawrence is that what he wrote for money seems loftily above the covenant of the commercial. He was professional in the other sense: that writing was a thing he professed, as other men profess religion, and the mountain could parturiate and produce lions or ridiculous mice, according to what was needed: the lions and the mice, as vessels of life, had to be accorded the same kind of reverence, and not even an article for the *Daily Mail* ought to be ridiculous. When Lawrence was writing not for money but to keep open the lines of communication, as in his thousands of letters, the verve, flow, fire and conviction are not less striking than in more considered writings. Indeed, these latter are closer to informal communications than to Parnassian utterances. The poems often sound like personal letters raised to a high level of intensity, and so do the personal letters. Lawrence was essentially a man who wrote, and the only form which he did not practise was the film scenario.

It has been remarked by those who knew him that Lawrence could write anywhere and at any time – withdrawn at a table during a party, on his feet in Orioli's bookshop in Florence. He never whined about distraction or writer's block; he got on with his trade or, to be fanciful, went daily down into the mine of his creative unconscious. He belongs to that Edwardian tradition of steady application to the craft which was discredited by Bloomsbury. Bennett, Wells, Conrad and Ford Madox Ford wrote much because it seemed morally right to do so. Virginia Woolf, E. M. Forster and T. S. Eliot either elevated creative costiveness to a virtue or interpreted silence as a kind of Quakerish waiting for the dove to descend. As a writer who himself has written much because he has had to, I feel strongly drawn to this professionalism in Lawrence. Like him, I was prevented by a medical prognosis from pursuing my trade as a teacher and so had to earn a living through writing. It seemed to me, as it must have seemed to him, reasonable to sit down at a table every morning and fulfil a minimal daily quota of a thousand words. This adds up to 365,000 words in a year, or five seventy-odd-thousand-word novels. Such industry could be taken for granted in Lawrence's day; today it is, thanks to the Bloomsbury legacy, suspect.

Lawrence, then, having written unremittingly for a quarter of a century, had probably written enough. If we think of him as old but vigorous in, say, 1961, it is as we think of George Orwell, cured of Lawrence's own condition, around in 1984 – both alive less as writers than as prophets interested to see how far their prophecies have been fulfilled. This prophetic aspect of Lawrence is not one that ought to interest us greatly – we would prefer to think of him as an interpreter of his own time, like Bennett or Ford or the Wells of *Tono-Bungay* and *Mr Britling Sees it Through* – but it seems inescapable. His prophecy was not, of course, prediction in the manner of the other Wells; it was prophecy in the older sense of speaking with an assumption of divine authority. If you speak a thing to the stiff-necked often and loud enough it has a chance of getting through. Lawrence's preaching about our need to see ourselves as part of the cosmos has, in a sense, been fulfilled in our concern with the biosphere or the ecology. The proto-industrial world he abhorred has been replaced by a cleaner one ruled by electronics. The science he distrusted has been the means of a kind of Laurentian regeneration.

During the First World War Lawrence saw, and was horrified by, the power of the state to subdue the individual will. He died three years before Hitler came to power, but he saw Italian fascism in action and did not like it. His own power-hunger, thwarted in marriage, given a fictional satisfaction in *The Plumed Serpent*, had little to do with the reality of politics. He foresaw what this reality would be in *Fantasia of the Unconscious*, with his vision of 'a new German twilight sleep':

... into the sleeper are inculcated the most useful and instructive dreams, calculated to perfect the character of the

young citizen at this crucial period, and to enlighten permanently the mind of the happy mother, with regard to her
new duties towards her child and towards our great Father-
land.

Lawrence's ravings about the ravening teeth of necessary tigers
and the salutary spillings of blood, which belong more to his
private letters than his public utterances, need not be taken too
seriously. His final political statements in *Apocalypse* are reasonable. He was not as anti-democratic as he liked to think; he was
merely honest enough to state openly that we all need living
models of superior energy and genius, that there is a *canaille*
around, and that politicans are, for the most part, inferior animals.
A writer so reviled by official authority was not likely to think
otherwise. Like Orwell, and with the advantage that Orwell
never had – that of actually belonging to a class that dropped its
aitches without effort – he stood for a tradition of British Nonconformist decency that was more and more being thwarted. If
he fought for this tradition from abroad, and not on the road to
Wigan Pier, he did not fight any less effectively than Orwell.
Unlike Orwell, he was not inclined to romanticise the working
class. In his own father he had had a daily experience of its vices
and virtues. It was not mere soft putty for the moulding of the
capitalists. If he had a romantic vision at all, it was of a British
lion whose claws had been clipped. The vision was even Miltonic;
it was certainly Blakean. When, at public gatherings or meetings
of the Women's Institute, Sir Hubert Parry's setting of certain
verses of Blake are sung, few of the singers realise that the 'dark
satanic mills' are churches and the building of Jerusalem is the
restoration of the creative imagination and a fine free sensuality
to a people over-institutionalised. They are, in effect, singing of a
Laurentian world, but one unmarred by Laurentian puritanism.

This puritanism would have made Lawrence shudder at his
realisation in the 1960s that he had become a prophet of the so-
called sexual revolution. As Philip Larkin puts it –

> Sexual intercourse began
> In 1963 . . .
> Between the end of the *Chatterley* ban
> And the Beatles' first LP.

The two big literary events of 1961 were the lifting of the thirty-year proscription of the unexpurgated *Lady Chatterley's Lover* and the publication of the first instalment of the *New English Bible*. People queued for both books. They were cognate in that they tried to demystify entities long shrouded in obscure language, those entities being God and sex. They proved together that demystification is not always a good thing. Whether readers of the *NEB* gained a clearer notion of the Christian message is still a matter for debate; *Lady Chatterley's Lover* was certainly, for the most part, misunderstood. It had always been a subject for music hall sniggering (introducing, as with a comedian named Bob Monkhouse, a non-existent character called Lord Chatterley), and the sniggering did not grow less. The novel was taken as an encouragement to talk more openly about copulation and, by those who had not read it, as a sort of New English Bible of the new religion of promiscuity. That it is an exaltation of fidelity and even chastity has been wilfully ignored. Here is a new Milton blessing Adam and Eve as they conduct their 'rites mysterious' of connubial love, and the popular approach to it has been more appropriate to some long-hidden Victorian memoir of indiscriminate fornication. Lawrence, prophet as he was, should have expected this. In the same way, Vladimir Nabokov should have expected that the term *nymphet* would be misapplied, and *Lolita* become a common noun for any over-developed teenage sexpot.

It is unfortunate that the name D. H. Lawrence should, in the common mind, be associated with only one book, and that one far from his best. We all suffer from the popular desire to make the known notorious. The book I am best known for, or only known for, is a novel I am prepared to repudiate: written a quarter of a century ago, a *jeu d'esprit* knocked off for money in three weeks, it became known as the raw material for a film which seemed to glorify sex and violence. The film made it easy for readers of the book to misunderstand what it was about, and the misunderstanding will pursue me till I die. I should not have written the book because of this danger of misinterpretation, and the same may be said of Lawrence and *Lady Chatterley's Lover*. Sex can be written about scientifically, and then it becomes an aspect of biology. Attempt to write about it in human terms, and you can produce only the dysphemisms, or dysglot, of pornography or the euphemisms, or euglot, of a legitimate erotic work like *The Rainbow* or *Women in Love*. If Lawrence is primarily the author of *Lady C.*, it is mainly his own fault.

To the serious reader, Lawrence is something else. To F. R. Leavis, his chief critical champion, he stood for 'life'. It is apparently possible to make a distinction between imaginative writers who purvey that commodity and those who are more concerned with 'art'. Henry James was annoyed at the young Hugh Walpole's praise of the 'life' in Dostoevsky, manifested in a 'mad jumble, that flings things down in a heap' and wrote to him:

> Don't let any one persuade you – there are plenty of ignorant and fatuous duffers to try to do it – that strenuous selection and comparison are not the very essence of art, and that Form *is* not substance to that degree that there is absolutely no substance without it. Form alone *takes*, and holds and preserves, substance – saves it from the welter of helpless verbiage that we swim in as in a sea of tasteless tepid pudding, and that makes one ashamed of an art capable of such degradations. Tolstoy and D. are fluid pudding, though not tasteless, because the amount of their own minds and souls in solution in the broth gives it savour and flavour, thanks to the strong, rank quality of their genius and their experience. But there are all sorts of things to be said of them, and in particular that we see how great a vice is their lack of composition, their defiance of economy and architecture . . .

James, as we know, dismissed Lawrence in his article on the younger generation of novelists in the *Times Literary Supplement* of 19 March 1914: he was said to 'hang in the dusty rear' of writers like Gilbert Cannan; the real novelists were Conrad, Edith Wharton, Compton Mackenzie and his self-proposed but rejected catamite Hugh Walpole. The rank broth of the later Lawrence would have disgusted James even more than the earlier. James, in whom there is much art but little sex (we do not count Roderick Hudson 'swinging his tool'), may be taken as a fair antithesis to Lawrence, in whom there is much sex but not much art of the Jamesian variety. 'Life' probably means sex.

Art and 'life' are not, of course, incompatible. There is plenty of ordinary human vitality in Joyce's *Ulysses*, much of it spinning around sex remembered, enacted, anticipated, and *Ulysses* is the supreme example in our age of the novel as art, or even artifice. It may be said that there is so much 'life' in the book that it had to be controlled by a rigorous set of cunning devices to prevent the vitality becoming mere strong rank broth. The devices come under the heading of symbolism, and the employment of symbolism marks the 'modernist' writer: the writer, in effect, draws attention to his work as an artefact functioning as an autonomous engine whose parts can be taken as metaphors of life, but which would function under its own steam even if the real-life referents were withdrawn. Push symbolism far enough and you arrive at surrealism. It is felt that Joyce's final work, *Finnegans Wake*, lends itself to the kind of interpretation which may safely ignore its plot, its characters, and its theme of incest, and concentrate on its wordplay and its structure. Lawrence was not like Joyce. Perhaps Richard Aldington was right in finding between them an antithesis powerful enough to imply a fundamental metaphysical opposition between being and becoming, static essence and fluid existence.

Lawrence ought not to be 'modernist', but he is ('in his own eccentric way,' says David Lodge, cautiously). As a poet he was at first hard to classify, as is indicated by his being published in both Georgian and Imagist anthologies, but he is seen clearly now – and the confirmation is in Michael Roberts's *Faber Book of Modern Verse* – as belonging to the free-verse-and-colloquial-language symbolists. As a novelist he does not represent a deliberate rejection of fictional modernism so much as an uncritical acceptance of what was already there. What was good enough for Thomas Hardy, and even George Eliot, was good enough for him. Conrad and Ford had announced the death of the omniscient narrator (consequent, it has been suggested, on the death of God), and they agonised about the narrative point of view, the subjective time-shift, and the exploitation of narrational ignorance and error, but Lawrence is content – and more so in his later work than in his earlier – to walk around his characters in full visibility, enter whichever of their minds he has a mind to, and address the dear reader as a fellow-conspirator in a plot to destroy fictional form. He was the father of what Richard Aldington was to call the jazz-novel, the novel in which you blow what you wish on your trumpet with only the sketchiest adherence to an inherited melodic and harmonic pattern. The modernism of Lawrence's fiction lies, as with Joyce's, in the narrowing of the gap between poetic and prose statements, the forcing on the critic of the novel an approach previously reserved to the lyric poem.

This does not mean that Lawrence wrote poetic prose in the manner of Ruskin or Pater. Rather he brought an intensity of image and rhythm to his *récit* which suggests poetry while remaining prose. Dickens was always ready unconsciously to break into blank verse at moments of high tension, but Lawrence avoids the movement of verse while retaining the heavy emotional charge traditionally associated with it. He repeats words, admits the reader to the process of finding them, gives an impression of clumsiness. There is more 'fine writing' in Joyce than in Lawrence (look at the first chapter of *Ulysses*), and Lawrence's exploitation of the ill-formed sentence – a high poetic content qualified by a deliberate looseness of shape – is in the service of rendering the jerky illogicality of life. The poetic subject-matter itself is a deeper layer of human consciousness than fiction had previously been equipped to admit. Lawrence's contribution to the novel lies in his having found a technique for such deep-level mining. Joyce in *Ulysses* touches preverbal areas of consciousness and shows the naked libido at work. In *Finnegans Wake* he dares to dive into the sleeping mind. But he is committed to human identity in a way that Lawrence is not, and it is probably fair to say that his experimentation has been acceptable only because of that solid traditional element in his work. Humphrey Chimpden Earwicker's initials are stitched into the fabric of Joyce's dream-prose like a desperate monogram, a gesture of fear of the loss of identity. Lawrence's characters sink easily into the world of 'otherness', where human life accepts that it is also natural life, and identity – 'the screaming of the ego', as Huxley puts it – is quelled.

The condition for Lawrence's being able to merge human entities with trees, flowers, animals, ultimately the cosmos, was his primary endowment as a poet of nature. Joyce and Lawrence very neatly oppose each other as apostles of, respectively, the urban and the natural worlds. To Joyce the city is cosmos enough; Lawrence wants everything except the city. A writer's subject-matter is usually a product of his early environment, and as Dublin made Joyce, so Eastwood made Lawrence. He eventually learned of a bigger natural world than the Nottinghamshire countryside and never made the Wordsworthian mistake of identifying a benign rural English God of nature with the Lord of All. It was left to Aldous Huxley to write an essay demonstrating that Wordsworth did not fit into the tropics, but Lawrence knew all about volcanoes, earthquakes and malaria. On the other hand, he did not forget that strange duality of the mining town and the rural ambience: in Australia he homed to it instinctively. A man of the cosmos, he remained a miner's son.

Scions of the working class, like Professor Hoggart, are disposed to hear in Lawrence a voice of that class, and the uneasy wraith of British social division hovers over any discussion of his work, life and temperament. Virginia Woolf praised *Sons and Lovers* but, with the rest of Bloomsbury, was to reject Lawrence as she rejected Joyce: that phrase she used of *Ulysses* might also have been applied to any of Lawrence's works: 'the book of a self-taught working man . . . of a queasy undergraduate scratching his pimples.' It is unworthy language, and variants of it are still to be heard in reference to both writers. But Joyce was Catholic, Irish, an alumnus of University College, Dublin, and excusable because outside the pale. Lawrence, who took no degree at the University College of Nottingham (only the wife of one of its professors), who despised Cambridge and had no interest in Oxford, committed an unforgivable sin: he emerged from a miner's cottage in the Midlands to become one of the great writers of his age. This, I think, still rankles in some quarters. I myself, brought up in a pub, a graduate of Manchester, have to avoid treating Lawrence as the patron saint of the provincial underdogs whose bark was first notably heard in John Osborne's *Look Back in Anger*. One does not delimit the achievement of a great writer by referring to his origins. William Shakespeare was another Midlander who did not go to Oxford.

There is another limitation being placed on Lawrence's literary and prophetic importance, and that is provided by the forces of women's liberation, who object to his doctrine of male dominance both in the sexual act and what is left of the marital sphere when the sexual act is over. Well, it was a woman who dominated Lawrence and, as one of the fruits of victory, outlived him. At least Lawrence preached the importance of sexuality and taught sexual tenderness. He engaged in the battle of the sexes but, at his most typical, was above it. Apart from the exalted diversion his books supply, we need his philosophy and ought to try to learn from his courage – the courage of his own contradictions. We need his paganism tempered by puritanism. We need his perpetual reminder that all literature is subversive. And, whatever life is, we need the eloquence of his allegiance to it.

Bibliography

All Lawrence's works, with the exception of *Mr Noon*, are published in London by William Heinemann. *Mr Noon* is published by the Cambridge University Press, which has undertaken an annotated edition of Lawrence. I quote in my text from the Cambridge edition of Lawrence's letters, which (1985) has arrived at Volume III and the years 1916–21. I have pursued the epistolary Lawrence from 1921 to 1930 in Harry T. Moore's edition, published, in two volumes, by William Heinemann. The following books, not all of which are in print, are memoirs of Lawrence or are otherwise germane to the subject.

Aldington, Richard: *Portrait of a Genius, But . . .*, Heinemann
———. Introduction to *Apocalypse*, Heinemann
Bedford, Sybile: *Aldous Huxley: A Biography* (Volume I: 1894–1939), Chatto, Collins
Brett, the Hon. Dorothy: *Lawrence and Brett*, Secker and Warburg
Brewster, E. and A.: *D. H. Lawrence: Reminiscences and Correspondence*, Harcourt Brace
Carswell, Catherine: *Savage Pilgrimage*, Harcourt Brace
Chambers, Jessie (E. T.): *D. H. Lawrence: A Personal Record*, Jonathan Cape
Ford, Ford Madox: *Mightier than the Sword*, Viking Press
Gray, Cecil: *Peter Warlock*, Jonathan Cape
Hart-Davis, Rupert: *Hugh Walpole*, Macmillan
Lawrence, Frieda: *Not I, But the Wind*, Heinemann

Luhan, Mabel: *Lorenzo in Taos*, Secker and Warburg

Murry, John Middleton: *Reminiscences of D. H. Lawrence*, Jonathan Cape

———. *Son of Woman*, Jonathan Cape

A selection of titles
available in ABACUS paperback:

FICTION

CRUSOE'S DAUGHTER	Jane Gardam	£3.95	☐
EVE	Penelope Farmer	£3.95	☐
ELBOWING THE SEDUCER	T. Gertler	£4.50	☐
SAUL'S BOOK	Paul T. Rogers	£3.95	☐
KENNEDY FOR THE DEFENSE	George V. Higgins	£3.50	☐
PENANCE FOR JERRY KENNEDY	George V. Higgins	£3.95	☐
THE KINGDOM OF THE WICKED	Anthony Burgess	£3.95	☐
SNAIL	Richard Miller	£3.95	☐

NON-FICTION

CHECK YOUR EGOS AT THE DOOR	Garry Trudeau	£2.95	☐
THAT'S DR SINATRA, YOU LITTLE BIMBO	Garry Trudeau	£2.95	☐
THIS SPACE TO LET	Ray Lowry	£2.95	☐
SCHUMACHER LECTURES 2	Satish Kumar (Ed)	£3.95	☐
THE TRUE ADVENTURES OF THE ROLLING STONES	Stanley Booth	£3.95	☐
THE FIRST DANCE OF FREEDOM	Martin Meredith	£3.50	☐
BEYOND THE DRAGON'S MOUTH	Shiva Naipaul	£3.95	☐
T. S. ELIOT	Peter Ackroyd	£3.95	☐

All Abacus books are available at your local bookshop or newsagent, or can be ordered direct from the publisher. Just tick the titles you want and fill in the form below.

Name _____

Address _____

_____

Write to Abacus Books, Cash Sales Department, P.O. Box 11, Falmouth, Cornwall TR10 9EN.

Please enclose cheque or postal order to the value of the cover price plus:

UK: 45p for the first book plus 20p for the second book and 14p for each additional book ordered to a maximum charge of £1.63.

OVERSEAS: 75p for the first book plus 21p per copy for each additional book.

BFPO & EIRE: 45p for the first book, 20p for the second book plus 14p per copy for the next 7 books, thereafter 8p per book.

Abacus Books reserve the right to show new retail prices on covers which may differ from those previously advertised in the text or elsewhere, and to increase postal rates in accordance with the PO.